THE
WINTERTONS
UNMUZZLED

THE
WINTERTONS
UNMUZZLED

The Life & Times of Nick & Ann Winterton,
Two Westminster Mavericks

SARAH WINTERTON

Biteback Publishing

First published in Great Britain in 2016 by
Biteback Publishing Ltd
Westminster Tower
3 Albert Embankment
London SE1 7SP
Copyright © Sarah Winterton 2016

ISBN 978-1-84954-744-4

10 9 8 7 6 5 4 3 2 1

A CIP catalogue record for this book is available from the British Library.

Set in Baskerville

Printed and bound in Great Britain by
CPI Group (UK) Ltd, Croydon CR0 4YY

*Dedicated to my parents, Sir Nicholas and Lady Winterton,
Mr Macclesfield and Mrs Congleton, Nick and Ann, Mav & V*

"I love argument, I love debate. I don't expect anyone just to sit there and agree with me, that's not their job."

MARGARET THATCHER

CONTENTS

FOREWORD

Nicholas and Ann spent over a quarter of a century together in Parliament, an extraordinary tenure that covered four Prime Ministers, two recessions and a number of scandals. Throughout all the chaos of parliamentary life, with the long hours, the late nights, and the prolonged periods away from family and home, the Wintertons were a beacon of dedication and marital fortitude. The popularity they still have among their former constituents bears testimony to their legacy of fighting tirelessly on behalf of the people who had elected them.

I first met the Wintertons at the wedding party of one of their constituents. Sitting at the same table as Nicholas, I, and indeed the rest of the table, was struggling to get a word in edgeways. Ann finally rescued us, appearing at the table and announcing that she was taking Nicholas off for a 'de-pomping'. Whatever she did, I never saw any evidence that it actually worked!

As their whip, I got to know Nicholas and Ann tremendously well, although trying to get them to toe the party line was a task far harder than any I have undertaken. They were both members of that rare band of MPs who were utterly unbiddable, grounded in the concerns and welfare of their constituents. They wore their bloody-minded independence as a badge of honour, invariably refusing to follow the whip or vote in any way but with their principles. In short, they had the courage of a lion and lioness.

In many ways this made my job easy. I knew not to waste my

time trying to convince them to vote with the government. And I knew that if I needed to speak to both of them I could call late and catch them together. This was one parliamentary couple who were tightly bonded together. Not for them the scandals of modern parliamentary life.

Of course, this independence, so prominently displayed from the start to the finish of their careers, meant that they were never ministerial fodder. Instead, they took with gusto to the select committees, being a constant thorn in the government's side. And they campaigned vigorously against the European Union, from their fervent denunciation of the Maastricht Treaty, to Nicholas even using Tony Blair's final PMQs to demand a referendum on our membership of the European Union. On this, as with so much else, they have been vindicated.

This book remembers the Wintertons' colourful careers with tremendous affection, and a good helping of humour. It is unlikely we will ever see a couple such as Nicholas and Ann in Westminster again, and the place is worse for it. The independence of Parliament, the veneration of constituents, the elevation of principle above promotion, defined the Wintertons. It is for these qualities that they should be remembered.

Rt Hon. David Davis MP

1.

EVERY CONSTITUENCY
SHOULD HAVE ONE

Who would be a back-bench MP? It looks a plum job, from the outside. There is never any shortage of applicants. People from all walks of life aspire to be elected to the House of Commons and sit on those famous green benches, at the heart of national life. But there can be very few professions where the rewards come with so many attendant risks. There are Hollywood stuntmen who lead a less perilous existence.

You do your job, sit on committee after committee, stick up for your constituents, try to make thoughtful contributions to the public debate, and you barely register on the political Richter scale. It can be grinding, thankless work – and not massively well paid, despite perceptions to the contrary. Only if you blot your copy-book in some spectacular way can you expect to graduate from the inside pages to the front pages.

Just ask yourself this simple question. When did you last pick up a newspaper, read a story about a back-bench MP you had never heard of, and end up thinking *better* of that MP? It just doesn't happen. You are more likely to find yourself chortling at some tale of greed, duplicity or goatishness. Backbenchers who keep out of trouble are about as newsworthy as bears who shit in the woods. It's not their role to be newsworthy. Their role – and, in fairness, some of them do it superbly – is to keep the rest of us entertained with their frailties.

For better or worse – worse, I would say – most people are not particularly interested in politics. They just see it as a spectator sport. The men and women sitting behind their party leaders at Prime Minister's Questions are mere ciphers, like the Arsenal fans sitting behind Arsène Wenger at the Emirates Stadium. It is a high-wire profession, building up the backbenchers with dreams of promotion, then bringing them tumbling down to earth. What was that? That was the career of the Member for Much Waffle, brought to a premature end after an indiscretion in a club in Birmingham. *Crash!* Another one bites the dust. The Member for Boring-on-the-Hill has unwittingly insulted Polish taxi drivers. There are probably hundreds of his constituents who are grateful for his exertions on their behalf, but who will remember those exertions now? His name is mud, and mud sticks.

Booby traps await the unwary backbencher at every turn. You think you are someone important. You think you have made it. You think of yourself as a pillar of your community. But, in a cynical world, it can prove a pretty wobbly pillar. Yes, there are those constituency fund-raisers where you are cheered to the echo. Yes, there are those periodic appearances on national television. Yes, you have mastered social media, send twenty tweets before breakfast and have acquired followers in Bermuda, Afghanistan and New Zealand. But being in the public eye comes at a price.

Send a foolish tweet or email and your reputation will be trashed. Claim £20 on expenses for a taxi and, if you have not kept the receipt, the knives will be out for you. As for sex... Don't even think of straying from the straight and narrow. There is nothing Fleet Street likes more than an MP caught with his trousers down. Preferably a Tory, of course. The story always reads better if the trousers are pinstriped and tailor-made.

In the perfect world – as viewed through the warped lens of Fleet Street, that is – the MP caught with his trousers down will be discovered *in flagrante* with another MP from the same party. The ultimate double-whammy. When it was revealed, years after the event, that Edwina Currie had conducted an affair with John Major, you can imagine apoplectic Fleet Street editors screaming at their reporters, 'Why didn't we know at the *time*? The story's no good now.' The foxes escaped the hounds on that occasion. But not all foxes are so lucky. British politics is part blood sport, part pantomime, with the poor back-bench MP cast as the villain.

Between 1983 and 2010, I can exclusively reveal, the Tory MPs for the neighbouring Cheshire seats of Macclesfield and Congleton conducted an intimate liaison, meeting in cafes, pubs, even churches. Scandalous behaviour! Unfortunately, they were married at the time, which spoiled the story. Nice one, Mum and Dad.

'Mum and Dad' because the MPs in question, Nicholas and Ann Winterton, are my parents, and I am very proud to be their daughter. As politicians, like all politicians, they knew triumph and disaster: good days, bad days and bloody awful days. They had quite a bumpy ride, particularly in the latter stages of their careers. Sometimes one of them would attract bad headlines. Sometimes the other would. Sometimes they both would, and for a few mad days, the Wintertons would be spoken of in hushed, disapproving terms, as if they were the Krays or the Borgias. But if a daughter doesn't stick up for her own parents, through thick and thin, who else is going to?

My father might never have been elected an MP if another daughter, in another era, had not forgotten that simple precept. When he stood as the Tory candidate at the 1971 Macclesfield by-election, his Labour opponent was a product of Roedean, one of the most exclusive girls' public schools in the country. Embarrassing! But not half as embarrassing as the fact that, when outed as an Old Roedeanian, she publicly criticised her parents for sending her to the school. My father was appalled, and so were the voters of Macclesfield. They might have elected a socialist, at a pinch, but not one capable of such rank filial disloyalty. You will not catch me making the same mistake. I am a fully paid-up member of Team Winterton, family cheerleader-in-chief, proud to celebrate my

3

parents, not just because of what they achieved as individuals, but because of what they achieved together.

They retired as MPs in 2010, and either one of them would make a worthy subject for a rollicking, incident-packed biography. They were among the leading back-bench MPs of their generation, in the thick of the action during a hectic period in British politics. But to appreciate the Winterton story to the full, you need to remember that it has two protagonists, equals in every respect, not least financial.

In an age when the pay gap between men and women remains scandalously high, here is a husband and wife who, for more than a quarter of a century, were paid *exactly the same*, down to the last penny. How many other couples could say the same? One in ten thousand? Probably not even that. That financial equality underpinned what was already a strong relationship, rooted in mutual respect. And, my God, it needed to be strong. Politics is a brutal business and has broken many a marriage. My parents were determined not to fall into *that* trap. Sink or swim, they were in the same boat, each grateful to have the other by their side.

They were fortunate, as they were the first to admit, to be Members of Parliament at the same time, overlapping as MPs for more than a quarter of a century. They knew the pressures the other was under – pressures of time, pressures from the party whips, from their constituents and from the media – so they had no excuse for trotting out the line that has sounded the death-knell for many a relationship: 'You just don't understand, do you?' They were bonded for all eternity by the superglue of parliamentary life.

Even for me, it is hard to think of one of them without the other: they just dovetail so perfectly, like bacon and eggs or Morecambe and Wise. I have heard one of Dad's constituents liken them to the Queen and Duke of Edinburgh, which is stretching things, and another liken them to the Beckhams, which is stretching things even more. But the point is that they were, and are, a team.

In Cheshire, they were known simply as Mr Macclesfield and Mrs

Congleton, rooted in their local communities, recognised wherever they went, synonymous with the parliamentary constituencies they represented. At Westminster, Macclesfield and Congleton fused into one: part double-headed bulldog, growling in unison, part pantomime horse, the object of amusement and affection.

A back-bench Labour MP once joked in a debate that Nicholas and Ann Winterton were Westminster's answer to the Washington double-act performed by Bill and Hillary Clinton. There were sage nods of agreement, until someone muttered from a sedentary position, 'And who's the Monica Lewinsky?' My parents laughed louder than anyone. They love that sort of parliamentary horse-play. They hate it when politicians take themselves too seriously.

Here are the Wintertons in action together during Prime Minister's Questions, in a vignette captured by the *Daily Telegraph*'s parliamentary sketch-writer in 1995:

> Sitting immediately behind Mr Nicholas Winterton (Con, Maccle-sfield), keeping a respectful distance, like a loyal Bedouin wife on a trek across the desert, was Mrs Ann Winterton (Con, Congleton)...
>
> After 30 years of marriage, they still flirt with each other like teen-agers. Time and again, Ann leant forward to whisper something to Nicholas and, time and again, he leant back to whisper something to her. It may have been pure domestic trivia. Perhaps Nicholas was asking if he could have steak for dinner and Ann was asking if he had remembered to buy eggs and bin-liners. But the affection which passed between them was genuine, unbounded, heartwarmingly transparent...
>
> And the fact that they sit for neighbouring constituencies only makes their relationship more charming. Leander had to swim the Hellespont to be with Hero. Romeo had to scale Juliet's balcony. Pyramus could only talk to Thisbe through a hole in the wall. But if Nicholas and Ann want to be together, they just meet in a lay-by on the A536.
>
> Bolshie and unpredictable in their politics, and notoriously out

of favour with the whips, the Wintertons are also, paradoxically, the acceptable face of the Conservative Party...

Amen to all that. The piece captures my parents to a T. Detested by some, revered by others, but never silent – certainly not both of them at the same time, which would have been a biological impossibility – the Wintertons of East Cheshire, aka 'those bloody Wintertons', became one of the great parliamentary double-acts; colourful bit-part players who could steal the show at any minute.

They were not everyone's cup of tea, but they didn't give a damn. They never chased the shimmering mirage of popularity. They were true to themselves and what they believed in. Best of all, they did it with smiles on their faces, which cannot be said of most back-bench MPs. To the corridors of power, they brought a real sense of fun and mischief. Getting elected to the House of Commons – both of them! – was the adventure of a lifetime, and they were determined to enjoy it.

They were outsiders, gatecrashing the best club in London. They had been born and raised in the West Midlands. Their constituencies were in the north west. Neither of them had been to university. And yet here they were, surrounded by chinless wonders who talked about their childhood nannies, owned castles in Kent and had been chums since Oxford. What larks! Wouldn't it be fun to let off a stink-bomb in the bar?

If they had the truculence of teenagers, they were grown-up in their politics: they said what they thought, gave straight answers to straight questions and did not believe in talking down to people. On the website www.theyworkforyou.com, which has a wealth of geeky statistical information about MPs, one discovers that Dad's speeches in Hansard, like Mum's, are 'readable by an average 18–19-year-old, going by the Flesch–Kincaid grade level score'. Fascinating! David Cameron's contributions, by contrast, can be read by an average 16–17-year-old. Even more fascinating! Is that why there was a whiff of the school playground about Prime Minister's Questions when Cameron was at the helm? Boris Johnson's can be read by an average 17–18-year-old – although presumably only by one who can read Latin and French and the other languages into which Boris tends to stray. Like turnips, Tory politicians come in all shapes and sizes, which is what makes them so fascinating.

My parents, as this memoir will demonstrate, were Tory politicians and not Tory politicians. They were one-offs or, as Boris would say, *sui generis*. Come rain or shine, they fought the good fight with gusto, however footling or esoteric the issue. Neither of them was the kind of grandstanding politician who is only interested in the limelight. They enjoyed the small beer of politics – particularly, of course, if it happened to be real ale made from British hops. They were the kind of uncomplicated patriots whose patriotism sometimes gets sneered at, but whose passion for their country never wavered. Dad once introduced a Bill to stop pubs with traditional names such as 'The Red Lion' or 'The Admiral Nelson' renaming themselves 'The Rat and Parrot' or 'The Mottled Oyster'. The Bill never got on the statute book, but it was the thought that counted. On another occasion, he fought to stop the traditional British custard pie being regulated out of existence by the EU – a campaign that earned him the undying gratitude of the National Association of Master Bakers, Confectioners and Caterers, who made him an honorary vice-president. He has had the custard pie vote in his pocket ever since.

Pub names? Custard pies? Who are these Cheshire backbenchers whose praises I am singing? Stand-up comedians from the provinces? Wrong! They were, in their idiosyncratic way, what politics is all about. Or should be all about. Miss the point of their story, misunderstand their struggles, and you will never grasp the essence of parliamentary democracy, that fragile English flower, battered by the four winds.

Soulmates politically as well as romantically – they first met as teenagers at a pony club, which is so corny you couldn't make it up – my parents were much, much bigger than the sum of their parts.

They became the first ever Conservative husband-and-wife team of MPs at Westminster, which was a notable achievement in itself, a triumph of guts and determination over centuries of prejudice. There have been other Tory husband-and-wife teams since, but it was my parents who broke that particular mould. And it was my intrepid mother, for whom the word 'feisty' might have been invented, who deserves most of the credit.

By the time Dad had been in the House for ten years, she had started to get itchy feet. Why should she be stuck in Cheshire, looking after the kids, while he buggered off to London and had all the fun? She wanted to come to the party. She wanted her *own* constituency!

Old habits die hard. Even after Margaret Thatcher had smashed the glass ceiling with her handbag, wives of Tory MPs were not expected to become MPs themselves. It would have been like letting the servants put their feet up in the drawing room. They were expected to look decorative, open the odd jumble sale in the constituency, and keep the home fires burning while their husbands were hundreds of miles away, probably in the arms of their mistresses. But Mum, a classic grammar schoolgirl made good, was not interested in playing second fiddle. She had things to say and she wanted to say them. As she had done when she was a girl, becoming a joint master of foxhounds while she was still a teenager, she blazed a trail for her sex. And she did it without wearing tacky shoes or spouting a word of feminist clap-trap. Quite a lady, with a bit of the devil in her.

The Tory old guard was never totally comfortable with her – you could say the same of Margaret Thatcher – but she just told them where to stick it, using the sort of crisp Anglo-Saxon expletives she had deployed in her fox-hunting days. She could never match Margaret Thatcher's intellectual gifts; she had not been to university. But she could match her determination. At heart, like her leader, she was always the plucky girl from the state school taking on the posh boys from Eton.

One of the gorillas from the Tory whips' office once tried to bully her over some trivial incident, but my mother was having none of it. She told the gorilla to back off or she would insist on a personal meeting with the Prime Minister. The gorilla backed off.

Unlike the Iron Lady, my mother had a real sense of fun and merriment. Laughter was never far from her lips. But she also had the same feral tenacity – pretty much a prerequisite for a woman in a parliament in which, when she was first elected, women were outnumbered by nearly thirty to one. It is worth repeating that statistic because it is just so mind-boggling: *thirty to one*!

Dad, now Sir Nicholas, a Deputy Lieutenant of Cheshire, was in some respects a more conventional figure, the product of a top public school and the Army. A Tory grandee. A knight of the shires. A conservative with a small c as well as a big C. But he, too, had a gloriously semi-detached relationship with his party. Any Tory whip who assumed he would just troop meekly through the Conservative lobby, whatever the issue, was in for a nasty shock. He was his own man, wayward and unpredictable, an odd mixture of Mr Toad and Dennis the Menace.

'If you have not upset the Establishment at some point,' he once told an interviewer, 'you have not been doing your job as a Member of Parliament.' He was prouder of being a non-conformist than he was of being a Conservative. It spoke to something deep in his personality. He probably had caveman ancestors who made nuisances of themselves in the Stone Age, scrawling graffiti on the cave walls or protesting against bison quotas. Once a rebel, always a rebel.

All government ministers have to budget for a certain amount of criticism from their own backbenchers. That is what parliamentary democracy is all about. But most MPs will pull their punches when they are taking issue with someone on their own side. Not my father. He would lay into underperforming Tory ministers with a savagery that would take their breath away and would leave his party colleagues tut-tutting and shaking their heads. Matthew

Parris of *The Times*, having observed Dad on the warpath, dubbed him 'Mr Angry of Macclesfield, the puce-faced, finger-stabbing Cheshire Snarler', and joked that he breakfasted on Rottweilers.

Dad once told an interviewer that he had achieved what he had achieved despite the fact that he was a Conservative, not because of it. He was not being big-headed: he just treasured his independence. And I am sure it is no coincidence that the three Conservative politicians he most admired – Winston Churchill, Margaret Thatcher and Enoch Powell – had a similarly uneasy relationship with their party. Churchill defected to the Liberals before returning to the Conservative fold. Thatcher was ousted by the Tory old guard, who eventually found her too hot to handle. Powell was so far out of sympathy with the party leadership that he ended his days in the political wilderness. Dad would never have kidded himself that he belonged in such distinguished company. But, as he has told me many times, history is a great teacher. He knew that only political pygmies offer unswerving loyalty to their party. And the Britain he loved was not a land of pygmies.

To all but the most dedicated students of the Westminster village, politics is a game played on the front benches: a ritual joust that comes to a head every week at Prime Minister's Questions. The poor backbencher is just part of the chorus line. So most people living south of Watford have never heard of Nicholas and Ann Winterton. They are not even the best-known Conservative husband-and-wife team from Cheshire. That honour falls to Neil Hamilton, the former MP for Tatton, and his wife Christine, who became minor TV celebrities for a while, horsing about on game shows. But the Winterton story – rousing, even inspirational – has real human meat on it.

It is more comedy than tragedy, and it is a heartwarming comedy, with feel-good moments amid the pratfalls. It is a tale not just of political rough-and-tumble, but of perseverance, hard graft and honest sweat: two decent human beings trying to make a difference, sticking their heads above the parapet when it would have been easier to settle for the quiet life. I am hopelessly biased, of course, because I am their daughter. But I hope, when other people read their story, they will start to glimpse the flesh-and-blood human beings behind the lazy stereotypes of Fleet Street.

As a double-act – and they were as inseparable as Tweedledum and Tweedledee, practically joined at the hip – the Wintertons were passionate, combative, public-spirited, everything a back-bench MP should be. By the time they retired, they had become the longest-serving husband-and-wife team in the entire history of the House of Commons, with a combined service of sixty-six years – quite a feat when you remember that the average length of service for an MP is just seven years. Boisterous, obstreperous, occasionally eccentric, they were part of the furniture of the House, from the sepia-tinged days before Parliament was televised to the days of Twitter, iPhones and the 24-hour news cycle.

In the dog-eat-dog world of Westminster, where promising careers crash and burn and the faces change with terrifying rapidity, they were great survivors, re-elected time after time, usually with increased majorities. In October 1971, when my father was first elected, Britain had not yet joined the Common Market, as it was then known; Bobby Moore was still captain of the England football team; Rod Stewart's 'Maggie May' was top of the pops; and colour television was in its infancy. His final intervention in the Commons, before he retired at the 2010 election, was a question to Ed Miliband, who was just a babe in arms in 1971. His parliamentary career spanned seven Prime Ministers, from Ted Heath to Gordon Brown. He fired straight questions at all of them and if he did not like their answers he told them so.

I was still a toddler when he was first elected, still a schoolgirl when my mother followed him into Parliament in 1983. Cynics might say, after Oscar Wilde: 'To have one Tory MP for a parent may be regarded as unfortunate. To have two begins to look like carelessness.' But I have never been cynical about politics, or about life in general. When Mum joined Dad at Westminster, it felt like the icing on what was already a pretty special cake. I was still at boarding school the day she was first elected, but I can remember as if it were yesterday the little surge of pride I felt when Matron whispered the good news to me at breakfast.

Some people are born into politics. Some have politics thrust upon them. I suppose I fall into both categories. Apparently, I screamed and screamed and screamed at my christening, as if it had just dawned on me that being a Winterton would condemn me to a life dominated by all things political, from obscure by-elections to the latest opinion poll. But I have taken to being a Winterton like a duck to water.

Born into such an unusual family, my childhood was fun, action-packed, wildly unpredictable. Every day was different. Moments of high political drama – like the Falklands War and the toppling of Margaret Thatcher – were interspersed with moments of low comedy – like the time Rory Bremner rang our home number and pretended to be John Major. Poor Mum swallowed it hook, line and sinker. She was always too trusting for her own good.

Inevitably, there were sacrifices. During the week, my parents would be at Westminster, only returning home on Friday night. Even at the weekend, there is nothing remotely normal about the home life of a Member of Parliament – as I can testify from bitter-sweet personal experience.

A simple trip to the supermarket to buy groceries would turn into a three-reel comedy. One man would want to bend Dad's ear about the NHS. Another would moan to Mum about the traffic lights on the A54, as if she was personally responsible. Then someone in the check-out queue would mention Europe, or immigration, or law and order, and Dad would be off like a jack-rabbit, talking for England. A lot of it passed over my head, particularly when I was young, but I never became disengaged or cynical about grassroots politics. Being an MP was good. Being an MP was cool.

And Mum and Dad, though I say it myself, were fine specimens of the breed. A lot of backbenchers, whatever their party, are wimps, all talk and no trousers. They mind their Ps and Qs, stay out of mischief, crawl to their party leaders and keep their eyes trained on the main prize – promotion to the front bench. They are lobby fodder, meekly doing what they are told by the party whips. My parents, bless them, were made of sterner stuff. Much sterner stuff.

The casual observer of Parliament might look at my father's CV, note that he was a backbencher for thirty-nine years, note that he never held a frontbench ministerial position and think, 'Bloody hell! He must have been useless.' (He was briefly allowed to speak from the front bench as opposition agriculture spokesman, but only after ten o'clock – a bit like a swear word that is only permissible after the nine o'clock watershed on television.) Some of the Tory MPs who have made it to the frontbench have barely been able to get up on their hind legs without making fools of themselves. They would embarrass a rotary club in Watford. So what kind of gibbering halfwit must my father have been not to be called off the substitutes' bench?

The casual observer might then ponder the case of my mother – who did have two short stints on the front bench in opposition, but was never a minister – and reach a similar conclusion. If she was deemed no better than Whatsherface, the one with the short skirts and hyena-like cackle, she must have been *seriously* incompetent.

Well, the casual observer would be wrong, utterly wrong, and one of my main objectives in writing this book is to try to explain why. Success and failure in politics are infinitely more complex than is generally acknowledged.

Here's a challenge. Think of the single most useless government minister you can ever remember. Their party doesn't matter. Nor does their sex. Just try to picture them at their mumbling, bumbling worst, ducking and weaving, talking rubbish on stilts. The kind of also-rans who would still be making the coffee if they were working in your own office. Now get on the net and spend five minutes researching their parliamentary careers before they graduated from the back benches to the front bench. I can guarantee that you will find that they never said boo to their party leadership. Not once. Not even when their party leadership had lost the plot and made a complete hash of something.

My parents *did* say boo. Loudly and often. They have many sterling qualities, but the ability to suck up to people in the hope of securing advancement is simply not one of them. They have too much self-respect. My mother has some hilarious stories about her fox-hunting days when, if a certain member of the Royal Family joined the field when moving off from the meet, some members of the hunt would try to ride alongside him in the hope of exchanging a few words. That was not Mum's way.

And it was not Dad's way either. Anyone else with his track record would look back over his career and think wistfully, 'If only I had played my cards better *then*, I could have ended up in the Cabinet.' But he just doesn't approach politics like that. Compared with a politician like George Osborne – the master card-player of his generation, forever shuffling his pack, calculating when to play his aces and jokers – he had something artless about him. He lived for the political moment.

And where is George Osborne now? That's the great irony. He is yesterday's man, gone like the dew off the rose, not just because he ended up on the losing side in the EU referendum, but because his slick brand of politics – presentation-led, not substance-led – increasingly turned off voters. Again and again, he would pop up on our TV screens on a building site, in his hard hat and viz-glo jacket, as if to say, 'Look at me! The Chancellor for the working man! Not stuck behind my desk in Whitehall, but getting out and about, meeting real people!' But the trick wore thin. People started to see through the photo opportunities. They hankered for politicians who could call a spade a spade – something my father has been doing all his life, even when it cost him politically.

Almost from the day he entered the House, he was a maverick, a paid-up member of the awkward squad. One of his nicknames at home is Mav, in tribute to his erratic voting record: one minute trooping through the lobbies with his fellow Tories, the next with Labour or the Ulster Unionists. But he never rebelled for the sake of rebelling: he had clear principles and followed them, even when the whips were twisting his arm so hard it threatened to snap.

'Nick Winterton is ideologically all over the place,' mused John Major in his memoirs. 'If he had formed a government of his own, he would have had to splinter off as a maverick against himself.' Major, an ex-whip, probably thought that was an elegant put-down. But there are a lot of long-haired lefties who have never voted Conservative in their lives, who would read that passage and think, 'I agree with Nick! Tell me more about this bolshie bugger who got up John Major's nose.'

Dad got his knighthood in the same honours list as Sir Mick Jagger, which felt entirely appropriate. Two bolshie buggers! I like to think that the Whitehall mandarins drawing up the list that year had been long-haired lefties in their youth.

Fleet Street was never sure what to make of my father. They wanted to put him in the pigeon-hole marked Tory Right-Winger. He ticked a lot of the boxes, and numbered Enoch Powell and Ian Smith, the man who declared UDI in Southern Rhodesia, among his political heroes. But he was too big for that pigeon-hole, or any other pigeon-hole, and the smarter journalists could see that. At one point in his career, to his great amusement, *The Guardian* declared him 'a serious hero of democracy', which was like the *Daily Telegraph* showering bouquets on Ken Livingstone or Tony Benn. On many social issues, particularly when it came to defending his beloved NHS from spending cuts, he was a screaming liberal. Rumours of impending cuts only had to come trickling out of Whitehall for my father to react like an angry rhinoceros, charging head first at the minister responsible.

In 1990, in a typical intervention, he savaged the Health Secretary Kenneth Clarke for failing to ring-fence community care funds, accusing him of 'gross irresponsibility'. Clarke was generally regarded as so far to the left of the Tory party that he was in danger of toppling off the end. But trapped in his ivory tower in Whitehall, he had failed to notice what my father, with his extensive local knowledge, had seen with his own eyes – that the human cost of government spending cuts was just too great. 'We are gambling with the welfare, and indeed the lives, of the weakest and most vulnerable people whose care is our responsibility,' he wrote. Nye Bevan couldn't have put it any better.

His priorities as a constituency MP mirrored his priorities at Westminster. Asked to name his three proudest achievements as Member of Parliament for Macclesfield, he cited his support for Macclesfield District General Hospital, the East Cheshire Hospice and the Rossendale Trust, a charity providing care and support for people with learning disabilities. For forty years, he made a mockery of the theory that Tories do not have a social conscience.

I never felt prouder of him than when my son Jack was born in Chelsea and Westminster Hospital in 2009. One of the midwives looked at my nametag and said, 'Winterton? You're not related to Sir Nicholas Winterton, are you?' She knew him as the author of a major report on maternity services in his days as chairman of the House of Commons Health Select Committee, and as an indefatigable champion of her profession. He is actually an honorary vice-president of the Royal College of Midwives, which must merit a place on a list of 101 Weird Things You Didn't Know About Male Tory MPs.

Another little-known fact about my father is that he had the distinction, while chairing that inquiry into maternity services, of being the first chairman of a Commons committee to allow a woman to breastfeed her baby while giving evidence in public. Hard facts about the NHS had to be punctuated with contented gurgling noises from the baby. 'I wasn't totally comfortable with the situation,' he admits. 'Breastfeeding in public isn't really my bag. But there she was, giving evidence, and her baby was clearly hungry, so what could I do? I listened to her evidence and averted my gaze, like an officer and gentleman.' Just another comic moment in his roller-coaster career.

Looking back, my brothers Robert, Andrew and I had a privileged childhood. Not because we came from a wealthy family – back-bench MPs are quite modestly remunerated, whatever some people think – but because we had a privileged vantage point. Yes, our parents were away from home a lot and we were packed off to boarding schools. But any disadvantages in having two MPs for parents were far outweighed by the many bonuses. How many children get taken to tea in Downing Street? Or have the chance to roam like alley cats around the Houses of Parliament? Or go to receptions in the Speaker's State Apartments? Or go to the State Opening of Parliament on their birthday? Our parents had ringside seats at the great events of the age and were always happy to share insights and titbits of gossip not vouchsafed to the general public.

The fly in the ointment, always, was the nagging fear of my parents attracting the wrong kind of publicity – the kind that can catapult a hard-working back-bench MP into the spotlight, shredding reputations and putting families under strain. Politics can be a bruising profession, and as every observer of politics knows, the good guys are almost as likely to get bruised as the bad guys. Times without number, my eye was caught by a newspaper headline – MP IN PUB BRAWL or SHAMING OF TOP TORY – and I felt a little tic of anxiety before reading the story and thinking, 'Phew! It's someone else.'

For most of their careers, despite some rocky times, Mum and Dad escaped the Fleet Street lynch mob largely unscathed. They were lucky, in one respect: they plied their trade in a gentler age, before the coming of Twitter and the other bullying social media of the twenty-first century. You could get away with more then. Things were less likely to be blown out of all proportion to make easy headlines.

Browsing through old files, I came across the following delight-fully po-faced transcript of a TV news bulletin in September 1983:

'Mr Winterton's home near Congleton is empty this week. He and his wife Ann are in the Bahamas with a parliamentary delegation as guests of the Bahamas Tourist Board.'

The Bahamas! Yikes! Just two simple, factual sentences. But can you *imagine* the kind of kerfuffle that would follow such a news item today? The howls of outrage? The Gadarene rush to judgement? The vicious trolling of my parents? The paparazzi pictures of my mother in a bikini and my father in a Hawaiian shirt, downing a rum punch? Things were not so frenzied then – or so unfair to the individual.

There were some pretty hairy moments, like the time my father was sued for the little matter of $250 million by an American businessman. Mum's weakness for the kind of jokes that go down well at rugby club dinners, but look terrible in print, twice got her into hot water. Very hot water. On the second occasion, I had to mount an SAS-style operation to smuggle her out of her London flat under the nose of waiting reporters. And there were times when the Tory in-fighting about Europe became so bitter and demented that life was not much fun for anyone. But they had thick skins. They needed to. If they had retired in 2005, as they nearly did, their legacy would have been secure, their reputation intact. A long record of distinguished public service, etc. etc.

As it was, they fell victim, like scores of other MPs, to the expenses scandal that dominated the 2005–10 parliament and engulfed them in a tsunami of public anger, not just about expenses but about an entire political class. There has probably never been a worse time to be a back-bench MP. A once respected profession suddenly lay in the gutter. Hysteria was in the air, and even MPs whose actions, calmly considered, merited no more than a rap on the knuckles, were treated like petty criminals in rural China, paraded in shame through the marketplace.

Mum and Dad have been in the firing line for years. They knew that abuse went with the territory, and they had learnt to shrug it off. But when they heard that their own grandchildren had suffered abuse at school, simply for being called Winterton, it was a very bitter pill to swallow. Had the game been worth the candle? Was all this casual mud-slinging the reward for their decades of public service?

It was a wretched time for the entire family. When the expenses furore was at its zenith, I only had to say that my name was Winterton to attract disapproving glances. Winterton? Winterton? Weren't there some Tory MPs called Winterton who… Nobody could remember what it was that these dastardly Wintertons were supposed to have done, but their names had featured in shrill headlines in the *Daily Telegraph* and *Daily Mail,* so they must be wrong 'uns, mustn't they? The logic of the madhouse.

The low point for my parents came in 2008, when David Cameron, their own party leader, described the arrangements they had made for reclaiming rental payments on their London flat as 'indefensible'. Indefensible? What a joke. A parliamentary committee examined the matter and largely absolved my parents from blame. A barrister with two days' experience could have defended them without breaking a sweat. But try telling that to a panicky young party leader in the run-up to a general election. That glib 'indefensible', which Mr Cameron had the cheek to repeat, was like a slap in the face, and my parents feel the sting of it to this day.

I will be revisiting the expenses saga, acting as counsel for the defence, as it were, and I hope readers will give me a fair hearing and try to look at the issues dispassionately. The dust has settled now, and it is easier to put things in perspective. But at the time, as recriminations flew, *nothing* was in perspective. It was a hysterical time, as if the Salem witch trials had come to SW1. You could hardly open a newspaper without references to hands in the till and snouts in the trough. Nobody took the trouble to look at the *facts*: the smears were far more fun. And with MPs' standing at an all-time low, every other lapse in behaviour, however minor, was magnified. *Chez* Winterton, after years of rolling merrily along, taking the rough with the smooth, it felt as if the wheels were coming off.

My father copped it in the press, after a casual observation about first-class rail travel. Then he copped it again after giving a female

Labour MP a playful pat on the bottom in the Tea Room. The MP did not object – she and Dad got on well – but other people objected on her behalf and, although what goes on in the Tea Room would normally stay in the Tea Room, the feminists of Fleet Street had a field day. The tarnishing of Brand Winterton was complete. Mum and Dad limped through to the 2010 general election, but as they rode off into the political sunset, it was with very mixed feelings.

In their pomp, they had been effervescent, bubbling with optimism, classic glass-half-full types. They could see the funny side of anything and everything – including, most importantly, them-selves. It was never difficult for me and my brothers to tease them when they were in danger of taking themselves too seriously. Now they were suddenly downcast, angry, prey to bitterness. I would hear them bravely recite the old mantra, that they had no regrets, and know that they were determined to move on with their lives, without bearing grudges or feeling sorry for themselves. But some of the wounds – particularly the ones inflicted by fellow Tories – still festered. My heart went out to them. It was as if they were acting out Enoch Powell's famous dictum that all political careers end in failure.

But what a shame it would be if the many good things they did in politics were wiped out by a few isolated incidents, many of them exaggerated or distorted in the press. The purpose of this book is not just to put the record straight, where necessary, but to celebrate two remarkable backbenchers whose hallmark – call it bolshiness, call it a refusal to be bullied – is in increasingly short supply on the green benches of the House of Commons.

My parents were in the House so long, made so many speeches, asked so many questions, sat on so many committees, came to the rescue of so many constituents, were witness to so many great events, that a year-by-year chronicle of their careers would run to several volumes. This memoir, perforce, is no more than a highlights reel: a tale of triumphs and disasters; of parliamentary battles won and lost. I have not even attempted a chronological narrative, preferring a more thematic approach. But I have tried to capture my parents' qualities as human beings and, by looking back on key episodes in their careers, show how individual politicians – not just titanic figures like Winston Churchill and Nelson Mandela, but ordinary men and women with ordinary gifts – can make a real difference. I have also tried to dig beneath the cynical stereotypes and put flesh and blood on that much-maligned individual – the jobbing backbench MP, beavering away in obscurity, trying to articulate the hopes and fears of tens of thousands of people.

The story of one Cheshire family is also, if this does not sound pompous, a modern political morality tale. I would hope the book will shed light on what sort of people we want to go into politics in 21st-century Britain. Cynical careerists or public servants?

It has become a commonplace of political punditry – a commonplace to which Mum and Dad would heartily subscribe – that far too few of our senior politicians have had a life outside politics. They have come straight out of university, become researchers, then special advisers, perhaps dabbled in politics in Brussels, then won election to the House of Commons with a CV from which experience of the real world is largely absent. Most of them have never visited a farm or factory, let alone run a small business. And it shows, frankly, the moment they open their over-educated mouths in the House of Commons. They sound like keen sixth-formers, not products of the working world.

But there is another, related, problem which is arguably just as serious. The men and women queuing up to become MPs are not just the products of a narrow upbringing: they are power-hungry to an extent that would once have been unthinkable. They are ambitious for themselves rather than ambitious for their country. Up the greasy pole of power they climb, barely looking at the ground below, losing touch with their roots.

In an interview he gave in 1996, marking the twenty-fifth anniversary of his election to Parliament, Dad made a telling observation about the changing face of British politics:

When I was first elected, 20 per cent of my fellow MPs were career politicians wanting to be ministers or even Prime Minister. The other 80 per cent had come into politics through the sheer challenge of being a backbencher and constituency MP. Now it is the other way round.

Cynics would probably say he was living in the past. They would liken Winterton & Winterton of Westminster (Backbenchers of Distinction: No Committee Too Small) to one of those old family firms which fail to keep up with changing times and are eventually swallowed up by the competition. Who cares about mere back-benchers? They are just glorified spear-carriers. But I think the cynics would be wrong. In fact, I know they are wrong.

Change is not always synonymous with progress, and only someone with an exceptionally narrow view of politics would welcome the supplanting of the old-style 'good constituency MP', admired across the political spectrum, by the career politician, power-crazed and ruthless, forever eyeing the next rung up the ladder.

Everyone who has ever watched Prime Minister's Questions will have been irritated by those toadying government backbenchers who ask the Prime Minister to agree that the government is doing a splendid job blah blah – toadies who mysteriously end up on the front benches in the next reshuffle. My parents would never have stooped so low. They would have thought it a blatant abuse of Parliament.

There is a nice story told about my father which could equally have been told about my mother. A man was stopped in the middle of Macclesfield by a reporter and asked whether he would be voting Conservative at the next general election. 'No way,' he said indig-nantly. 'I've never voted Tory in my life. I'll be voting for Winterton.'

Needless to say, that is *not* the sort of story the Tory party hierarchy wanted to hear. By 2010, the leadership had become heartily sick of my parents. But in a funny way – certainly in Cheshire – they were *bigger* than their party. Bigger because their constituents knew instinctively that, whatever the political weather in Westminster, they would always put their constituents first. Bigger because there was more to Brand Winterton than simply being card-carrying Conservatives.

For every enemy they made, they must have made a hundred friends, and this family memoir, in which Macclesfield and Congleton will play as big a part as Westminster, will explain why. I would like to think the book will not just salvage the somewhat tainted honour of the Wintertons, but revive respect for an endangered species of politician: the man or woman who belongs to a political party, but is not the pawn of that party; who retains their independence, serves their constituents and votes according to their conscience, without fear or favour.

When David Cameron stood down last summer, his final quip at his final Prime Minister's Questions ('I was the future once') was a deliberate echo of a dig he had made at Tony Blair ten years before. It was a rueful, self-deprecating admission that he was just another here today, gone tomorrow politician. I was tempted to give the line another tweak, with reference to my parents. 'They were the past once.' And they *were* the past once: political has-beens from another era, their values derided, but now, post-Brexit, a cause they had championed for years, people with things to say about the future which might be worth listening to.

I have been intrigued by politics all my life. I live and breathe politics. I find the interplay of issues and personalities endlessly fascinating. I am also a Winterton. I inherited the bolshiness gene from my parents, and it has shaped my entire life. 'You're in danger of turning into a trade union leader,' one of my bosses once told me. She meant it as a warning that I was being insubordinate. I took it as a compliment: an acknowledgement that I was prepared to stick up for and protect my team, come hell or high water, the way my parents stuck up for their constituents.

At one point, I nearly followed my parents into the House of

Commons. In 2001, when the Tatton constituency was looking for a successor to Neil Hamilton, who had been defeated at the 1997 election, I considered putting my name forward. Three Tory MPs called Winterton representing adjoining seats in Cheshire would have been quite a coup. We could have formed an awkward squad without parallel in the annals of the House of Commons. They would have had to build a separate division lobby to accommodate our idiosyncratic views. But I thought better of the idea, went into political strategy and communications instead, and the Tatton Conservatives plumped for someone called George Osborne who, at 29, was even wetter behind the ears than me.

But if Parliament needs its high-fliers, its big beasts, what it needs just as badly is MPs rooted in their communities whose loyalty to those communities is paramount; who relate to ordinary people and, when asked a question, just say what they think, in plain English, without clearing the answer with No. 10 first.

Every constituency should have one, though alas, not many do. It is the careerists, the time-servers, the party hacks, who get advancement. But Macclesfield and Congleton *did* – thanks to the magnificently bloody-minded couple who brought me into the world.

2

JOHN WAYNE RIDES INTO MACCLESFIELD

As a child, I could not keep up with my father. Not many people could. There was something elemental about him, a zest for life, an energy that seemed unquenchable. The world tends to think of back-bench MPs as sedentary figures, occasionally tottering to their feet to catch the Speaker's eye. But my father was not, and is not, a sedentary man. Well into his late twenties, he played rugby for the Sutton Coldfield 1st XV. 'What position?' I once asked. 'Left wing. That fooled 'em!' He was also a stalwart of his local tennis club. And, unlike so many MPs, he did not abandon his sporting interests when he entered the House.

Asked to list his hobbies for a political reference book, he came up with the startlingly homogenous quintet of 'squash, tennis, swimming, jogging and skiing'. A parliamentary pentathlon. Let other MPs affect an interest in the novels of Marcel Proust or obscure German landscape painters. His own hinterland was much simpler, rooted in vigorous physical exercise. When the House of Commons gym opened in the 1980s, he was one of the first MPs to sign up. He liked to keep himself trim, burning off a few hundred calories before heading off to chair a committee meeting.

He was slightly built, and no more than average height, so he did not naturally dominate a room, but he had fire in his belly and people could feel the heat of it. You did not want to cross him, whether you were a Cabinet minister or a traffic warden. Even the law-abiding squirrels of East Cheshire would feel the full force of his fury, peppered with an air-gun if they strayed onto his precious bird-feeder. Out walking, Dad never ambled, he *strode*, as if perpetually in a hurry. He looked like what he was – a man who had decided to do something with his life.

Parliament flattens politicians, turns three-dimensional human beings into characters from a cartoon strip. On television, one middle-aged male MP looks pretty much like another. The suit has become the uniform of an entire profession. All the viewer sees is a lot of grown men shouting and a sea of grey. 'They are all the same!' cries the voice of cynicism. The human nuances are missed.

But, growing up in his shadow, I could hardly miss my father's nuances. He was all nuances, as gloriously, indelibly individual as a character in Shakespeare or Dickens. A very simple man in some ways, the sort who looks people in the eyes and says what he thinks, he was a highly complex one in others. The more I got to know him, the more I became conscious of hidden emotional deeps, little psychological riddles.

A lot of the time, he would come across as a true-blue, flag-waving pillar of the British Establishment. But then, out of nowhere, he would suddenly give the Establishment a good hard kicking. He was a mass of contradictions. One minute he would be starchy and strait-laced; the next he was like a naughty schoolboy himself, trying to sneak illicit goods into the dorm while Matron wasn't looking. I have seen him in all seasons and all moods, but never quite got the measure of him.

When he was first elected as an MP, at a by-election in 1971, one on-looker joked that 'a blond John Wayne' had ridden into Macclesfield. It was a shrewd observation. The comparison might have been meant ironically, but it had a germ of truth. To the leafy lanes of Cheshire in the '70s, that somnolent pre-internet world where nothing moved faster than a cow, Dad brought verve, passion and a dash of heroism, braving the brickbats of political life the way John Wayne ducked Apache arrows. He was a man in a suit, but he was also so much more.

MPs have had such a bad press lately that we have lost sight of the chivalrous instincts that – far more than personal vanity, I would suggest – brought people like my father into politics in the first place. In the fractured landscape of post-war Britain, where politicians across the board wanted to build a better country, even if they disagreed about how to do it, the flame of idealism still flickered.

Tory or Labour, most rank-and-file back-bench MPs – certainly the ones of my father's generation whom I have met – were fired by a genuine sense of public duty. They saw the chance to make a difference, and to stand up for the little people, the men and women whose votes had taken them to Westminster. If they had not got into the House of Commons, they would probably have tried to serve their communities in other ways: as JPs, perhaps, or as parish or district councillors, or simply as umpires of their village cricket team. The notion of service – perhaps it was a legacy of their parents' generation, who had been called to make such heroic sacrifices for their country – was central to their entire worldview.

In the middle of Bristol – well worth a detour, for anyone visiting the city – there is a statue commemorating the great eighteenth-century politician Edmund Burke, inscribed with words he used in his first election address: 'I wish to be a Member of Parliament to have my share of doing good and resisting evil.' What a modestly worded manifesto! Have my share... That was Dad in a nutshell. He did not imagine himself on the steps of 10 Downing Street, cheered by enormous crowds. He just wanted to do his bit in a good cause.

It sounds rather banal, put like that. But that really was the way most ordinary MPs – men and women who had grown up in the grey post-war years, with memories of rationing still fresh – used to think. They knew that, compared with defeating Hitler, the challenges facing them at Westminster were quite prosaic. More houses. Better schools. More roads. Better health care. But that didn't matter. They just wanted to build a better Britain for themselves and their families, brick by patient brick.

One must not romanticise the past. Then as now, there were some complete bastards in the House of the Commons, and there always will be. Politics brings out the worst in people as well as the best: it can be a cut-throat business. But having watched my father at close quarters, and seen what makes him tick, I am sure I am right to emphasise the strong streak of chivalry in his make-up. Miss the chivalry and you miss the man.

For forty years, day in, day out, he could not see a constituent in trouble without wanting to ride to their rescue. Being a county councillor and then an MP brought him into contact with a bewildering range of humanity: a few crooks, a few crackpots, but often people whose plight was genuinely desperate and who needed his help.

He has never forgotten the case – very early on in his political career, when he was a county councillor in Warwickshire – of the daughter of a local family who was suffering from progeria, an extremely rare genetic condition which causes children to age prematurely. She was still at primary school but, because of her frail physical condition, the head teacher felt she would be safer receiving individual education at home. The girl herself, who was as bright as a button, was desperate to stay at her local school with her friends and lead as normal a life as possible. My father, after visiting the family in their home and talking to both the parents and the daughter, was convinced that the interests of the child were paramount and waded into the case with fervour. He got his way, and the girl remained at the primary school. At such moments, he felt a genuine sense of fulfilment: quiet pride in a job well done. Helping people in Warwickshire and Cheshire made the dog days of politics – the long hours, the interminable committee meetings – worthwhile.

For all the fact that he was a conviction politician, with trenchant opinions, he did not give a damn whether the people who came to him for help were Tory, Labour or Liberal Democrat voters, or did not support any party at all: they were *his* constituents, his responsibility. One of his best-known contemporaries at Westminster was the Rev. Ian Paisley, who was famous for that same even-handedness. Even Paisley's worst enemies, who regarded him as a religious bigot, acknowledged that he dealt with problems raised by Catholic constituents as assiduously as he dealt with ones raised by Protestants. And when my father was able to help constituents get something they could not have got without his efforts, he derived more pleasure from that than anything else. It might be something seemingly trivial, but that was irrelevant. Small things can often make big differences.

He learnt that lesson very early on in his political career, when he was a county councillor in Warwickshire. One of his most cherished memories of that period was helping a boy from an impoverished mining family get the uniform grant he needed to get a place at the Queen Elizabeth Grammar School in Atherstone. When he visited the family in their home, the father was slumped in an armchair in a string vest, begrimed with coal dust, the mother ironing and the daughter of the house holding hands with her boyfriend on the sofa. But he was so touched by the sight of a studious eleven-year-old boy doing his homework at the kitchen table amid the chaos that he resolved to do something about it. The boy not only got his place at grammar school, thanks to the uniform grant, but went on to become a doctor. He never forgot what my father had done. In fact, the two men stayed in touch for a number of years. My father's life has been packed with so many similar episodes that they could fill a book in their own right.

In his very last week in Parliament, in 2010, my father found himself lobbying – successfully – on behalf of the son of one of his constituents who had gone to work in Qatar, but then been refused permission to leave Qatar, thanks to the Qatari government's no-torious insistence on exit visas. The case was light years away from the kind of bread-and-butter issues, such as housing and traffic calming and school places, with which he was used to dealing. But at the bottom of it, as always, was a fellow human being in trouble who had come to him for help.

In the Commons, he could be a tub-thumper, a no-frills orator. In Macclesfield, he had to strike subtler notes. On one occasion, he found himself in the home of some constituents whose teenage daughter had got pregnant while living in a squat. He had to take the girl into a separate room, leaving the door open, so that her parents could not object, and much as a good GP would have done in the same situation, cross-examine her gently and delicately about whether she wanted to have the child. (In the event, she did, married the father and, with Dad's help, they got the council housing they needed.) He did not learn those skills at Westminster.

As a constituency MP, he was part social worker, part trouble-shooter, quick on the draw when he spotted an injustice. The spirit of the old Wild West coursed through his veins, and for him, polit-ics was one long game of Cowboys and Indians. Not surprisingly, classic John Wayne Westerns were among his favourite films.

In personality, he was, and is, hopelessly old-fashioned: a dinosaur from his regimental tie to his perfectly knotted boot-straps. Does he mind being called a dinosaur? Not a bit of it. He is the proudest brontosaurus in the forest. In fact, he regularly attends meetings of a group called 'the Dinosaurs': like-minded souls from the distant past. They sit around in a cave in London, aka the Carlton Club, talking about the good old days, before new-fangled inventions like wheels.

Dad's tastes and habits haven't changed in fifty years. He is a bacon-and-eggs man, not a cappuccino-and-croissant man. He stands ramrod-straight during the National Anthem. His musical education stopped with the Beatles. I *think* it was the Beatles – it might have been Dame Vera Lynn. (He also liked Jim Reeves, the American country singer, and even went to a gig – except he didn't call it a gig, of course – by the Platters, early exponents of rock and roll in the early 1960s, to impress Mum.) He detests, absolutely *detests*, political correctness in all its forms. As for modern technology… Don't get me started on *that*.

There are probably men born in 1938 who know less about computers than my father, but I have yet to meet one. He will go to his grave without having sent a single email, which some people would say was taking small-c conservatism too far. He will peer at a BlackBerry or iPad as if it was a ticking bomb. He has to have social media explained to him very slowly, in words of one syllable. But if he were less old-fashioned, would I love him so much? It is his pre-Twitter innocence, a boyishness of outlook that is refreshingly untouched by cynicism, which is his most endearing quality.

For a seasoned politician, who should know the rules of the political game by now, he can be extraordinarily naïve, the complete reverse of image-conscious. When he was an MP, he just said what he thought without worrying about how his words would look in the next day's newspapers. I don't know if anyone has ever kept a tally of British politicians who have given straight answers to straight questions with the greatest frequency, but N. Winterton would come close to the top of the list.

A word he uses a lot when talking about politics and politicians is 'genuine'. Does so-and-so look you in the eyes and deal with you in a straightforward way? Or is there something slippery about them? Hidden agendas lurking beneath the surface? When he thought someone was genuine – like Roy Mason, the former Labour Northern Ireland Secretary, celebrated for his plain talking – he respected them for that, even if they were political opponents. I once asked him how many of the 650 MPs in the House of Commons passed his genuineness test. 'About 100. If that.' Which is pretty depressing, when you stop to think about it.

He once astonished his fellow MPs during a debate by admitting that he was wearing a second-hand suit – a hanging offence in the Conservative Party, which likes to out-do Labour in matters of haberdashery, and regards even off-the-peg suits as plebeian. (He had been given the suit by a fellow county councillor whose husband had died and, as it was a good-quality suit, decided to save himself a few bob, as is his wont.) He added that he hoped to pass the suit on to one of his sons, which made the Wintertons sound like ragged paupers in a Victorian novel and probably made my brothers cringe in embarrassment. But that's just how he was: candid and unpretentious.

At the time of the 1971 by-election I was still a baby, so I have no memory of the occasion, obviously. But Dad has kept the photograph that appeared on the front page of *The Times* the morning after the election, showing the victor with his arms held aloft like a prize-fighter and his beautiful young wife by his side. There is an onlooker in the background shielding his eyes, as if dazzled by the sheer brilliance of this charismatic young couple. You can almost smell the giddy optimism of the times. Dad was thirty-three, young for an MP, but looks even younger, a thrusting politician from a new generation.

Some idiot apparently tried to heckle him at the count, when the result was announced, but Dad was having none of it. 'This is a *victory*, whether you like it or *not*!' he bellowed. Returning insults with interest has been a hallmark of our family ever since. You don't mess with the Wintertons. You'll get a bloody nose if you try. In fact, Dad's propensity to fight fire with fire has been one of his most enduring characteristics.

There is something choleric, even splenetic, in his make-up. He can be as fiery as raw cayenne pepper when provoked, and many a minister at the despatch box has been wrong-footed by the ferocity of the Member for Macclesfield's interventions. One reporter in the House of Commons Press Gallery drew his readers' attention to 'the crimson Winterton face, lightly covered with apoplectic perspiration'. I must have seen that face a thousand times.

There was a telling moment at a political meeting in the 1971 by-election campaign, which may amuse Tory-ologists. A bespectacled man in a grey suit sidled up to my mother and asked if he could have a word. It turned out to be Sir Geoffrey Howe, the Solicitor General. Howe was later a major player in the Thatcher administration, of course, and one of the big political beasts of the 1980s. But he was such a mumbling orator that Denis Healey famously likened being attacked by Howe to being savaged by a dead sheep. And what did the future dead sheep mumble into my mother's ear during the 1971 by-election? 'I do think mumble mumble that you should mumble mumble tell Nicholas mumble mumble not to shout.' Nick Winterton not shout? Mum had married a man with a carrying voice – if you set a Winterton speech to music, it would be scored *fortissimo* – and that was how she liked it. One of his Tory contemporaries joked that he was 'a megaphone populist'. We have always been what you might call a decibel-rich household.

Dad had fought and won two more parliamentary elections, in February and October 1974, before I really began to connect with this mysterious male figure in my life: a whirl of energy, always on the move. My earliest memories are of clinging on to the leg of a man in a suit, trying to slow him down, as he careered around Macclesfield and the surrounding villages. It was hopeless. Dad was always leaving me behind or wondering off without me! I did lose him sometimes, but was quick to learn my address off by heart and where to find the 'lost children' tent or police from very early on in life!

Off he would stride, dragging me in his slipstream, to greet some old biddy I had never seen before, like a long-lost friend. 'Mrs *Johnson*!'

Their ensuing conversation would pass so far over my head that it might as well have been in Serbo-Croat.

'…something be done about it?'

'Something *is* being done about it, Mrs Johnson. Only last week I managed to persuade the under-secretary of state… It's all there in black and white in Hansard…'

'…just doesn't seem fair. Not after what happened last time.'

'I couldn't agree with you more, Mrs Johnson… Ted Heath never quite managed to… Of course, the trouble with people like Shirley Williams… Only in Brussels… That's why…'

There were many Mrs Johnsons in my childhood, although I must have been five or six before I learnt the right collective name for them. Constituents. Try saying that when you are a lisping girl at primary school. All children have to share their father with someone else, someone whose demands on his time they come to resent. It might be their mother. It might be their siblings. It might be their father's scary new girlfriend. In my case, it was the 70,000-odd voters of Macclesfield, some of them very odd indeed. Who *were* all these people, bewildering in their variety, who seemed to command so much of Dad's attention?

From the age of three or four I knew, because Mum told me, that my father was 'someone important', and that was why he spent so much time away from home. When the House of Commons was sitting, he would drive down to London on a Sunday night, returning late on Friday afternoon. Little by little, the 'someone important' achieved sharper focus, and I started to understand what an MP was, and what he did. But a lot of it was still quite vague. To the usual riddles of childhood, such as where babies come from and why some teachers are grumpier than others, there were added dozens more. Why Big Ben? What did the Home Secretary do? What were Bills and who paid the bills? Could women play this game called politics? Who was the sinisterly named Chief Whip?

In the 1970s, the televising of parliament still lay years in the future, so back-bench MPs were shadowy figures, respected without being understood. I certainly would never have boasted about Dad's job in the playground at the village school. I would have been met by uncomprehending gawps. An engine driver would have had more cachet. As for what he did at the weekends, charging hither and thither, on foot or by car, meeting people, talking to people, shaking hands with every Tom, Dick and Harry in Cheshire, it was a mystery. Little by little, I was being inducted into a strange world, simultaneously scary and exciting.

When we are very young, we think our own childhoods are normal because they are all we know. But by the time I was eight or nine, I had no such illusions. Life as the daughter of a Member of Parliament was lots of the things, but it was emphatically not normal. The stage on which our lives was played out was just too crowded. There was a supporting cast of thousands, all jostling for attention, all bound up with their own problems and a fair proportion of them barking mad. Or so they seemed to me as a child, struggling to keep up, struggling to make sense of my life. There I would be, desperate for a pee on a route march around the constituency, and some old fart I had never met would ask Dad a question about the Common Agricultural Policy, and he would be off. Aaaaagh!

I was a painfully shy girl, so I found talking to strangers an ordeal at the best of times. To talk to hundreds and hundreds of them, as Dad did, chatting nineteen to the dozen to a man on a bicycle or a woman with a shopping bag, was unimaginable. One thing that amazed me – and still amazes me – was his knack of remembering names. To this day, you can show him a photograph of a prep school rugby team and he can put a name to every face, after more than half a century. He has a highly retentive mind – a priceless gift in a politician. Forget some small but significant detail and you can be sure of one thing in politics – your opponents will *not* have forgotten it.

You would not describe my father as a smooth-talker, a charmer, a ladies' man, but he was extremely engaging, at ease with people of all backgrounds, and as ready with questions as he was quick with answers. If John Wayne was a man of few words, the strong, silent type, my father was a man of so many words that there ought to be a psychiatric term for his condition. 'God gave me a mouth and I have used it,' Dad told one interviewer. Has anyone ever informed the Almighty of this strange bequest?

He could talk for Britain and, Britain and Britishness being two of his pet themes, he regularly did. Did my attention sometimes stray when the Member for Macclesfield was in full flow, itemising everything that was wrong with Brussels/socialists/Robert Mugabe/ the NHS? You bet it did! If it had not strayed, I would have gone stark raving mad. I cannot put it any better than the journalist on a local paper who, after having his ear bashed by Dad on numerous occasions, paid him a wry compliment: 'Nobody could accuse Nicholas Winterton of reticence. If you asked him a question on Shrove Tuesday, he would still be talking on Good Friday.'

Queen Victoria famously said of Gladstone: 'He speaks to me as if I were a public meeting.' I know how Her late Majesty felt. Get Dad on to politics and, even at the kitchen table, he does not talk, he orates, structuring his arguments and using rhetorical questions to make his points. 'Do I believe that, when Margaret Thatcher took on the miners, she considered that she was acting in the national interest? Yes, I do. Do I believe, on the other hand, that mistakes were made which, with the benefit of hindsight...' You can boil a kettle, eat a bowl of muesli and read the *Daily Mail* cover to cover during some of his longer orations.

In family folklore, one episode that has lingered down the years, and grown with the telling, is the time my father took my brother Andrew – who was seven or eight at the time – on a drive around the constituency. He stopped outside one constituent's house and, with the immortal words 'I'll be back in ten minutes', locked Andrew in the car. Social services would have had his guts for garters nowadays – the windows were shut and the poor boy could hardly breathe. Two *hours* later – by which time Andrew had read a book, scratched his nose till it bled, familiarised himself with the contents of the dashboard and generally lost the will to live – Dad returned with a sheepish grin on his face. We saw a lot of that sheepish grin, particularly in election years.

Politicians are famous for liking the sound of their own voices, of course, and you would have to say that Dad fitted the stereotype like a glove. He once raised £2,000 for charity after keeping silent for 2,000 seconds, but only after he had been physically gagged – he could not have completed the challenge otherwise. But his garrulousness had a kind of innocence about it that was ultimately more attractive than off-putting. He just couldn't help himself. He was all emotion, wearing his heart on his sleeve in a way that was quite rare among Englishmen of his generation.

As a country, we are world-famous, particularly our men, for being laconic and emotionally reserved. That was particularly true in the years after the war, when the stiff-upper-lip attitudes that had helped win the war were still widely admired. But Dad hadn't read the script. He didn't believe in being stoical, biting his lip, suffering in silence. He let it all hang out, like a Frenchman or an Italian – *not* that he would welcome the comparison. In true dinosaur tradition, he is inclined to be suspicious of dinosaurs with foreign accents.

My brother Andrew – now fully recovered from his trauma in the locked car, although he still twitches when Dad says he will be back in ten minutes – maintains that my father's natural loquaciousness was the key to his success:

> He was an instinctive politician, which put him in a small minority. What he thought, he spoke, straight out, without mincing his words. It was a rare gift, and one he shared with Mum. The trouble with 90 per cent of politicians today is that they are too circumspect. They look at every issue, and every question, and calculate what is in it for them. They choose their words with extreme care, terrified of being misconstrued. Dad was never calculating in that way. He went with his heart and trusted his own instincts, even at the risk of putting his foot in his mouth.

That knack of straight talking – or shooting from the hip, to use another John Wayne analogy – is intrinsic to any understanding of my father. It was in his DNA. He aligned himself four-square with Margaret Thatcher, who once described herself as 'a politician of instinctive reaction'. Dad loved that line.

In 1992, when Madonna's sexually explicit coffee table book *Sex* was published, to a chorus of disapproval, he was even quicker on the draw than the Vatican in calling for it to be banned. 'This is a vile, obscene and pornographic book,' he opined. 'Filth of this kind should not be sold in our shops.' Did he solemnly read the book cover to cover before coming to that conclusion? Did he linger over the picture of Madonna hitchhiking naked in Miami? Or the images of bondage and sado-masochism? I hope not! He just didn't like the sound of it, and went with his gut instincts. And if you told him that *Sex* is now regarded, in some quarters, as a bold post-feminist work of art, he would embark on one of the throaty rants that have made life in the Winterton household so entertaining over the years.

Other politicians of his generation might have been cleverer, more wily, more sophisticated, but very few were as fluent in the way they communicated with the man in the street. His own father – whom I never met – had been an auctioneer in a long-established family firm in Lichfield, and no doubt that contributed to his breezy, confident manner. I marvelled at his confidence because I had none of that confidence myself. But it could also be quite exhausting to someone living in his shadow.

The trouble with instinctive politicians is that they use up so much energy on politics that there is not much energy left for anything else. As I traipsed around donkey derbies and church fetes, and Dad was button-holed by constituent after constituent, and they talked, and talked, and talked, a small worm of resentment started to grow. What about *me*?

Anyone who follows British politics will be familiar with the West Lothian question. In Macclesfield, there is also the Winterton question, one I have asked my father many times. 'Who matters more? Your family or your constituents?' Like a good politician, he has been ducking the question for years. Or he might just give a helpless shrug and say, 'Can't they *both* matter, darling?'

Divided loyalties have been the story of his life, and have coloured our relationship since the day I was born. Mum has never forgiven Dad for being late in picking her up after she had given birth to me at the local hospital because he was attending a meeting of a Warwickshire County Council committee. She felt that some things were more important than others and that – not for the first or last time – he had got his priorities wrong. I would probably have been christened Agenda or Any Other Business if she had not put her foot down.

I am certainly not trying to suggest that he was a bad or neglectful father. I was lucky enough to grow up in a close-knit family, where everyone got the chance to have their say, and Sunday lunches – the weekly gatherings of the clan – were glorious, raucous affairs, with a minimum of three members of the family talking simultaneously at any given moment. Considering that there is a spread of ten years between the three children, the Wintertons are a remarkably cohesive tribe, loyal to each other through thick and thin. An attack on one Winterton is an attack on all Wintertons.

One of my proudest memories of my father is of the time, late in his career, when Mum was in the dog-house and some wet-behind-the-ears journalist invited Dad to join in the chorus of denunciation. 'I will *not* criticise my wife,' he shouted, purple in the face. 'Would you criticise *your* wife?' If it had been Dad in the dog-house, Mum would have been equally vociferous, but not purple in the face. You will not find a more ferociously tribal family than the Wintertons of East Cheshire.

As a social institution, a way of life, family mattered hugely to him. In fact, you could say it was his bedrock. His own parents got divorced when he was still in his late teens – a much rarer occurrence than it is today – and he wanted better for his own children. His main business might have been in London, but he was emotionally bonded to hearth and home. When he drove home from Westminster on a Friday evening, his joy at seeing his nearest and dearest was touchingly evident. On many Fridays he would come laden with Smurfs, which he had picked up at a service station on the M6. They came free with the petrol, but it was the thought that counted.

He was quite a strict father, by modern standards, although hardly a martinet. He liked a well-run household in which he could play the paterfamilias, the centre of attention. Orderliness was tantamount to an obsession. He wanted everything to be done just so, and was thrown when there were disruptions to his various routines. Every Sunday evening, he would religiously polish all his shoes, a hangover of his Army days – he had done National Service, mainly in Germany. His tiny study beside the garage was always immaculate – not a file out of place, although there were so many you could build a house out of them. But behind the strict, well-ordered façade, there was a marshmallow centre.

The daughter who becomes Daddy's little princess, and can do no wrong, is something of a cliché, but it has a germ of truth in my case. I was an afterthought, born six years after Andrew, the second son in the family, and not given the warmest of welcomes by my brothers – classic sibling rivalry. Apparently, I was brought home from hospital shortly before Andrew's sixth birthday, for which he had asked for a new scooter. 'I would prefer a scooter,' he declared, when asked what he thought of his new sister. My brothers only really took to me when I was a little older and would lie on my bed kicking my legs in the air. In fact, my first family nickname was Georgina Best, because I was such a good kicker. Lucky I was not mad on sailing boats, or I would have been Edwina Heath.

My brothers would probably say I was spoiled rotten compared with them. My 'apple of my father's eye' status was cemented when I began to take far more interest in politics than they did, listening meekly to his orations at the kitchen table while they were stifling yawns.

In those days, Sunday mornings in our Cheshire home normally meant church – the Tory party at prayer, as someone famously described the Church of England. For Dad, it was as much a chance to glad-hand constituents as to worship. He liked being asked to read the lesson occasionally at one of the local churches. He also had a lusty singing voice, and would give 'Jerusalem' or 'All Things Bright and Beautiful' plenty of welly, belting out the hymns as if they were the Gettysburg Address. But I remember Sunday mornings when, if I kept schtum in my bedroom and hid under the duvet, Mum and Dad would enjoy a lie-in and give church a miss. I liked that slightly erratic element in our lives.

Dad was certainly an erratic parent when it came to my schooling. Like my brothers, I was packed off to boarding school – first to Homefield, sister school to Bilton Grange in Warwickshire, where he had been at school himself in the 1940s, then to Malvern Girls' College. I was very happy at both, I hasten to add, and never saw boarding schools as the glorified prison camps of popular myth. But his visits, though not frequent, had a way of going comically pear-shaped. Something about the boarding-school environment seemed to bring out the schoolboy in him.

On one occasion, he tried to aid and abet me in smuggling not one, but twenty packets of crisps into my dormitory (I already had an 'illegal' torch that Dad had hidden inside my Kermit the Frog teddy). Matron put the kibosh on that one. He enjoyed a bit more success with my brothers' school, smuggling jelly babies to them concealed in boxes of toy soldiers. He had no time for the pettier school rules, treating them with the same disdain as he treated EU regulations on fishery quotas.

You would have thought that, as a pillar of the House of Commons, he would have been on his best behaviour on school speech day. Not a bit of it. The speeches would get under way, a soporific calm would descend, and the only other sound was the popping of corks from behind the shrubbery, where Mum and Dad and other parent rebels would skip the speeches and spend the afternoon getting sloshed on white wine and playing baseball on the games pitch. Similarly, when they grew bored of the Sixth Form Leavers' Ball, they took a few bottles into my school study with close friend Alice's parents – Jimmy and Stina Whitehead. My Dad, remember, was a man whose maiden speech in the Commons had been on the theme of law and order. Appalling behaviour! I had long since learnt the single most important lesson of my childhood – having normal parents is overrated. Better card-carrying mavericks any day.

In an eccentric-rich environment like the House of Commons, Dad did not really stand out from the herd: he was just another middle-aged man in a suit. But when I compared him with some of my friends' parents – worthy country solicitors and doctors, by-words for middle-class respectability – I came to treasure his ability to go off-piste occasionally. I loved his quirks, his foibles. The eminent backbencher, chairman of a dozen committees, would suddenly morph into Benny Hill, playing the clown, pretending that his glasses were steaming up if a pretty woman appeared on television. To this day, if you ring him in his study in the Cheshire family home – his bunker, as he thinks of it – he is likely to pick up the phone and say: '10 Downing Street'.

I suspect that, like a lot of outwardly confident people, he has an underlying shyness which he tries to mask with humour. You can never be totally sure when he is being serious and when he is joking. He is a master of the dead-pan, tongue-in-cheek English humour that takes a bit of getting used to, and can baffle non-Wintertons.

As I got older, and boyfriends started to appear on the scene, there were some hilarious misunderstandings, little private jokes that backfired. 'Just so long as he's not a long-haired Old Etonian with an earring,' Dad said sternly, as I prepared to introduce him to – you guessed – a long-haired Old Etonian with an earring. 'Well, he'll need a medical check before he comes anywhere near this house,' he snapped, pulling a face. I thought it was the long hair and earring he objected to, but the real killer, Mum told me, was the Eton connection. They had seen enough toffee-nosed Old Etonians at Westminster to last a lifetime.

The Old Etonian bit the dust, but other boyfriends fared no better when it came to getting on the elusive Winterton wavelength. I hoped a Swiss boyfriend might cut the mustard, Switzerland being outside the EU and thus not part of the Evil Empire in Brussels, but the prospect of my migrating to the land of lederhosen and cuckoo clocks set alarm bells ringing in Cheshire.

Embarrassment was heaped on embarrassment in the mid-1980s,

when Mum and Dad appeared together on a daytime TV show presented by Esther Rantzen. The theme of the show was supposed to be whether politics and family life were compatible. But Dad hadn't read the script. He spent half the show saying what a beautiful, talented daughter he had and touting for a husband for me. He didn't actually say, 'British men with sound Conservative views preferred', but he came within a whisker of it, assuring would-be suitors that his daughter was good at housework – which I am certainly not. However, I did get some offers after the show!

Marc, my long-suffering husband, the one who finally made the cut, is Dutch – an even graver sin than going to Eton, jested my father on first meeting him – and still has to put up with tongue-in-cheek questions about his countrymen's passion for cannabis and euthanasia. *The Sun* reacted to our engagement and jumped upon the fact that Marc is European:

> Husband and wife MPs, Sir Nicholas and Lady Winterton have received a set-back in their anti-Europe crusade. Their only daughter is to marry – horror of horrors – a Dutchman. For lovely Sarah's sake, The Whip hopes mum and dad don't keep harping on about how the English language was only invented so the Dutch could communicate with the rest of the world.

You'll be pleased to know that Marc is hanging in there and gives as good as he gets by reminding us that the Dutch Navy beat the British Navy at the Battle of Medway, albeit a very long time ago in 1667 and I do remind him that it was the only time. While he must find the Wintertons a challenge at times, he also finds us great fun, calling us the 'Wound-Up Wintertons', and I even see glimmers of my father in him on occasion – oh help!

Marc and I got married in a registry office, rather than a church – officiated by a former doorkeeper from the Houses of Parliament, which made Dad very happy – and had a service of blessing afterwards. I was worried Dad would be disappointed, cheated of the chance to walk his only daughter down the aisle. But in fact he confessed to Mum – quite revealingly, in retrospect – that he felt relieved. 'I wouldn't have been able to do it without crying,' he told me, with a tremor in his voice.

The only other time I remember seeing him in tears was after his mother died. I have only a few, blurry memories of her, but Dad was very close to her and has always cited her as a major influence on his life, a kind-hearted woman with a strong sense of right and wrong. Mum also remembers her very fondly: she had been a pillar of strength during the early years of their marriage.

There were tears, too, not that I saw them, when I was sent off to boarding school for the first time. Mum and Dad drove me and my hamster, Honey ('that bloody hamster', as Dad called it) down from Cheshire to Warwickshire, said their goodbyes, then got back into the car and – as I learnt years later – burst into floods of tears in the lay-by just outside of school. I knew them as good, loving parents. I never knew quite how good and loving they were. Although I must add that they did forget to pick me up from school once and luckily my friend Susannah McAlpine's parents took me home with them!

Some of my happiest childhood memories are of family holidays, first in Devon and Wales, then later in Portugal, where Dad, ever the clown, turned into a parody of the Englishman abroad. 'Where are your oven chips?' he would ask bemused Portuguese shopkeepers, talking slowly, miming a packet of frozen chips and raising his voice to make himself understood. If he did not get his beloved chips, he would sulk, and revert to the safety of melon and Parma ham. A galloping gourmet he was not. In fact, he regarded almost all non-English food with visceral suspicion. But it was good to see him unwind. Needless to say, given Dad's boundless energy, there was no loafing about on sun-loungers. Brisk walks or ridiculously competitive games of tennis were the order of the day.

Family skiing holidays in Austria were another golden thread in my childhood. We went to the same resort every year for almost ten years and, again, it was Dad's determination to prove himself a match for Johnny Foreigner which provided the comic relief. He once appeared on the ski slopes in the morning wearing a Union Jack hat, before toppling over and disappearing down a crevasse, so that the hat was all that was still visible, like a British flag staking claim to Antarctica.

When the Wintertons were together, with time on our side – which was all too rare, alas – there was no stopping the laughter, the teasing, the larking about, the *joie de vivre*. We did not have to play at happy families: the happiness was there naturally. Aside from the usual dose of family rows, it really was a laugh a minute: imperishable memories. But always, day in, day out, throughout my childhood, there was the competing tug of politics: not just the great national debates to which Dad was party, but grassroots issues such as bin collection and hospital car parks.

Every MP who has ever been elected has paid lip-service to the idea that he is the servant of his constituents, but there cannot have been many who took that responsibility as seriously as my father. It sometimes seemed as if he was not so much his constituents' servant as their unpaid lackey, on call twenty-four hours a day. 'I've got to go, people expect it,' he would snap, if it was suggested that a family birthday party was more important than sheepdog trials or a dinner at the Macclesfield Rugby Club. Birthday get-togethers were planned a year in advance so as not to clash with important constituency commitments.

If he had gone on his own, it would not have been so bad. But there were times when he expected the entire Winterton clan to be on parade and, the Wintertons being insubordinate so-and-sos, there was mutiny in the ranks. Probably the closest Mum and Dad ever got to divorce was very early on his political career, when he wanted to attend a bingo evening at the Liberal Club in Atherstone and, keen to make a good impression on the locals, insisted that Mum accompany him, with three small children in tow, all scrubbed up to look like characters from *Mary Poppins*. It was the evening from Hell and, to this day, Mum wakes up in a cold sweat with a shout of 'Sixty-six! Clickety click!' ringing in her ear. She has never been to bingo with my father again, preferring to sit at home with a good book.

And if the call of duty took Dad beyond Macclesfield, into another north-west constituency, or indeed anywhere in the UK, he answered it, every time, even at the weekends. Here he is at two o'clock on a Sunday afternoon in August 1979 – August, for heaven's sake – rallying the Tory troops at the home of a Mr and Mrs Freeman of Mustard Lane, Warrington. 'We Conservatives are faced with a heavy task, an awesome duty, a great opportunity … This is no time for faint-hearts or trimmers…' You can question the sanity of someone turning the air blue on a nice summer afternoon with this sort of stuff. You cannot question their integrity – or their selflessness.

Like a dutiful vicar – one of his friends once suggested he should have gone into the Church – he found it impossible to say no. Some weekends, he would have half a dozen or more constituency engagements, and be out till two in the morning. But if there were times when I resented his ordering of his priorities, I have come to admire that professional assiduousness more and more the older I get. It's a rarity.

Who would *you* want to represent you at Westminster? A career politician, inching his way cautiously up the career ladder, or someone who remembered your name, respected your views and would go the extra mile to help you? Being an MP, as my father so vividly demonstrated, is more than a job: it is a vocation. You are responsible, even if only in a small way, for tens of thousands of people. If those people are let down, whether it is by the government or local authorities or hospital trusts, it is your job to seek redress for them. If they are pissed off about something, it is your job to make sure their voice is heard. And you cannot do all that from an office in Westminster. You need to be there on the ground, listening, taking soundings, being a pillar of the community in good times and bad.

The Queen is sometimes quoted as saying: 'I have to be seen to be believed.' Whereas Queen Victoria had become a virtual recluse after the death of Albert, the young Queen Elizabeth realised that the survival of the Monarchy depended on her being visible to her subjects, day in, day out. Dad felt the same way about his constituents: he *owed* them his presence. In fact, if you were to imagine a Queen who was not just conscientious and hard-working and steeped in the traditions of public service, but also had trenchant opinions and a voice like a fog-horn on the Mississippi, you might end up with an approximation to my father.

Quite a few Tory MPs, and not just the Old Etonians, can be snobbish and cliquey, and not over-enamoured of their constituents, whom they secretly regard as a nuisance. But Dad always seemed happiest when he was dealing with normal people and their normal problems. He thrived on human interaction, meeting people face to face.

If a constituent wrote to him with a problem, he would jump in his car and pay them a personal visit, rather than communicating by letter or holding constituency surgeries. He had tried surgeries for a few years, but not found them very satisfactory. Why should his constituents have to travel into the middle of Macclesfield to see him? Shouldn't it be the other way round? Just out of courtesy?

His more hands-on approach may have been unconventional, but he was only applying theories that are as old as politics itself. The word 'ambition', I once discovered, comes from the Latin word 'ambitio', which means 'going around', and was how Romans described what we would now call canvassing. If Pompus Maximus Tossa wanted to be elected consul, he would hawk himself around the Forum, making sure the plebs knew who he was. Dad driving around Macclesfield was following the same script. He knew that, if he called in on Mr Hoskins, who had written to complain about the local bus services, he would not only make a good impression on Mr Hoskins, but on Mrs Hoskins, the Hoskins's teenage daughter Jane, Granny Hoskins in the attic and the Hoskins's next-door neighbours, the Ramsbottoms. Six votes in the bag already!

And you would have to say the theory worked a treat. In 1971, when he was first elected, his majority was just 1,079, precarious to say the least. I have heard people in Macclesfield say that, if he had not been such an energetic candidate, the Tories would never have won that by-election. By 1992, it had swollen to a thumping 22,767, enough to fill Macclesfield Town FC's ground three times over. In twenty-one years, he had increased his majority by 21,000, or 1,000 a year, or twenty a week.

Even in 1997, when the party nationally was humiliated, he held on with nearly 10,000 votes to spare. Compare that with Michael Portillo, say, who sadly lost his Enfield Southgate seat in 1997, despite sitting on a majority of over 15,000. Other Tory MPs who had thought they represented safe seats got similarly short shrift from voters at that election. Perhaps they should have taken a leaf out my father's book and spent more time taking tea with Mr and Mrs Hoskins.

Drive around Macclesfield with him today and, every five minutes or so, he will say, 'I turned the first sod there' – one of those wonderfully old-fashioned English expressions that still pepper his conversations. His scrapbooks are filled with pictures of him, spade in hand, turning the first sod at new golf courses, new leisure centres, new hospitals. He was the sod-turner's sod-turner, the master spade-man of Macclesfield. He just loved being involved with new enterprises from the outset, particularly if he had been instrumental in lobbying for the necessary funds beforehand. And the locals appreciated that involvement. They really did. Every sod turned meant yet more votes for the sod-turner at the next election.

I have already told the story of the constituent who told a reporter he had never voted Conservative, but would vote for Winterton. Dad's personal standing in his constituency was such that, as election followed election, the word 'Conservative' on his election leaflets got smaller and smaller, while the words identifying *him* – The Right Man for Macclesfield, etc. – got bigger and bigger. That wasn't vanity. It was a recognition that a successful back-bench

MP cannot ride on the coat-tails of his party leaders: he needs to *earn* his constituents' gratitude by working tirelessly on their behalf.

After the 1983 general election, there was a storm in a teacup when an article in *Private Eye* alleged that my father had set up a secret slush fund in Macclesfield, contrary to election law. He had done nothing of the kind. He had simply established a small 'Nicholas Winterton Fighting Fund', properly audited, which did what it said on the tin. The £3,600 in the fund's bank account represented donations from well-wishers who wanted my father as their Member of Parliament, but were damned if they were going to give a penny to the Macclesfield Conservative Association. No law whatsoever had been broken.

Being an effective constituency MP is not a one-man or one-woman job, of course. An MP, particularly at election time, needs not just a small army of unpaid party workers, but a good agent – an important cog in the political machine whose role is often overlooked. Dad was particularly lucky in this respect. He was blessed with a series of excellent agents whom he regarded as personal friends. They included Gillian Rogers in Meriden, his very first agent when he was a county councillor; Arthur Moss in Newcastle-under-Lyme, a parliamentary seat he twice contested unsuccessfully; and Frank Horsfield DFC, Marguerite Shorter and Elizabeth Gilliland in Macclesfield, all of whom worked tirelessly for the cause.

My father was not just generous with his time, but had a naturally outgoing, inquisitive personality. He was a born mixer, at ease with people of every class, colour, creed and background. During election campaigns, he would go on an extended pub crawl of the constituency, sitting in pubs and working men's clubs sporting a bright blue rosette, happy as Larry, talking, talking, talking... A man in his element. The fact that, under election law, he was strictly debarred from bribing voters with drinks only deepened his contentment. His constituents could buy him a half of bitter if they were so inclined. But his money had to stay in his pocket. Result!

Whatever Dad's other faults, he is devoid of snobbery. He takes people as he finds them and doesn't put them in arbitrary pigeon-holes based on their social backgrounds. One of the minor tragedies of his final Parliament was the way an off-the-cuff remark he made about MPs needing to travel first-class between Westminster and their constituencies – so that they could do their paperwork in peace, basically – was reported as if it was a disdainful comment on the riff-raff who travelled standard class. That just wasn't the Winterton way.

He was not the kind of up-his-own-arse Tory MP – and I have met a few in my time, some of them so far up their own arses they couldn't find their way out again – who keeps constituents at a distance because he feels a cut above them. Quite the reverse. He was hungry, even ravenous, to spend time with them, listen to their concerns, argue with them, share a drink and a joke with them. That was what politics meant – and why, for my father, it became such a full-time occupation.

He was not an out-and-out intellectual, but he had a magpie mind, picking up little nuggets of information – about history, about geography, about different industries and how they worked – which would stay with him for years, and become the grist to his political mill. His Macclesfield constituency was part rural, part industrial, so he could relate to farmers and textile manufacturers alike. But he had also spent his early political years in areas where coal-mining was still part of the cement that bound communities together. He had been down mines. He knew and respected miners. Compared with the three most recent Conservative leaders – representing Folkestone, Witney and Maidenhead, respectively – he had a political hinterland that was as much working class as middle class.

His very last question in the House, in April 2010, was to the Labour energy secretary and future leader, Ed Miliband, pressing for the development of clean-coal technology as the best guarantor of the country's energy supplies. Miliband, who himself represented a mining area, Doncaster, was happy to salute a fellow MP who had been 'a fighter not just for coal but for manufacturing industry in general' and would be 'much missed in the House'. Party rivalries suddenly dissolved in a happy confluence of shared values and priorities.

But how much effort and energy it took to take up so many cudgels on so many other people's behalf! My brother Robert – who was never locked in a car for two hours, but feels as if he might have been – puts it very succinctly: 'Politics was Dad's life.' It was, and remains, such an all-consuming passion that it is almost impossible to imagine him in another profession. People used to say the same of Margaret Thatcher. 'No hinterland,' her critics muttered. Out of office, she shrivelled, became listless and apathetic. She had no other interests to fall back on, and that was her tragedy.

You would not call Dad tragic in the same way, but since he retired in 2010, I have noticed definite withdrawal symptoms. If you ask Mum, she will say she wished she had retired at the previous election, in 2005, before the shit hit the fan. There is a part of Dad that wishes he was still in the House, sitting on the green benches, tabling questions, chairing committees, staying on and on and on till he was Father of the House, the longest-serving MP. Who wants to be retired when you can happily work till you drop?

He misses the cut and thrust of Westminster more than he cares to admit. Even more, he misses the life of a constituency MP: the glad-handing, the problem-solving, the human dimension of politics. To go from being Mr Macclesfield to being just another man from Macclesfield has been a painful adjustment.

Enoch Powell was once asked after he had retired as an MP whether he missed the House of Commons. 'Not really,' he replied. 'What I most miss is my constituents.' Dad would have understood that perfectly. The ties binding an elected politician to the people who voted him into power – and the challenges and responsibilities that come with those ties – are the essence of democracy.

'It's in my blood,' he once said. I have got to know scores of MPs over the years and come to realise that, in matters political, there are two basic human types: the addicts and the non-addicts; the ones who inhale and the ones who do not inhale. Poor Dad, bless him, inhales. In fact, he has been taking great steaming gulps of the stuff, day in, day out, for more than fifty years.

3.

DOGS, SLIPPERS AND
COCKTAIL PARTIES

When did my father catch the political bug? What were the stepping-stones on the road to Westminster? It is a long story, but Dad being Dad, I have heard it a hundred times.

To set the scene, the Wintertons were a long-established auctioneering family in the West Midlands. There have been Wintertons putting lots under the hammer since 1864. The latest in the dynasty is Richard Winterton, who can be seen wielding his gavel on TV shows such as *Bargain Hunt*. The auctioneering proceeds paid the bills, but the Wintertons also had a long tradition of public service. They were an interesting clan, active on many fronts. One of my father's cousins, Father Gregory Winterton, converted to Catholicism, became Provost of the Oratory in Birmingham and was instrumental in advancing the cause for the beatification of Cardinal Newman.

Dad's paternal grandfather, Harry, became Mayor of Lichfield and was later made a freeman of the city after nearly fifty years of service to the community. He sounds a colourful character, as he does his wife, whom Dad remembers dressing up as a witch and chasing her grandchildren around the garden at Westgate in Lichfield.

I never met Dad's father Norman, although you can get a flavour of him from old family photographs. He was quite slender, with a pencil moustache, and a snappy dresser, judging by his double-breasted suits. Dad likes to tell a story about him beginning 'He danced with Queen Ena of Spain', which sounds as if it should be the first line of a dirty limerick. He looks pretty self-assured, from his photographs, and no doubt he passed some of that on to Dad.

But it was Dad's mother Veronica who first pointed him in a political direction. She was a dyed-in-the-wool Conservative from a solid middle-class Tory family – her father was a doctor in Leamington Spa – and served as a parish councillor and diocesan church councillor in the village of Longdon, near Rugeley, in Staffordshire. It was hardly classic Tory territory – Rugeley was then a mining town, with a solid Labour base – but Dad has fond memories of accompanying his mother when she went canvassing on the doorsteps of the Pear Tree estate.

It must have been an odd experience, knocking on the doors of complete strangers, working class to their boot-straps, and asking them if they were going to vote Conservative. But he loved the element of adventure, the thrill of the unexpected, the battle for hearts and minds. A seed had been sown.

He always shudders if asked if he was ever a Young Conservative – *not* a breed whom he holds in high regard, probably because they spend half their time getting pissed – and until his mid-twenties remained interested in politics without becoming an out-and-out activist. 'I had always been Conservative and thought the party, even at its worst, was the best of a bad bunch, but had never been a member,' he later said of his early years. To an energetic young man, the ultra-traditional Conservative Party of Harold Macmillan, Anthony Eden and Sir Alec Douglas-Home – an Old Etonian hat-trick to make the most committed Tory blush – must have had as much appeal as a visit to the dentist.

To this day, some Tory MPs behave as if they have been put down for the House of Commons at birth, but my father spent his formative years living and working in the real world – a badge of honour he wears far more proudly than if he had gone to Oxford or Cambridge. It was his life experiences that shaped the way he thought about politics, not anything he had read in books.

He grew up in a large-ish country property, Lysways House, which was a wing of Lysways Hall, in the village of Longdon Green, between Lichfield and Rugeley. In addition to his mother and father, the cast-list included his sister Susan, who was eighteen months younger than him, and a pedigree bull mastiff called Raymond which had been given to him as a Christmas present. 'A magnificent specimen,' Dad will tell people to this day, when he is in sentimental vein. And Raymond certainly was a superb-looking animal, although he was to end his days in unfortunate circumstances.

To cut a long – and for my father, quite traumatic – story short, the neighbours who lived in Lysways Hall had two wire-haired terriers with whom Raymond came into conflict. One of them bit Raymond on the nose as a puppy and, some years later, Raymond decided to get his own back and the terrier had to be put down. Raymond rushed towards the other terrier when she got into our garden, and the terrier collapsed and died – although not, my father insists, through any fault of Raymond, who never touched the other dog. The long and the short of it was that my grandparents, keen to stay on good terms with their neighbours, had Raymond put down without telling my father – a loss he felt keenly, for obvious reasons. Still, the episode had bequeathed him an invaluable lesson in life – always get your retaliation in quickly. At Westminster, he enjoyed releasing his inner Raymond, so to speak (Raymond is also his middle name), and took no nonsense from the terriers snapping at his heels.

Like many other middle-class children of that era, Dad was packed off to boarding school at the earliest opportunity. At the age of six or seven, after his mother was hospitalised for a few weeks, he found himself imprisoned without trial at a small Catholic establishment, St Bede's, where boys could get off lessons by the simple expedient of saying that they had to go to confession. Dad, recognising a good thing when he saw one, went to confession as often as possible, no doubt regaling long-suffering priests with interminable tales of non-existent sins.

The rest of his education was comparatively uneventful. His parents belonged to the professional middle classes rather than the landed gentry but, like thousands of similar families – including Mum and Dad later – put a high premium on education. They would always rather send their children to good independent schools than splash the cash on fast cars or foreign holidays. So, after the Catholic interlude, Dad was sent to Bilton Grange prep school in Warwickshire, then to Rugby School, immortalised in *Tom Brown's Schooldays*. It was possibly a notch or two below Eton and Harrow in the social pecking order, but still the leading public school in the Midlands. He didn't tear up any trees academically, but horsed about in Gilbert and Sullivan productions and excelled at the game that gave the school its name. There is a wonderfully evocative picture of him playing rugby at school, ball in hand, running like the wind and executing a perfect hand-off.

There were few clues to his future career in politics, beyond his membership of the school debating society. His House Master in Stanley, 'Bopper' Chase, wrote in one school report: 'Winterton, N. must always be given responsibility because he responds to it well.' But how much responsibility could Winterton, N. be trusted with? Then as now, he seems to have had an errant streak. On one occasion, he helped a younger boy with his Latin homework by lending him a crib and, when his 'crime' was discovered, was summoned to see the headmaster, Sir Arthur fforde. It could potentially have been a flogging offence, but the headmaster, bizarrely, offered him a glass of non-alcoholic sherry. It no doubt helped that fforde, like Dad's stepfather Kenneth Cole, was a former partner at Linklaters & Paines, the London solicitors.

On becoming a prefect – in this respect, nothing had changed since *Tom Brown's Schooldays* – my father was given the authority to administer corporal punishment to younger boys, using a carpet slipper. Only in England... The same thing happened to Douglas

Hurd, later Tory Foreign Secretary, at Eton. Hurd discharged his duties with such enthusiasm that he acquired the nickname Hitler Hurd. No such stigma attached to my father although there was an amusing twist: one of the junior boys he had occasion to beat at Rugby – or *thinks* he had occasion to beat; his memory is a bit hazy – was Ian Lang MP, who served as Scottish Secretary in John Major's Cabinet. Whoops! Lang, now Lord Lang, was Dad's fag at Rugby, responsible for cleaning his shoes and his study so the old school pecking order was well and truly reversed at Westminster.

Dad was in the Rugby School Combined Cadet Force, was promoted to Sergeant, and thoroughly enjoyed the whole experience. He has particularly fond memories of a CCF summer camp in Pembrokeshire, when he and his friends got the chance to fly in one of the famous Sunderland flying boats, which were based at Pembroke Dock. A few months after leaving school, he joined the Army to do the two years of National Service that were then compulsory. He did his basic training with the Royal Scots Greys at Catterick in North Yorkshire. 'It was quite a change of lifestyle, being billeted with twenty other young men you had never met before,' he remembers. 'They came from every walk of life and included some "Teddy boys", who arrived all cocky and confident, but quickly changed their attitude and buckled down. You had to get on and work together because, if you did not, you were in trouble – one of life's great lessons, which has stood me in good stead ever since.'

After being selected for officer training, he went to the Mons Officer Cadet School in Aldershot, where he and his fellow cadets were licked into shape by those gruff, no-nonsense, non-commissioned officers who are the glory of the British Army. Dad has particularly vivid memories of one of them, RSM Smy, with whom he got into conversation at a cocktail party and tried to match in the drinking stakes, dry martini for dry martini. Alas, the young Winterton's head for alcohol was no match for the older man's. He left the event, passed out and was discovered by a patrol party in a flower-bed. He was taken back to his billet, but could not be revived, even under a cold shower. The next morning, on drill parade, he was still feeling like death warmed up, but struggled through, winning the grudging approval of RSM Smy who, naturally, was looking as fresh as a daisy. 'Luckily, my commanding officer never found out, as it would have been a black mark on my record,' says Dad. 'Let's just call it one of those life experiences that shape a man.'

He was growing up fast and, after a tough period at officer cadet school, was posted to Germany with the 14th/20th King's Hussars, an armoured regiment, holding the rank of second lieutenant. His duties took him all over Germany – Hohne, Lemgo, Celle, Detmold and Berlin – but the undoubted highlight was serving as a tank troop commander in Berlin. It was a fantastic opportunity for a young man, and Dad remembers horse riding in Grunewald forest, sailing, even playing rugby in the Olympic stadium, where the 1936 Olympics had been held. Throw in the theatre, the opera and the Berlin nightlife and you have a treasure trove of memories to last a lifetime. No picture in the family photo album gives Dad more pleasure than the one of him standing in a tank in the middle of West Berlin, looking as if he has just licked the Nazis single-handed.

He was stationed at Smuts Barracks, next to Spandau prison, where several former Nazi prisoners, including Albert Speer, Hitler's armaments minister, were still imprisoned. Memories of the war were fresh, West Berlin was still divided into French, American, British and Soviet zones and, although relations with the locals were generally good, there were occasional minor diplomatic incidents, at least one of them sparked, indirectly, by my father. On Remembrance Sunday in 1958, he was charged with firing the traditional salute, blank shells from the 20-pound gun on his Centurion tank at the beginning and end of the two minutes' silence. All went according to plan, until the German staff of a neighbouring cemetery office came rushing out holding coffee cups filled with plaster and dust. The ceiling of the office had fallen in during the salute due to the reverberations of the gunshots and, although my father was absolved from blame, the Army had to pay for the damage.

On another occasion – a Saturday afternoon, after a convivial lunch – he went riding in Grunewald forest and decided to attempt a series of jumps which were used during drag hunts, which were quite common in Berlin in those days. His horse got the bit between its teeth, set a cracking pace, and Dad was on cloud nine, whooping and hollering, until disaster struck. The horse slipped at a corner, my father was unseated, and the episode ended in ignominy, with the horse bolting and Dad vainly pursuing it on foot. It was a German policeman who eventually caught up with the animal. 'Typical British officer,' he muttered, handing my father the reins in the middle of a main road into central Berlin.

Every day was different, comic incidents abounded, and Dad still has very fond memories of the period, not least because, after the cloistered world of public school, the Army brought him into contact with people from every walk of life: from a happy-go-lucky commanding officer who knocked back half a bottle of whisky before lunch with no ill effects, to grizzled troop sergeants who had fought in the war and had the seriousness, laced with humour, of the breed – Sergeants Wallace and Tasker come to mind. They were the backbone of the British Army, whose help and advice was vital to young officers. Abdul, the Turkish head waiter in the officers' mess, only added to the experience. He was still there, years later, when my brother Robert was also posted to Berlin with the Army, and found himself in the same Smuts Barracks in Spandau where Dad had been posted.

When not larking about, Dad acquired some useful life skills, such as how to make a bed properly. 'My hospital corners were immaculate,' he remembers with pride – *not* a boast you would hear from a modern philosophy student at the LSE. He also mastered the art of spit-and-polish shoe-shining, a subject on which he can still talk for ten minutes without irrelevance or repetition. (Punch-line: 'You can always judge a man by his shoes.')

Like Parliament, the Army is a much misunderstood institution. From the outside, it can look like a simulacrum of the British class system, with rigid dividing lines between officers and other ranks. But what Dad remembers about his Army days is a sense of camaraderie that completely transcended class barriers. One callow young English soldier in barracks in Germany is much like another.

In his final year at Rugby, he had been a prefect, a big fish in a small pond. Now he was having to start again at the bottom, which is how it should be in life. To my father, it is only by learning the ropes with due humility – whether it is in a school, a regiment, a commercial company or the House of Commons – that one can progress up any career ladder.

Throwing himself into Army life with his usual gusto, he acquired the reputation of 'a soldier's officer': someone ready to muck in with other ranks, and always prepared to stick up for his men. On one occasion, he had to defend one of his troopers at a court-martial after he had been caught selling booze from the NAAFI to the locals. It was a formative experience. Courts-martial, unlike some other courts of law, do not tolerate waffle. Dad had to make his points in a clear, economical, cogent way – one of the first skills the budding politician has to master.

The Army suited him down to the ground and, but for family commitments, he would probably have stayed in the Hussars for longer than the compulsory two years. He has kept in close touch with the regiment ever since, did his stint with the Army Emergency Reserve, is a member of the Cavalry and Guards Club in London and was as pleased as Punch when Robert, his elder son, followed him into the 14th/20th King's Hussars on a short service commission after graduating from the Royal Military Academy at Sandhurst.

After the thrills and spills of National Service, he had zero interest in going to university. He had got decent, if not spectacular, A-level grades, but academia was not his bag. Unlike today, when nearly half of school-leavers go on to higher education of some kind, only a dedicated minority took that route in the 1950s. Instead, he did management training with Shell-Mex and BP, then worked in the construction machinery business, gaining the sort of hands-on experience that would prove invaluable in later life. One of his politer nicknames at Westminster was Mr Manufacturing. In a parliament dominated by lawyers and trade union officials, he had an in-built advantage. He knew how small businesses worked.

Throughout the 1960s, he was the sales and general manager at Stevens and Hodgson, a company that had been started by his father-in-law, Bob Hodgson, after the war. Dad had married my mother in 1960, Robert was born soon afterwards, so he had his hands full for the next couple of years. Nothing could have been further from his mind than politics when, slap in the middle of Wimbledon fortnight in 1963...

As Dad tells the story, it was a sunny day and, not for the first time in his life, he was doing two things at once: one, mowing the lawn and, two, ducking into the house from time to time to watch Wimbledon. The door-bell rang and he went to answer it, not best pleased to be disturbed at the weekend. It was a local Tory activist, Peter Thomas, who was hoping to form a Conservative branch covering three villages in the area: Middleton, Curdworth and Wishaw. Would Dad like to come along to a preliminary meeting? So Dad went along and, on being asked to open his mouth, opened it. And kept it open. One imagines there were other Tory hopefuls trying to get a word in edgeways but, knowing Dad, they were wasting their time. Before he knew it, he had been elected first chairman of the branch.

After that, things happened quite quickly. Only eight years separated his election as chairman of a small local Conservative branch and his election to the House of Commons. It was not quite a meteoric rise, but it was exhilaratingly rapid, and Dad's eyes still shine when he remembers that heady period in his life, when anything seemed possible.

In 1967, he was asked to stand for Warwickshire County Council, taking on a strong sitting Labour candidate in the mining town of Atherstone. How simple politics was in those days! Nowadays a Tory candidate in a local election would be told to set up a Twitter account, spew out fatuous propaganda and tweet inane smears about his opponents. Or he would be given copious crib-sheets on the 'line to take' if challenged by journalists. He would barely meet any real voters face to face, listen to them, engage with them, discover what *they* wanted. My father's baptism into local politics – and remember, he was still in his twenties – was quite different. And not just different, he would argue. *Better*.

'Just come and meet me at the Red Lion, and we'll take it from there,' his agent, Gillian Rogers, told him. A quick pint and, like a driver with L-plates, he was on his way, scouring the streets for Tory voters. At first, it was a bit like a game of Hunt the Thimble. Gillian introduced him to eight known Conservative supporters and marked twenty more on the electoral register and he was then on his own. But he kept looking and discovered – not for the first or last time in his life – that there are far more Tories around than you think. They can be quite shy, and reluctant to come out of their burrows, but they can be coaxed out into the daylight if you ask them nicely.

And politics at the grassroots in those days, Dad insists, *was* nice. It was not vicious or acrimonious, but an honest clash of competing views, sincerely held: grown-ups talking to grown-ups. He could walk into the Miners Welfare Club any day of the week and get a cordial welcome. He never felt as if he was crossing enemy lines.

He remembers his margin of victory in the election to this day – 129 votes – and the sheer excitement of finding himself on the campaign trail, scrapping for votes, arguing on doorsteps, canvassing as many households as humanly possible. It was the first of his many electoral victories and, in some ways, the sweetest of them all.

The political gods were certainly on his side, as he still remembers with gratitude half a century later. On the very night he was elected, he was driving home from the count in the rain when he was dazzled by the headlights of an oncoming car, swerved and crashed, nearly ending what would have been the shortest political career on record. His car flipped over and by the time he had got out he was so disoriented that, when he accepted a lift from a passing lorry driver, he travelled two miles in the wrong direction before he realised it. His father-in-law picked up the battered car.

Still, he had made it and, growing in confidence the whole time, had an immediate impact on the council with his tooth-and-nail opposition to comprehensive schools, then a burning political issue. He raged against what he called 'compulsive mediocrity', earning plaudits from, among others, a teacher at Shakespeare's old school in Stratford-upon-Avon.

County councillors tend to be quite long in the tooth, with a significantly higher average age than MPs. Still in his twenties when he was first elected, my father must have stood out like a sore thumb: not so much the new boy as the only boy in an assembly of the grizzled and middle-aged. But he talks of his days as a county councillor every bit as fondly as he talks of his days in the House of Commons. It was a political apprenticeship, not just a stepping-stone to higher things, and he learnt something new every day. About people. About rules and regulations. About husbanding limited resources. About what was possible and impossible.

He also met some remarkable people in the course of his official duties – none more remarkable than the legendary Group Captain Sir Douglas Bader, who came to present the prizes at Atherstone High School in the Atherstone ward, which my father represented. The school had an outstanding and brilliant headmaster, Mr Kirkpatrick. Bader's heroics as a fighter pilot in the Second World War, and the fact that he had overcome the loss of both legs, made him one of the most admired figures in the whole country – his story memorably retold in the movie *Reach for the Sky*, starring Kenneth More.

There were a few steps leading up to the podium from which Bader was to present the prizes, and my father – making a mistake which hundreds of others had made before him – offered to give him a helping hand. 'Bader wouldn't hear of it,' he remembers. 'In fact, to watch him climbing those steps without assistance, very slowly and very determinedly, was one of the most inspiring things I have ever seen.'

A little over a year after being elected a county councillor, Dad was selected to fight the parliamentary constituency of Newcastle-under-Lyme. It was normally a rock-solid Labour seat, but when it became vacant in October 1969 following the death of the sitting MP, Stephen Swingler, Dad managed to trim the 12,000 Labour majority to just over 1,000. He stood for the same seat again, without success, at the general election the following year, losing by a relatively narrow margin.

You could say his political career had hitherto followed quite a conventional path. It is common for aspirant MPs to cut their teeth in constituencies where they have little chance of winning, before graduating to safer seats. But Dad's determination to be his own man, even if it meant ruffling feathers at Conservative Central Office, was already apparent.

At the outset of the 1969 by-election in Newcastle-under-Lyme, he was asked by a vice-chairman of the national Conservative Party, who was responsible for by-elections, whether there were any leading Tory politicians he would like to invite to address meetings on his behalf. 'Well, yes, there is one,' said Dad, without batting an eyelid. 'Enoch Powell.' Cue a long, frosty silence. As Dad tells the story, it sounds like a Bateman cartoon: The Man Who Mentioned Enoch. The vice-chairman, who had previously called him 'Nicholas', did a loud snort and started addressing him as 'Winterton'.

This, remember, was only a year after Powell's controversial Rivers of Blood speech to a meeting of Tory activists in Birmingham – a speech which Dad had witnessed at first hand. The speech has become so much part of British folklore that one assumes it must have been pretty combustible stuff. In fact, Dad remembers driving home from the meeting in Birmingham with a friend, and the subject of the speech did not crop up once during an hour-long journey. It was only the next morning, when a few choice excerpts from the speech were splashed across the front pages by the national press and reported on TV and radio, that the repercussions began – repercussions which can be felt to this day.

Powell was summarily sacked from the Tory front bench by Ted Heath, the party leader, and had soon achieved pariah status. But, the issue of immigration aside – which I will come to later in the book – Dad recognised something in Powell which he aspired to himself: the ability to connect with ordinary voters by plugging in to *their* concerns, not by speaking down to them from on high.

I have made fun of his incessant talking, but he was also an excellent listener, which made him a far more effective grass-roots politician than those who analysed issues in a more cerebral way. Like Enoch Powell – or among today's Conservatives, Boris Johnson – he had the common touch.

Enlisting Powell into his camp for the Newcastle-under-Lyme by-election certainly did Dad's electoral prospects no harm. At the first meeting, which Powell was due to address, there was such a big turnout, not to mention protesters massing outside the hall, that the guest speaker nearly had to be smuggled into the meeting through a back window. By the time of the second meeting, at the Westlands High School, there were almost as many people outside the school as in the hall, including protesters from Keele University. The topic of immigration, for better or worse, had struck a raw nerve.

Powell was also responsible, incidentally, for the alliterative election slogan 'Westminster Wants Winterton'. Years before the creation of the World Wide Web, fliers featuring three huge Ws were circulating in Newcastle-under-Lyme, giving the acronym WWW an early outing. It is still the closest Dad has got to engaging with the internet.

His two failures to get elected as MP for Newcastle-Under-Lyme were his only failures at the polls in his entire career. But you will not hear him say a bad word about Newcastle, one of those down-to-earth Staffordshire towns with a rich industrial heritage, embracing everything from hatting to coal-mining to porcelain manufacturing.

The seat has been held continuously by Labour since 1923, and no Tory candidate has come closer to winning it than my father, who twice pushed the Labour candidate, John Golding, very close. Golding was on the right of the Labour Party and, by one of those delicious parliamentary ironies, even fonder of his own voice than my father. He holds the all-time record for the longest ever speech in a House of Commons committee – an impressive 11 hours and 15 minutes. (I have known Dad speak for 11 hours and 47 minutes, on the subject of tattoos, but that was in the family kitchen, so it does not really count.) Golding was notionally moving an amendment to the Bill to privatise British Telecom, but was so successful in his delaying tactics that the Bill had to be deferred until after the 1983 election. It was one of the legendary parliamentary filibusters.

In the course of his campaigning in Newcastle, my father also formed a warm and enduring friendship with Dr Jock Brown, the chairman of the local Conservative Association. With his kindly, weather-beaten face, Brown was one of those salt-of-the-earth Scottish GPs who could have been a character in *Dr Finlay's Casebook*. 'If all Tories were as sensible and level-headed as Jock,' I have heard my father say, 'we'd never fight about anything.'

Guy and Christine Cavenagh-Mainwaring, of Whitmore Hall, were also great supporters and became good, lifelong friends. My father became a godfather to their daughter, Fleur, who had been taken out canvassing with her parents as a baby – Tories start out young, which is one of the secrets of their success – strapped into a carry-cot in the back of the car.

If Dad fell short in Newcastle-under-Lyme, he did not have to wait too long for another opportunity. In early 1971, the sitting Tory member for Macclesfield, Sir Arthur Vere Harvey, chairman of the 1922 committee, was elevated to the House of Lords, precipitating a by-election. Dad, naturally, threw his hat in the ring. He was still a county councillor in Warwickshire, where the family was based, but Macclesfield was so close to Staffordshire, the county where he grew up, that nobody could accuse him of being a carpet-bagger, trying to represent a constituency about which he knew nothing. Vere Harvey was elevated to the House of Lords because the Prime Minister, Ted Heath, did not want an anti-EU Chairman of the 1922 Committee. Vere Harvey became a lifelong friend.

He was young, he was brimming with self-confidence, and it was only when he saw the list of other young Tory hopefuls vying for the Macclesfield seat – an all-star political cast, jam-packed with high-fliers – that Dad felt up against it. Douglas Hurd, Leon Brittan, Nigel Lawson, Norman Lamont... A future Foreign Secretary, a future Home Secretary and *two* future Chancellors of the Exchequer! Bright young things, with impeccable pedigree, brains the size of Cheshire and brilliant futures ahead of them. Never in the history of the Conservative Party can so much Oxbridge-educated fire-power have found its way on to the same constituency longlist. And poor Dad hadn't even gone to university.

The exact details of the selection meeting have got lost in the mists of time, but knowing the personalities involved, I can envisage the whole occasion as if I was there. Dad opened his God-given mouth and *talked*, straight from the heart. He was fluent. He spoke with passion and honesty. He gave straight answers to straight questions. The others – cagier, more lawyerlike, terrified of putting their foot in it – froze on the big stage. Next to John Wayne, all guns blazing, they must have seemed like grey young men in suits.

Don Porter, who was the Young Conservatives' representative on the panel, and later became national chairman of the party, remembers the whole occasion vividly:

> I was so convinced that Nicholas was the right candidate that I had put a cross against his name on my ballot paper before the others had finished making their presentations. He was the perfect man for Macclesfield, which has a reputation for plain talking, along with a strong non-conformist streak. We did not want a smooth metropolitan type who would not have been on our wavelength at all.

As other candidates fell by the wayside, the race for the Maccle-sfield nomination came down to two men: my father and Peter Temple-Morris, a silky, Cambridge-educated barrister and an exact contemporary of my father. Temple-Morris would later became the Tory MP for Leominster, in Herefordshire. But, as my father gleefully recalls, he badly misread the mood in Macclesfield in 1971.

In those shamelessly chauvinist days, candidates were expected to turn up with their wives, who would be assessed for their suitability as Spouse of the Member of Parliament, like marrows at a village fete. The unwritten rules of the beauty content were scarcely subtle. Stay-at-home mothers preferred. Flashy dressers rejected out of hand. Career women tolerated, but viewed with slight suspicion. (This *was* 1971.)

Mum – sensible, supportive, in touch with rural concerns – fitted the part perfectly, while poor Mrs Temple-Morris, a charm-ing aristocratic Iranian lady, was simply not up to snuff as far as Macclesfield was concerned.

'What part do you plan to play in the social life of the constitu-ency?' she was asked by one panel member. 'I would throw the odd cocktail party,' came the reply. *Not* the answer the Tory faithful of Macclesfield were looking for. Cocktail parties? They didn't give cocktail parties. They were more interested in someone who could draw the raffle at church fetes and fade into the background at the Dog and Duck.

Peter Temple-Morris was then asked how his wife would cope with looking after his children during his absences at Westminster: 'That will not be a problem,' he responded, with his customary suavity. 'We have a nanny.' Oh dear, oh dear. Another schoolboy error.

Disapproving scowls passed across the stolid provincial faces of the farmers and teachers and housewives and district councillors on the selection committee. My father's heart danced. Game, set and match to Winterton.

A *nanny*? Who needed a nanny? *He* didn't need a nanny.

He had Mum.

4.

THE GIRL AT THE
PONY CLUB

Anyone reading the official report of the hunting debate in the House of Commons on 18 March 2002 could be forgiven for feeling frustrated.

Mrs Ann Winterton (Congleton): When I was first taken hunting as a child by my mother, I never expected that one day I would be standing at the despatch box to defend the right of the individual to take part in one of the greatest of our traditions. Hunting and ponies definitely played a part in my eventually standing for Parliament, because it was while I was a member of South Staffordshire Pony Club that I met my hon. Friend—

Mr Deputy Speaker: Order. Before the hon. Lady gets too far into her remarks, may I say to her that we are discussing a very narrow motion on how we shall proceed this evening. This is not the time for a broader debate.

Oh, come *on*! Who is this unnamed Deputy Speaker and how dare he call a halt just as the debate is hotting up? That is the trouble with Hansard, as the official report is called. It leaves out all the best bits.

Suppose a Labour frontbench spokesman has been gibbering like a baboon, hurling insults at Boris Johnson, making obscene hand gestures and generally whipping the backbenchers behind him into a frenzy of indignation. All you will read in Hansard the next morning is the catch-all euphemism '*Interruptions*'. It doesn't quite do justice to proceedings, does it?

Those frustrated by the Deputy Speaker's intervention on this occasion included the late Simon Hoggart, *The Guardian*'s parliamentary sketch-writer, who grumbled:

> Mrs Winterton had started a Mills and Boon novel… She was galloping back down memory lane to that blissful time when she first set eyes on Nicholas Winterton, her future husband… MPs craned forward. Would she describe his steaming thighs and throbbing fetlocks as his hot breath scorched her cheek?

Hoggart continued in the same merry vein, imagining Dad whinnying and pawing the ground with his hoof.

The story of how my mother met my father at the South Staffordshire Pony Club might not have appeared in Hansard, but no history of my family would be complete without this colourful chapter, still fondly remembered after more than sixty years. The setting is light years from the House of Commons, but the characters are as vivid as the most flamboyant Cabinet minister.

Like bankers and estate agents, back-bench MPs tend to get tarred with the same brush. They are cast as cartoon villains, their villainy self-evident. It is only when you take the trouble to look at their lives in the round that they start to emerge as what they are: ordinary human beings with as many quirks and wrinkles as their constituents. And nobody will ever get to grips with my parents without factoring in the four-legged friends who have shaped their lives.

The walls of their house in Cheshire are festooned with so many hunting prints, riding crops and other horsey memorabilia that it is like wandering into the weighing room at Aintree. They tell of a passion, not a hobby. In fact, the Winterton story without horses would be like the Jeremy Clarkson story without cars. To the names of Ted Heath and Enoch Powell and Margaret Thatcher must be added the names of May Day and Volant and Big Ben and Lark-spur and others too numerous to mention. The equine supporting cast is key to the narrative – far more so than Europe or expenses or other parliamentary side-shows.

The main stage for my parents' political career may have been in London, but their roots were rural, provincial. They not only met on horseback, but put their children on horseback as soon as they could sit upright and, for much of their lives, owned horses of their own. My brothers and I grew up with horses grazing out-side our bedroom windows. We loved each and every one of them. When Mum and Dad wanted to move furniture from their house in Cheshire to their flat in Westminster, they used a horse-box with straw on the floor. Can you imagine the Blairs or the Camerons doing the same?

But back to the pony club and that first, momentous, meeting. It was early 1956. The year of Suez, but also a time of innocence. Slap bang in the middle of the decade which, for many Tories, has come to symbolise the England they love, a land of lost con-tent, presided over by Dixon of Dock Green. And where better to observe that vanished England than a pony club set deep in the English countryside?

By the time I was a teenager, the horsey set in the English shires had acquired a far raunchier image, thanks to Jilly Cooper novels with women in tight jodhpurs on the covers. But back then, the pony club belonged to childhood, as surely as ice-cream vans and conker fights and bucket-and-spade holidays. It was a wholesome, uncom-plicated world, immortalised by the cartoonist Norman Thelwell, whose drawings of plump schoolgirls on underperforming horses delighted a generation.

Spawned in England in the 1930s, and now to be found all over the world, pony clubs were not only a great way for children from horse-owning families to meet, but offered children whose parents did not own horses an opportunity to learn to ride, as well as to look after and feed ponies, clean the tack etc. In many rural areas, pony clubs were an important part of the social fabric, appealing to people of all classes, binding communities together.

In an article in the *Daily Telegraph* in 2016, waxing lyrical about a childhood dominated by ponies, the writer Marina Fogle seized on this point: 'Pony clubs were classless. In a uniquely British way, the older your tack, the hairier your pony, the more threadbare your hacking jacket, the better you were respected. It was the girls who arrived with fancy ponies in shiny horse-boxes who never lasted long.'

Anyone who thinks only Conservative supporters own and ride horses is missing the point by a country mile. The riding fraternity is a far broader church than that, and has been part of English rural life for centuries. You will never catch horsey folk talking party politics: they are more likely to be discussing the runners and riders for the next hunt ball. A love of horses – like a love of sport or music – transcends arbitrary social divisions, such as what school somebody went to. Indeed, one of the tragedies of the fox-hunting debate, and the ban that eventually resulted, was the way that genuine concerns about animal welfare got entangled with class war politics of the most blinkered, ignorant kind. Half the Labour MPs who tramped through the division lobbies to support the legislation banning fox-hunting had barely seen a horse in the flesh, let alone taken the trouble to understand fox-hunting. But I digress.

Most pony clubs are affiliated to local hunts, and it was at the South Staffordshire hunt's first meet of 1956 that my parents met. Dad was still a boarder at Rugby School, so his attendances at the South Staffordshire Pony Club had been quite limited up to that point. But he was a keen and energetic horseman and, like teenage boys through the ages, starting to take an equally keen interest in the opposite sex.

There was certainly no danger of him missing the girl galloping confidently past him, as if she had been born on horseback. He was seventeen at the time, and she was fourteen, but what stood out a mile was that this slim young girl was not just an extremely accomplished rider, but quite possibly – blast and dammit – a better rider than him! He cantered after her, stung into a response...

'She had a good seat,' Dad recalls, selecting his words with care. Mum's first impressions were rather less favourable. She didn't think much of Dad's seat. In fact, she didn't think much of him at all: he just seemed rather bumptious. It certainly wasn't *Romeo and Juliet* on horseback. More a case of *Pimply Rugby Sixth-Former and Juliet* on horseback.

Still, at least their paths had crossed, and they crossed again at subsequent meetings of the pony club. Dad was well and truly smitten by now, but getting nowhere fast with his conversational sallies, so he took out his frustration by hurling a cream bun at Mum while she was cantering past – much as he would later hurl barbed questions at ministers who were cutting NHS budgets. Subtlety has never been his strong suit.

If he had missed, there might have been no Winterton story to tell: Dad would probably have abandoned the chase and married some milksop called Millicent. But his aim was as true as Cupid's arrow and the bun landed flush on Mum's hacking jacket, to general amusement. The only person not laughing was Mum's mother, who insisted that Dad dismount and clean the mess on the jacket, which he duly did. At which point, the scales suddenly fell from Mum's eyes. Flowers or chocolates would have been more romantic, but a man who could throw a cream bun with such precision was not to be sneezed at.

Soon, in the vernacular of the day, they were courting. Dad helped Mum with her Latin homework, which always goes down well with a Latin-challenged girl, then started taking her to the pictures, as they were known. Their first date was a double bill at the Odeon in Sutton Coldfield: a John Wayne Western, followed by *Rock Around the Clock*, featuring Bill Haley's smash-hit song of the same name. It was so popular with teenagers that cinema audiences, including the one in Sutton Coldfield, started dancing in the aisles. Mum was all for joining in the dancing, but Dad refused point-blank. This noisy modern music was ghastly. What was wrong with Gilbert and Sullivan?

It was a strange relationship, in some ways. The three-year gap in their ages was far from typical among teenagers of that generation. And there were other, bigger hurdles to cross. In the hurly-burly of the pony club, where all that really mattered was staying on your horse and ducking cream buns, social distinctions counted for nothing. But the fact that Mum and Dad occupied slightly different rungs on the English class ladder gave their courtship an extra edge.

If the Wintertons were old middle class, a solid, professional family going back generations, the Hodgsons were new middle class, upwardly mobile. Or, to put it another way, Dad was middle-middle and Mum was lower-middle – a seemingly subtle distinction but one of huge significance in the class-conscious Britain of the 1950s.

Everyone meeting my parents always comments on how well-matched they are. With some couples, it does not take five minutes to work out who wears the trousers in the relationship. With Mum and Dad, it really is impossible to say. Sometimes she defers to him, sometimes it is the other way around. They have matching coffee cups – his says FATHER OF THE HOUSE, hers says CHIEF WHIP – which give a nice humorous twist to that natural parity. They are a team, and an unusually well-balanced one; equals in every respect. But, as I have slowly come to realise over the years, it was not always like that.

Mum at the age of eight or nine seems to have been quite like me at the same age. Not exactly crippled by shyness, but lacking in social polish and unsure of herself in unfamiliar situations. A diffident member of the diffident sex. And her subsequent marriage to Dad would take her a long way out of her comfort zone. She was 'marrying up', as people used to say, which is always far more stress-ful than marrying down. Like thousands of women in the same situation, she was treading on egg-shells, petrified of committing some unforgivable *faux pas*, like saying 'toilet' or pouring tea the wrong way.

By the time she became an MP, in her early forties, she exuded such natural self-confidence that it is hard to think of her as gauche or tongue-tied. Although she never styled herself a feminist, she had the combativeness of the breed, the determination to stand up for herself, the irritation at being patronised. When the Tory whips tried to bully her, as they often did, she swatted them away like flies. She was nobody's pushover and she certainly wasn't going to let the braying ex-public schoolboys who dominated the parliamentary party call the shots. As Margaret Thatcher found, the *real* class war at Westminster was often not between Labour and Conservative, but between the two wings of the Tory party – the one born into a world of privilege, the other not.

In 2017, the great fault-line running through the party, even after the EU referendum, is Europe. For most of the second half of the twentieth century, it was class. Class is a national obsession anyway, but it reached its apogee in the Conservative Party in that period. There was a perpetual tension between a patrician tradition, embodied by Old Etonians like Harold Macmillan and Alec Douglas-Home, and a meritocratic tradition, of which Ted Heath and Margaret Thatcher, products of grammar schools, were the standard-bearers. Within the parliamentary Conservative Party, riven with petty snobberies, it mattered *hugely* where you had been to school. My parents – a grammar schoolgirl and an ex-public schoolboy – straddled the class divide as best they could. But it was never easy, and the impact of class on their respective careers – particularly my mother's – should not be underestimated.

When she looks back on her earlier life, she often talks about feeling terrified in social situations where she felt out of her depth. On the outside, she was calm and composed. Inside – and how many successful career women would say the same – she was a mass of nerves, scared of failure. Women may be the more competent sex, in a myriad ways, but it is men who have been endowed, over-endowed, with the confidence gene. My mother had to *achieve* confidence. She was not born with it.

One of the things that helped her grow in confidence, interestingly, was politics. Canvassing with my father during his early forays into politics, she found herself knocking on doors, talking to total strangers and realising that, against expectations, she was rather good at it. 'The fact that you had to talk to all sorts of people, and make a connection with them, was an education in itself,' she remembers. 'Talking to people is always a great confidence-builder.' Courage in life can take a thousand forms. There have been men who have fought in battle who would blanch at the thought of knocking on a stranger's door and starting a conversation, 'Can I interest you in supporting your local Conservative candidate, Nicholas Winterton?' My ballsy mother had no such inhibitions.

I never really knew my father's parents, but I saw quite a lot of my mother's. They played a significant part in my childhood, and I can remember them both vividly. It was hard to miss them: they were such colourful, larger-than-life characters.

Politically, you would say they were to the right, but not card-carrying Conservatives. 'They probably looked down on politics slightly,' my mother once told an interviewer. 'They certainly were not active in party politics. They had too much else on their plates.'

Bob Hodgson, Mum's father, was the youngest of five children brought up by their widowed mother on a smallholding near Wearhead, County Durham. He attended the village school and left at the age of fourteen to start work. There was no further education available in those days and, anyway, he needed to work to help support the family. He had always been interested in cars, motorcycles and machinery of every description and, in order to make money, bought second-hand vehicles, sometimes ones that had been involved in road accidents, which he renovated in his spare time and then sold on.

He also worked for a time on the machinery down the local pit, but vowed to himself that he would never do so for longer than was necessary. Later, he gained more experience working in quarries, where he learnt how to handle dynamite – a skill which came in handy years later when he wanted to enlarge his business premises by blasting down a bit of the sandstone bank at the back of the site. Nowadays, he would probably be prosecuted under article 337(2) of some obscure EU regulation. He would have heartily detested the modern workplace with its nit-picking dos and don'ts. He believed in hard work, common sense and the personal touch. He was the ultimate entrepreneur.

By the end of the 1930s, work prospects in the north east were so bleak that Bob Hodgson took the plunge and, to better his prospects, moved from County Durham down to Birmingham, where he initially drove buses to earn his living. Later he set up a small construction machinery, Stevens and Hodgson, close to what is now Spaghetti Junction.

He met my grandmother at a tea dance on New Year's Day and that, as they say, was that. She was a nurse at the Selly Oak Hospital at the time, and one of the daughters of a very large Scottish family. There were initially twelve children, six boys and six girls, of whom ten grew to adulthood. The boys went into farming and the girls into nursing before their careers took them in different directions. My mother has idyllic memories of family reunions at harvest time, with the men helping in the fields while the women made hearty ham sandwiches and steaming jugs of tea. She loved having so many cousins to play with and is still in touch with some of them today.

Bob Hodgson was always 'Grandad' to me and my brothers, but my grandmother did not want to be 'Granny', so she ended up as 'Mama Pat', a name coined by my elder brother Robert. She had actually been christened Ellen Jane and nicknamed Nellie, but hated both names, so when, at the start of her nursing career, a boyfriend suggested that she 'looked like a Pat', the name stuck.

She was quite compact, physically, and took great pride in her appearance, getting her hair and nails done every week without fail. If Bob Hodgson was his own man, Pat Hodgson was one of those gloriously ripe characters around whom stories naturally accumulate. I remember her as a husky-voiced chain-smoker – Benson & Hedges were her weed of choice – with a rebellious streak and a heart of gold. My brothers have fond memories of her surreptitiously giving them their first taste of tobacco – even, on one occasion, waving a cigarette playfully in front of a baby's face. I remember her kitchen full of Jack Russell terrier puppies, and only ever eating apple sauce when I stayed with them. She was also comically accident-prone. Once, when testing a new car, she accidentally hit the accelerator and drove the car straight through the dealer's showroom window. It might have been a premonition of future Winterton car crashes at Westminster.

Both Bob and Pat Hodgson loved horses and Grandad often gave me medication meant for the horses when I had tummy ache or toothache, citing 'what's good for my horses is good for my granddaughter'. Grandad had had dealings with them when he was young, and so had my grandmother, mainly with the pony that pulled the milk float. They never did things by halves, so it was perhaps inevitable that, when they were on holiday in Devon one summer, they should have acquired not one horse, but two. Then the mare, Black Beauty – what else would conservatives with a small c have called her? – turned out to be in foal, completing an equine hat-trick. The ponies were kept on some rented land a couple of miles from home, where my mother was taken to ride every weekend, whether she wanted to or not. It was the first three-line whip in her life and just about the last one she took seriously.

With two such doughty and idiosyncratic parents, it is perhaps not surprising that my mother was a quick developer. She might have been shy when she was eight or nine, but her natural ability in the saddle helped build confidence in other parts of her life. In the classroom, she was just one of the crowd, getting average grades and coasting through lessons. On horseback, it was a different matter. She had found something at which she could excel and she revelled in the attention that brought.

She was only eleven when she competed at the Royal Windsor

Horse Show and was voted best rider in one of the show pony classes. Her prize was a pair of tailor-made jodhpurs from one of the grandest London shops. She remembers her father taking her down to London by train for the fitting. It was one of the high points of her childhood. She had no inkling when she was being measured for the jodhpurs that the master tailor doing the honours – one Bernard 'Jack' Weatherill – would later become a fellow Tory MP and Speaker of the House of Commons. A small world indeed.

Her first name was Jane, but she was always known by her second name, Ann. She was the oldest of three daughters and was followed by Elizabeth and Janet, who were four and seven years younger, respectively. They all attended local grammar schools – Erdington, in Mum's case – and all competed successfully on horseback, initially in show pony classes and then progressing to the hunting field. The Hodgson girls were stalwarts of the aforementioned South Staffordshire Pony Club, and Mum actually got through to the national finals of the Pony Club One Day Event Championship, where she finished fifth on Hallowe'en – a mare she had first ridden in Ireland, after skipping school one Friday afternoon to fly across the Irish Sea to try her out on a day's hunting. Incidentally, the finals that year were held on the Highgrove estate, then owned by the Macmillan family, who were well-known in the UK political scene.

There was nothing remotely normal or conventional about the Hodgsons. They believed in living life to the full, bucking trends, taking risks, not fading meekly into the background. Living life in the fast lane seems to have been in the family DNA. Elizabeth Hodgson went on to became a successful rally driver, competing in her Mini in the RAC Rally, then teaming up with the legendary Pat Moss-Carlsson, with whom she won the Ladies' Prize in the Monte Carlo Rally. Janet Hodgson enjoyed equal success at three-day eventing and was a member of the UK team, including Princess Anne, which competed in Kiev in 1973 – when the Hodgson name was plastered all over the front pages after she fell and smashed her face, but gallantly remounted to complete the course. Her most successful horse was Larkspur, known as Fred at home, whom Grandad had bought unbroken out of a field in Ireland. He and my grandmother had always had a good eye for raw, unbroken horses with long-term potential.

As for my mother, Bob Hodgson had vague hopes of her becoming a vet, but he was not a pushy parent, the sort who hovers over his children as they do their homework. His daughters might have got into grammar school, but as a self-made man, he did not really believe in the academic route to success – there was more to life than books. I have sometimes heard Mum say that she wished he *had* been a bit pushier: it might have made her buckle down more and, who knows, qualify as a vet or get some other professional qualification. But she clearly adored her father and treasured his ruggedly individualistic approach to life.

Throughout her teens, Mum continued to go from strength to strength in the saddle and, at the age of just seventeen – a national record – became joint master of foxhounds (MFH) for the South Staffordshire Hunt, encouraged every step of the way by her horse-mad parents. It was a challenging position, calling for both organisational skills and decisiveness. No job for a teenager, you would probably say. But my mother, as a lot of people could already see, was no ordinary teenager. She had something about her. She understood horses. More than that, she understood people.

One of the main jobs of the MFH is to maintain order and discipline during the day's hunting. The huntsman is assisted by whippers-in or whips – the origin, ironically, of the party whips in the House of Commons with whom Mum would later have so many run-ins. (What she wouldn't have given to set a pack of hounds on *them*!) Hunts are quite loose hierarchies, and the emphasis is on having fun, but there are some important unwritten rules and the members of the field are expected to stick to them. If some twerp who is new to hunting is about to ride over a field of wheat, they can expect a loud and expletive-laced bollocking from the MFH.

Mum had a carrying voice, which helped. In fact, readers of a literary bent may be put in mind of Bertie Wooster's Aunt Dahlia – 'an energetic chivier of the British fox, who could lift fellow members of the Quorn and Pytchley out of their saddles with a single yip, though separated from them by two ploughed fields and a spinney'. But she also had a natural air of authority, an old head on young shoulders.

The girl from the pony club had become a woman.

*   *   *

Like children through the ages, I have always been intrigued by the parents I never knew, the ones peeping back at me from old family photographs, taken when they were younger than I am today. Mum on horseback. Dad in school uniform. Mum as a baby. Dad clutching a rugby ball. Silent emissaries from a vanished age.

It can be hard to connect with those ghosts from the 1950s. Mum and Dad are not the lovey-dovey types, the sort who bore their children with blow-by-blow accounts of their wooing. Their love has a more matter-of-fact, unsentimental quality. But even though the Winterton story is not principally a love story, if you take away the love story, you lose half of the tale.

Ask anyone who knows Dad to describe him, and the word 'passionate' will crop up again and again. Beneath the veneer of middle-class respectability, he is a one-man volcano. I have seen him erupt in incontinent fury, like a Cheshire Victor Meldrew. I have also seen him bursting with so much pride – perhaps about something one of his children or grandchildren has achieved – that there is a tremor in his voice. If he is garrulous, it is not because he likes the sound of his own voice – though he is certainly extremely fond of it – but because he cares so deeply about whatever he is talking about, whether it is Winston Churchill or the iniquity of hospital car park charges.

As a teenage girl, Mum certainly felt the full hot blast of Dad's passion. That public school lout who had thrown a cream bun at her had hidden depths. In 1958, the year she became master of foxhounds, while still in the sixth form, Dad was doing his National Service in Germany. Did he forget the girl he had left behind in Warwickshire? He did not! Was he distracted for an instant by the local Fräuleins? He was not! As Mum recalls with a mixture of puzzlement and tenderness, he wrote to her every day for weeks. It was love-bombing on the grand scale, Luftwaffe-like in frequency and intensity, and would certainly raise eyebrows among Dad's fellow Tory MPs, some of whom have never written a love letter in their lives.

None of the letters survive, which is a shame, as they would have showed a very different Nicholas Winterton to the eminent committee chairman of later years. But Mum remembers them with wry amusement. He was such a prolific and enthusiastic correspondent that she found it hard to keep up.

One thinks of the 1950s as a grey, dour decade, but by the end of the decade, that stereotype was rapidly being challenged. One of Dad's most intriguing contemporaries – who did his National Service in Germany, with the US Army, at the same time as my father – was Elvis Presley. Like Dad, the King met his future wife, Priscilla Beaulieu, when she was just fourteen, and if Dad had had Presley's voice – or, for that matter, if Presley had had Dad's legislative skills – history might have been very different. Both men, in their contrasting ways, were screaming romantics, exulting in being far more emotionally unbuttoned than their fathers before them.

The daily plopping of letters from Germany on the doormat was certainly not wasted on Mum's parents. Bob and Pat Hodgson had always got on well with Dad, once he had outgrown his cream-bun-throwing stage. He had visited their house regularly and, after the separation of his own parents, which left him disoriented for several years, must have found the ambience of a warm, if eccentric, household reassuring and congenial. They were not paid-up party members, but they were certainly conservatives with a small c, and they liked the cut of his jib. One imagines them pondering the significance of the daily letters from Germany while Mum was out of earshot. So young Nick was serious in his intentions, eh? So be it. They could do a lot worse with a son-in-law.

Two years later, in 1960, Mum and Dad married and set up a home together. For the next decade and more, they would live at Stoke End farm in Middleton, between Sutton Coldfield and Tamworth. Children followed, then horses, then more children, then more horses. The big adventure that had begun at the South Staffordshire Pony Club had entered a new chapter.

In the same year, to cement the bonds between the two families, Bob Hodgson took on his new son-in-law as sales and general manager at Stephens and Hodgson. That, too, marked a new chapter – leading, though nobody could have guessed it in 1960, from Sutton Coldfield to one of the most famous buildings in the world.

5.

JOINING THE PANTOMIME

What kind of a woman is my mother? It is a question I often get asked by my friends, particularly when she has been in the news, sometimes in a less than flattering light. A lot of people outside politics feel they know Ann Widdecombe, even if they have never met her: love her or loathe her, she has become a familiar figure, her foibles well known. Ann Winterton – and no, she has no plans to make a spectacle of herself on *Strictly Come Dancing* – is a far more shadowy figure.

The two Anns, born in the same decade, make a fascinating contrast. In fact, you can learn a lot about politics – real politics, not the politics of easy slogans – by studying their respective careers. They were both elected Tory MPs in the 1980s. Their names have a superficial similarity. They hold identical, and unfashionable, views on a wide range of subjects, from hanging to abortion. On the face of it, they seem to belong in the same political pigeon-hole. But beware the trap that forever lies in wait for the political pundit – lazy stereotyping.

You only have to hear the two Anns debating the subject of fox-hunting – to which Ann Widdecombe is as implacably opposed as my mother is implacably in favour – to realise that these are strong women with minds of their own. You will only ever understand them if you approach them as individuals, warts and all.

It is years since Mum hunted regularly, but if you met her for the first time, you would probably be struck by some of the qualities that made her so feared by generations of Staffordshire foxes.

There is nothing soft around the edges about her. She is not one of those women who takes an hour to get dressed in the morning, or who uses her femininity as a means of getting her way. She has an air of quiet determination: if she has set her heart on something, she generally gets it. She also enjoys the thrill of the chase.

Mum can seem so very respectable on the outside – correctly dressed, impeccably mannered – but she has a streak of pure mischief, a devil-may-care attitude that my father, for all his contrariness, does not have to quite the same extent. It is as if she is still that plucky girl on a horse, hurtling towards the biggest, scariest fences, riding for a fall, but not *afraid* to fall. (She needed sixty-eight stitches after one tumble, when she was in her twenties.) Courage or recklessness? I am still not quite sure, even after all these years. But it is part of who she is and I would not want her any different.

In June 1991, there was huge amusement in the Winterton household when the local paper, *The Messenger*, reported that, in a survey of the most rebellious back-bench MPs in the House of the Commons, the Member for Macclesfield had come second – beaten only by the Member for Congleton! My mother had, in the scholarly assessment of *The Messenger*, 'pushed her outspoken hubby into the runner-up position'. Even her outspoken hubby – who does not like being beaten at anything, from skiing to tennis to snarling at Liberal Democrat canvassers – was chuffed.

'Always courteous, never diplomatic', was how someone once described my father. It could just as well have been a description of my mother. You can see why they were soulmates. The English are celebrated for not calling a spade a spade if they can possibly help it. Nobody told my mother. If she thinks someone is fat, she will say they are fat, not pussy-foot around with 'plump' or 'overweight'. Her natural kindliness and consideration of others – and she has a barrel-load of both – are not wrapped up in cotton wool.

She dresses well, but not flashily, and likes to keep herself fit, not out of physical vanity, but because she thinks it is the key to a healthy lifestyle. When the House of Commons gym first opened in the late 1980s, she signed up enthusiastically, like my father before her. 'There are some grossly overweight MPs with very florid complexions who look as if they are going to keel over at any minute,' she told an interviewer, forthright as ever. In Parliament, she campaigned for swimming lessons in state schools to be compulsory. In retirement, she has taken up pilates, walks all over Cheshire, and is as fit now as she was in her thirties.

Like my father, she is more complicated than she seems, a woman of contradictions and hidden depths. I used to tease her that she had two faces: her normal face, open and transparent, and her Member of Parliament face, polite but guarded, a mask for public consumption. If I introduced her to a boyfriend and she put on her Member of Parliament face, making the kind of small-talk she would make to a constituent, I knew he was in deep, deep trouble.

She is thick-skinned, and she has needed to be – politics is not for shrinking violets. But beneath the skin, she bruises much more easily than my father. One of the things you have to budget for as a Tory MP – other parties are the same, I hasten to add – is being stabbed in the back by other Tory MPs. When it happened to my father, he would be incandescent for a while, but then shrug it off, picking himself up and carrying on as if nothing had happened. He had the resilience of India rubber. My mother was the opposite: she could forgive at a pinch, but not forget. Again and again, she has caught me out with her enduring strength of feeling about many things, from farming to defence to pro-life issues.

Most of the time, my mother breezes through life with a huge smile on her face, determined to enjoy herself, incapable of taking herself too seriously. Sunny is her middle name. Some of her happiest memories of the House of Commons are not of taking part in debates of national importance, but of unwinding in the Tea Room, a place of laughter and gossip, where the partying could go on late into the night.

In one of her many hats, she was President of the Congleton Pantomime Society, which says it all really. While Dad was being wined and dined by the hearties at the Macclesfield Rugby Club, my mother would be listening to double-entendres from a balding accountant dressed as Widow Twankey. Politics *is* pantomime. There can be a paper-thin dividing line between Prime Minister's Questions and a drunken amateur performance of *Jack and the Beanstalk*, and Mum appreciated that better than any of her fellow MPs. Her merry laugh, as familiar in Cheshire as Westminster, can be heard across three counties.

But miss the other Ann Winterton, the one who is tough as an old boot beneath the bonhomie, and you miss my mother. Her natural merriment, although it makes her terrific company, is not indicative of a permissive attitude to life. Quite the opposite. She likes to work hard and play hard, have fun but not go off the rails. Traditional Christian morality is the foundation on which her whole life rests. She has more dos and don'ts than the dress code at Royal Ascot.

I love her when she is in party mood, letting her hair down, but I love her just as much when she is being a bloody-minded battler, sticking up for what she believes in, giving no quarter to her opponents. She does not give a damn whether she is in the minority or majority on a given issue: she just speaks her mind. Her sense of right and wrong – not to mention her impatience with people with no similar moral compass – runs deep and colours her whole life.

Hywel Williams, the former Plaid Cymru MP, hit the nail on the head when he referred to Mum as 'Congleton's crusader for family values'. Some Tory MPs who have championed family values have come a cropper, to general amusement. They have got on their soap-boxes, then been exposed as hypocrites in the *News of the World* by kiss-and-tell lovers. My mother – unless she had a fling with William Hague which I missed – has avoided that trap. She preaches family values because she believes in family values and, though never claiming to be perfect, worries about the various threats to family life that the modern world has thrown up.

Family values are a familiar Tory tune, of course, and if my mother had had her way, the party would have made much more of it. She made no bones of the fact that she thought the Conservative governments of Margaret Thatcher and John Major had let families down on a whole range of issues, tagging along with the liberal consensus of the day when they should have been taking a much stronger moral stance.

In January 1994, in a typically trenchant speech in the House, she reiterated her opposition to lowering the age of consent for male homosexuals from eighteen to sixteen – a burning issue at the time – and laid into the 'bleating agnostic bishops' who she thought were taking the Church of England to hell in a handcart. It was hard-hitting stuff and, even though I did not agree with all of it, it was amusing to think of the said bishops bleating into their cornflakes as they read their Hansards the next morning.

Is my mother a reactionary? You bet she is! And proud of it. Anyone who applied the R-word to Mum could expect an indignant snort and a lecture straight out of the Margaret Thatcher book of political homilies. 'I'm a reactionary because there is a lot to react *against*. If you see something happening that is wrong, or if you see the country going downhill, you have to *challenge* it.' She could not stand the creeping permissiveness of the age, with its toxic impact on family life.

Take drugs, about which she had zero tolerance as a parent and zero tolerance as a politician. In an age when casual drug-taking has become increasingly acceptable, and social liberalism has seemed like an unstoppable tide, she has been outspoken in warning against an unthinkingly *laissez-faire* approach. You see a lot of life as a constituency MP, and she had seen enough young lives wrecked by drugs – and talked to enough constituents worried sick about drug abuse – to know that here was an evil to be resisted, not a harmless form of recreation. She mugged up on the subject, mastered the finer details and was duly rewarded. Her first front-bench appointment came after the 1997 election, when William Hague asked her to be the Conservative spokesman on drug policy. She took up the brief with gusto and, while left feeling exasperated by the failure of policy-makers to grasp the nettle, was able to make some telling interventions on the subject.

In 1999, she came top of the ballot for private members' Bills, which gave her the opportunity to introduce a Bill on another subject close to her heart – euthanasia. It never got on the statute book – controversial private members' Bills generally get 'talked out' and founder for lack of time – but it gave her a chance to raise the profile of the issue. She cannot stand the way the sanctity of life has gradually been eroded by people with a sinister, narrowly utilitarian agenda.

My mother is not just tiger-like in her championship of the causes she espouses, but a stickler for propriety, in matters great and small. She once had the distinction of being thrown out of a Vancouver nightclub on a fact-finding visit by the House of Commons Agriculture Committee. (Don't ask what facts the Agriculture Committee was hoping to find in Vancouver. Some political riddles are insoluble.) What did she do? Get drunk? Snog the DJ? Not a bit of it. She just objected to the thoroughly un-British practice of queue-jumping at the entrance to the club. 'You're out of order, Miss,' said the twenty-stone bouncer, escorting her out to the street. Mum, steaming, took further exception to the 'Miss'. It was not Canada's finest hour.

Unlike Dad, Mum has mastered the internet and other modern communication tools. But you won't catch her squinting at her iPhone when it is bad manners to do so. She believes in the little social courtesies that meant so much to her parents' generation. Her neatly handwritten letters observe the conventions of an earlier age. Yours sincerely, this, yours faithfully, the other. Envelopes will be addressed to John Smith Esq., never to Mr John Smith, unless John Smith is a tradesman. The habits she acquired at grammar school have never left her.

She is equally conservative in matters of sexual morality. Though she was a teenager at the start of the Swinging Sixties, when other women her age were shedding their inhibitions as fast as their knickers, for her, the sexual revolution might as well never have happened. My brother Andrew always chuckles when he recalls bringing girlfriends to stay at the family home in Cheshire. First, the girlfriends would be frogmarched to bedrooms as far as possible from his. Then Mum would contrive to find a series of noisy household chores to do at two in the morning. It was a *cordon sanitaire* of genius, executed with military precision.

Her genius also extended to handling Dad. People who have known Mum and Dad for years say she acts as a calming influence on him. If Dad is talking through his hat, which is not unknown, his wife will be the first time to tell him. A lot of male politicians are not so lucky in that respect: they become domestic tyrants and, away from the house, their arrogance grows unchecked. Mum and Dad enjoy a much healthier equilibrium. Their affectionate sparring is a joy to see. Here is a specimen Winterton exchange in the local pub.

NW (to the waitress): I want the fish and chips.

AW: *Would like* the fish and chips. Really, Nicholas!

NW: Sorry, darling.

In matters of politics, they are such soulmates that it is very unusual for them to disagree about anything. Sometimes she is more outspoken than him, sometimes it is the other way around: they take it in turns to let off steam, like neighbouring volcanoes in Indonesia. But in the wider context of their lives, their careers have followed very different trajectories. One is a male politician. The other is a female politician. They are not the same thing.

In one of the televised debates between the rival Democrat candidates in America in 2016, there was a remarkable moment of candour from Hillary Clinton – not everybody's cup of tea, but certainly a standard-bearer for her sex and, like my mother, a female politician who had to emerge from her husband's shadow. 'I'm not a natural politician, like my husband or President Obama,' she admitted. 'I have a view that I have to do the best I can, get the results I can, make a difference in people's lives.'

Not a natural politician! With all that she has achieved! Perhaps what Clinton was hinting at was something with which my mother would probably agree – but which, in a PC age, when nobody dares makes sweeping generalisations about the sexes, rarely gets said. Some of the core skills of a successful politician – the pugnacity, the slick salesman-ship, the mixture of bombast and low cunning needed to out-argue an opponent – depend on traditionally 'masculine' virtues. Remember how often Margaret Thatcher was jokingly called the best man in her Cabinet? She was admired for beating the boys at their own game, not for inventing a different game, designed by girls for girls.

My mother, like many female politicians, had a more pragmatic, less overtly 'political', approach. Doing the best one can, trying to get results, trying to make a difference… It sounded humdrum when Mrs Clinton said it. But every woman who has tried to practise those virtues in their own lives – from the classroom to the family kitchen – will have nodded in agreement.

One of Margaret Thatcher's most famous maxims was: 'If you want something said, ask a man. If you want something done, ask a woman.' My mother gets that. Boy, does she get that – particularly when she is cooking lunch while Dad is lolling in a chair, deep in the *Daily Telegraph*, sounding off about the European Union. As someone else once put it, 'Men play the game. Women know the score.'

I joked earlier that Dad was addicted to politics, and that he has been inhaling it all his adult life. I am not sure Mum does inhale, certainly not to the same extent. As a constituency MP, she was hard-working and conscientious, just like Dad. It was a point of honour with her to reply to letters the day they arrived. She took the same satisfaction from helping constituents in trouble. She put herself out for people. She listened to their concerns. But she did not go charging around Congleton with the same indefatigable zeal as Dad charged around Macclesfield. If Dad talked nineteen to the dozen, she only talked thirteen or fourteen to the dozen. She was a more low-key politician – although an equally effective one.

Some politicians treat politics like a game of chess, planning several moves ahead. They think: 'Well, if I suck up to *him*, and make sure not to get the wrong side of *her*, and avoid signing *that* early day motion, in two or three years, at the time of next reshuffle…' My mother is the polar opposite. 'I don't think I have personal political ambitions,' she told an interviewer in 1994. 'I'm rather inclined to take life as it comes.' Even when life kicks her in the solar plexus she never loses her sense of perspective. She can have a bloody awful day, then start whistling 'Que Sera, Sera' in the shower.

As a constituency MP, watchful of her flock, you could not fault her. While Dad was steadily building up his personal vote in Maccle-sfield, Mum was doing the same in Congleton. On paper, this was a seat where the Liberal Democrats might easily have challenged the Tory hegemony, as they did in many other Conservative-held rural seats. In the 1999 local elections, the Lib Dems won thirty-eight out of forty-eight seats on the borough council, which had substantially the same boundaries as the parliamentary constituency. But at general elections, Mum went from strength to strength. The more Congleton saw of her, the more it liked her.

In 1992, when the Conservative vote fell slightly, hers rose slightly. In 1997, when the Tories nationally were hammered, she bucked the trend again – her vote fell by 7 per cent compared with a national average of 11 per cent. It was the same story again in 2001. With the party nationally gaining just 1 per cent, she increased her vote in Congleton by over 5 per cent, routing the Lib Dems in the process. And having canvassed with her at those elections, I can say categorically that the bare statistics do not lie: they are proof positive of a popular constituency MP with a knack for listening to the concerns of ordinary voters and articulating those concerns at Westminster. Her values were *their* values, and if she was not quite as fiercely dedicated a politician as my father, it probably did her no harm. To the man and woman in the street, she came across as normal, sane, grounded, one of them. They could imagine going to a pub with her and having *fun* – not something that could be said of many MPs.

She put herself at their disposal, if that makes sense. In her very first election address, she put her home address at the top of her signed message to voters. How many other MPs do the same? They like to keep their constituents at arm's length or, in some cases, cover up the fact that they do not live in the constituency, but fifty miles away. My mother was better than that. Approachability was her trademark.

Politics and life intersect in a myriad ways. That is what makes it so fascinating. Mum can be as trenchant in her political views as Dad, sometimes more trenchant, but she has managed – not that she would ever use such jargon – to achieve a better work–life balance. Family has always come before politics – which is just as well for me and my brothers, as we have all needed what might be called firm parenting on occasion. And it is Mum, 99 per cent of the time, who has provided it, simply because she has been around more.

The year 1971, in which Dad was first elected an MP, was a watershed for the whole family. Up to that point, despite Dad's increasing involvement in local politics, the Wintertons had been a bog-standard English family of the period, living under one roof, with the father going out to work and the mother staying at home to look after the children. That was the social norm and only a small minority of families departed from it.

Dad – and this was again the norm – paid Mum a weekly housekeeping allowance, which became something of a family joke. At one point, it was set at £32.50 and stayed there for years, even though it bought less and less. Dad, like a good Tory, did not believe in inflation-proofing. No Chancellor of the Exchequer in history was more resistant to the argument that a rise in food prices had a knock-on effect on family budgets. Mum had to fight like a tigress to secure various concessions and opt-out clauses. It was the perfect training for a future politician.

With Dad's election to Westminster, the rules of the game changed overnight.

Mum now had to bear the entire burden of the childcare during the week, while Dad was in London, banging on about Europe and drafting amendments to clause 23 of the Finance Bill. It is a moot point who had the harder task and, if I were a full-on feminist, I would probably labour the point at length.

Suffice to say that, in my formative years, I saw a lot more of Mum than of Dad. She was the glue that held the whole family together. Not only was she holding the fort on her own most of the time, the fort had to be moved sixty miles to the north, a major logistical operation in itself.

After his 1971 by-election win, Dad was naturally keen to relocate from Warwickshire to his Macclesfield constituency as soon as possible. So, after a few months' house-hunting, my parents purchased a family-sized house with a bit of land near the village of Astbury – the home where they still live. Relocating all the ponies and the children meant that there were an awful lot of Wintertons travelling up and down the newly completed M6 motorway.

For my mother, although she has never made a song and dance about it, the early years in Cheshire must have been quite hard going. She was moving further away from her parents, upping sticks in Warwickshire and having to start again from scratch – without her husband by her side most of the time. Day-to-day childcare was slowly getting easier. Robert and Andrew were already at boarding school, so for most of the 1970s, except during the school holidays, it was just me, Mum and the ponies during the week. She quickly made friends with parents of children of my age, some of whom remain good friends today. But integrating yourself into a new community can take time, particularly when you are living in an isolated property, with no immediate neighbours. There must have been some lonely half-hours when she wondered whether being the wife of a Member of Parliament was everything it was cracked up to be. Couldn't her husband have become a dairy farmer instead?

But here is where the steeliness of her days as a master of foxhounds stood her in good stead. Like Margaret Thatcher, she did not do self-pity, grumbling for the sake of grumbling, sitting around feeling sorry for herself. She was a level-headed, practical woman. She believed in soldiering on through thick and thin, making the best of whatever cards life had dealt her. Family life *chez* Winterton might have changed now that Dad was away half the time, but she was still determined to make sure that it was a warm, happy family, like the one she had grown up in.

She was never the sort of domestic goddess who rustles up pan-fried venison with chanterelle mushrooms and a red wine *jus*. It would have been wasted on Dad, who would have demanded to know what was wrong with bangers and mash. But she ran a tight ship. She planned ahead. Her engagement diary was as neat and tidy as an accounts book. If she had to be somewhere at 9.30 a.m., she would be there at 9.30 a.m. without fail. Shirts were ironed, floors cleaned, carpets hoovered. The table was always set for breakfast before she went to bed. A tight ship indeed.

Mum, ever the perfectionist, also wanted to do a good job as the wife of the local MP. That did not just mean doing the decent minimum: it meant doing a lot more than the decent minimum. She would be at Dad's side during important constituency engagements and, if two engagements clashed or Dad was unavailable, she would fill in for him. Her sunny, outgoing personality made her the perfect political consort. If a lot of my childhood memories of Dad involve him talking the hind legs off a donkey, my memories of Mum usually involve her chuckling or sharing a joke with someone. Ordinary Maxonians – as the people of Macclesfield are known – adored her. She was approachable. She was down-to-earth. But most of all, she was a lot of fun to be with.

When she first moved to the area, the idea that she might one day follow her husband into politics would have seemed ridiculous. It would have been like Jeremy Corbyn becoming Leader of the Opposition. An excellent joke, but a joke nonetheless.

To give some historical context, there were just nineteen women MPs – less than a hockey and lacrosse team combined – at the start of the 1980s, compared with 191 today. My mother never entertained any ambition to join them, and not many other people entertained it on her behalf. They could see that she had the human qualities to make a good MP. In fact, my father, prophetically, told an interviewer in 1982: 'My wife is a tremendous help to me in politics, and I sometimes think she would make as good an MP as I do.' But she was also, let us not beat about the bush, a woman. She should be dividing her time between the kitchen and the bedroom, not getting ideas above her station. Maxonians may be the salt of the earth, but when it comes to feminism, it is the day before yesterday's salt. They were behind the times and proud of the fact.

It would be nice to think that the election of Margaret Thatcher, first as party leader, then as Prime Minister, changed attitudes and paved the way for women like my mother. There may be a grain of truth in that. But, as Mum would be the first to admit, her graduation from wife of a Member of Parliament to Member of Parliament owed more to luck than anything else. She just happened to be in the right place at the right time.

In early 1983, a major review of the boundaries of parliamentary constituencies reached its conclusion, resulting in a redrawing of the political map of the UK. The implications for the Tories of East Cheshire were profound. Congleton, which had previously been part of Dad's Macclesfield constituency, was to be a constituency in its own right. Knutsford to the west, held by Jock Bruce-Gardyne at the 1979 election, was to go altogether, with parts of it being absorbed in the Tatton constituency and the rest in the new Congleton constituency.

The resulting game of musical chairs was complicated by the fact that Jock Bruce-Gardyne had never really been a big hit in Cheshire. A slightly aloof man with mutton-chop whiskers, he came from a Scottish landowning family, was 13th Laird of Middleton and had represented South Angus between 1964 and 1974. But he had been parachuted into the Knutsford seat without having much knowledge of the area. He had also blotted his copy-book by opposing the Falklands War, no doubt a principled stand but, in the context of the times, electoral suicide.

As the newly formed Congleton Conservative Association turned its mind to who it wanted to fight the seat for the Tories in the forthcoming election, expected in the spring, Bruce-Gardyne was the obvious first name on the list, but not the only one.

Dorothy Littler, a Macclesfield Tory stalwart, and later Mum's constituency secretary for many years, remembers what happened clearly:

> We had seen a lot of Nicholas and Ann in Congleton and were equally fond of both of them. Nicholas had been our local MP for the last ten years, and a damn good one. Ann had been a major figure in the constituency in her own right, always rock solid, always putting herself out for other people. They made a wonderful team and really connected with local people. So we just thought: 'Why not?' Let's have another Winterton representing us at Westminster. It will keep things in the family.

When Mum was first approached by local members of the Congleton Conservative Association, she poured cold water on the idea: she did not feel she had nearly enough experience of politics, or indeed *any* practical experience of politics. The leap from Cheshire housewife to Member of Parliament was just too daunting. When they approached her a second time, she was still reluctant. But then came the lightbulb moment, the sudden flash of realisation that, if she did not seize the moment, she might regret it all her life. As she told an interviewer years later, there was a voice in her head whispering: 'Why be such a wimp? How would you feel if some pinstriped young man who did not know the area won the seat?' She was always clear that she was not prepared to traipse up and down the country putting herself forward for other Tory seats. But this was Congleton, for heaven's sake, a town she could find her way around blindfolded!

Her mind was made up. Even though she had not formally been vetted by Conservative Central Office, as was the norm, she knew she would be able to count on strong support from local Tories. She could also see that, now that I had settled in at boarding school, the timing could not have been better. Perhaps most importantly, she saw the chance to graduate from second fiddle in the Winterton household to a co-starring role.

Most stay-at-home mothers who return to work once their children have fled the nest are so far behind their husbands in career terms that they can never hope to catch up. The beauty of Parliament is that it levels that playing field in an instant. A newly elected MP is the equal, professionally, of an MP of thirty years' standing.

I am not suggesting that Mum was nursing long-held grievances at playing a subordinate role in the home. That was not the way she tended to think. She was never a militant, bra-burning, equality-at-all-costs feminist. But I am sure that, subliminally, the idea of a career move which, at a stroke, would ensure her true parity of esteem with her husband was hugely attractive. It would be nerve-racking at first, given her inexperience, but it would also be the adventure of a lifetime, a chance to prove herself on the national stage, just as Dad had done.

'I wanted to make my own footprints in the sand,' she explained to an interviewer in 1994. 'And to be fair to Nicholas, who is the original male chauvinist pig, he was totally supportive throughout.' The chauvinist pig reference might have been made in jest – or partly in jest; that £32.50 housekeeping money still rankled – but her gratitude for his unwavering support came from the heart. Where other husbands might have had their noses put of joint, Dad was as enthusiastic as anyone when it looked as if his wife might become the parliamentary candidate for Congleton. One discouraging word from him and her confidence would have shrivelled. But he embraced the idea with all his usual gusto. Two Wintertons at Westminster! What a mouth-watering prospect. Between them, they could *really* shake up the Tory Establishment.

With Mum's hat in the ring, the final selection meeting became effectively a three-horse race between Mum, Jock Bruce-Gardyne and Bill, now Sir Bill, Cash, a familiar figure to Westminster-watchers. The bespectacled Staffordshire MP, who is still in the

House, is the only man I know who could beat Dad in a talking-the-hind-legs-off-a-donkey contest, particularly on the subject of Europe. He is a colourful eccentric, whom my parents hold in warm regard, but one surmises was a bit full-on for the good Tories of Congleton. If they had asked him about EU secondary legislation in 1983, he would still have been talking in 1984. And that would just have been his introductory remarks.

In the end, Mum won the nomination quite comfortably, opening the most exciting chapter yet in the Winterton story. All she remembers about the selection meeting was how incredibly nervous she felt as she answered questions. She knew she was up to the job. She knew that, in time, she could be a capable constituency MP. But she was also crippled by self-doubt. As she later confessed, 'There were many times in the selection process when I felt I might have bitten off more than I could chew.'

As the questions flew, the butterflies in her stomach were flapping hard. She was not a complete novice at public speaking: she had often had to stand in for Dad at constituency functions and, although she lost sleep beforehand worrying about them, had given a reasonably good account of herself. But now, with so much at stake, and in the full glare of public scrutiny, she became a girl again, petrified of failure. It must have taken guts and determination just to hold herself together.

Luckily, Dad was at her side every step of the way, as she had been at his side during his own career. He had briefed her meticulously on what to expect. He had driven her to the selection meeting and waited outside while she was put through her paces. He had even found some suitably inspirational audio tapes to listen to in the car: the wartime speeches of Winston Churchill and, if that did not do the trick, 'Land of Hope and Glory'.

Non-Tories might sneer, but I still smile when I think of Mum and Dad on that fateful car journey: the truest, bluest Tories in the land, as excited as schoolchildren. The South Staffordshire Pony Club trains its sons and daughters well.

6.

GROWING UP IN THE
TORY TRIBE

When Dad was a boy at Rugby in the early 1950s, the school
hosted a debate at which Ted Heath, then Tory Chief Whip,
spoke on one side of the motion, and Jimmy Johnson, the local
Labour MP, on the other. The debate itself was unremarkable. It
was the vote held at the end of that debate that Dad remembers
– an overwhelming Conservative majority. Tories: 120. Labour: 3.

One wonders who the plucky dissenters were. Were they expelled,
put on detention, flogged by the headmaster, sent for a quiet word
with Matron? And where are they now? Have they stayed true to
the socialist principles of their youth? Or are they now propping up
the bar with Nigel Farage? Nothing in politics is permanent.

But it is that overwhelming Conservative majority that really
tells the story. How on earth did Ted Heath, a notoriously wooden
speaker at the best of times, persuade so many young schoolboys of
the rightness of his case? Did the muse of oratory suddenly touch
him with the divine fire? Answer: almost certainly not. The boys
probably just voted for him because he was the one with the blue
rosette.

In the 1950s, as historians of the period never tire of pointing
out, the overwhelming majority of Tory-voting schoolboys came
from Tory-voting families, for whom voting Tory was as natural as
breathing. And the same was true of Labour-supporting families.
You were born on one side of the social divide and you stayed on

that side. Nothing had changed – apart from, of course, the replacement of the Liberals with Labour as the main party of opposition – since Gilbert and Sullivan's *Iolanthe* in 1882:

'Every boy and every gal
That's born into the world alive
Is either a little Liberal
Or else a little Conservative.'

In the Labour strongholds in the north, there were whole streets where you could not find a solitary Tory voter. And the same was true of the Tory heartlands in the south of England. Two-party Britain had reached its apogee. In fact, at the 1955 general election, over 95 per cent of the population voted either Tory or Labour, a figure that would be unimaginable today. Life – politically, at least – was very, very simple.

Nobody would pretend that the 1950s was a golden era in British politics. Politically, it was a rather bland decade, with the single, catastrophic exception of Suez. Europe – the subject of such ferocious arguments later – was just a continental land mass off the south coast of England. It was a place, not an issue. The big issue of the day, so far as there was one, was simply whether a Tory-led or Labour-led government offered the best economic future for Britain. Everyone had their own view, but their views were largely shaped by whether they had grown up in Surrey or Liverpool, a leafy suburb or a mining village.

There was the odd exception. Dad likes to tell the story of a miner he met on a visit to a colliery in Silverdale, near Newcastle-under-Lyme, who grinned from ear to ear when he heard Dad was a Tory, and embraced him like a long-lost brother when he met him at the pit-bottom. He even remembers his name, more than half a century later – Percy Scragg. But, generally speaking, the Tory-voting miner was as rare as the Labour-voting farmer. People knew where they stood and they knew where other people stood, so there was a bedrock of certainty which, on the whole, was probably good for the body politic.

Dad – like Mum, and like scores of other Conservative MPs whom I have met over the years – was born into a Tory family and imbibed Tory values with his mother's milk. They just made sense to him, and the older he got, the more sense they made.

He is a simple, straightforward man, the type who does not overthink things or see problems where none exist. Like a devout Catholic or Muslim, secure in his faith, comfortable in his own skin, he has never wavered in his basic convictions. If he was against something in 1965, the chances are he is still against it today – and probably even more strongly. The siren voices of the left – so seductive at times that they have come close to becoming the conventional wisdom of modern Britain, as peddled by the BBC – have fallen on deaf ears.

Mum is the same: a textbook case of a conservative with a small c, true to her roots, suspicious of change, loyal to the country she grew up in. At heart, she is still the girl at the South Staffordshire Pony Club, a bundle of laughs, at ease with England and English ways.

Pinning labels on the Wintertons is an exercise in semantic futility. If pressed, Dad will generally describe himself as a politician of the centre right, rather than an out-and-out right-winger. He likes to tell a story about my brother Andrew being interviewed by a newspaper when he was a teenager. 'My father right-wing? You must be joking. He's a liberal compared to me!' Or he will call himself a 'progressive traditionalist', insisting that he is not against all reforms: he just wants to satisfy himself that mooted reforms are sensible and practical, not just window-dressing. But he gets irritated by those lazy commentators who are determined to place every politician at some arbitrary point on a left–right spectrum. His personal political mantra never changes and is disarmingly simple. 'I'm a Tory.'

Of course, what exactly makes a Tory a Tory is a moot point, and one which cleverer thinkers than me have spent long hours debating. In my experience, there are almost as many sub-species of Tory as there are Tories, and the problem is compounded by the fact that, compared with Labour or Liberal Democrat supporters, Tories have little interest in existential discussion of such hifalutin issues. Conservatives can fight with each other like alley-cats. I have seen them do it, and it is not a pretty sight. But, north of Watford, they seldom argue about philosophical abstractions, like members of a student debating society. Their conservatism is more practical in nature, more a matter of instinct than ideology.

Harold Wilson famously said of the Labour Party that it owed more to Methodism than to Marxism. One could make a similar point about the Conservative Party. From time to time, it has rallied to the colours of political philosophers and gurus – Milton Friedman, for example, under Margaret Thatcher – but the more it wallows in abstract theories, the less Conservative it becomes. Tory-ism, as Dad likes to put it, is not a philosophical creed: it is a way of life.

John Major once waxed lyrical about a Britain of 'long shadows on cricket grounds, warm beer, invincible green suburbs, dog-lovers and pools-fillers … old maids bicycling to holy communion through the morning mist' – a Britain that would still be there in fifty years' time. My parents would have heartily agreed.

If they were vehemently opposed to the abolition of fox-hunting, it was not just because it had played such a large part in their own lives: it was because it embodied a way of life that had been passed down from generation to generation and was worth conserving on those grounds alone. They were against pit closures for the same reason – because they struck at the heart of communities which had owed their cohesion to a particular way of life. The Tory whips didn't thank them for saying as much, but they didn't give a damn. Their hearts – and their votes – were with the mining communities.

Sunday trading was another red line for them. They treasured the British Sunday they had grown up with – a day of rest and re-ligious observance, quite different in character from Saturday. Why sweep away centuries of tradition just so that people could spend Sundays buying bras and lawn-mowers? A free market was not the same as a free-for-all.

'If it ain't broke, don't fix it.' There is more wisdom in that old saying than in a thousand political textbooks. And it goes to the very heart of Tory-ism, even if it doesn't totally explain it.

I am an instinctive Tory myself, so I suppose I can recognise a fellow Tory when I meet one – but only nine times out of ten, and not if we have both been drinking. That is all I would say with any confidence, even after a lifetime of living in the Tory tribe, learning by heart all the little unwritten rules that bind the tribe together.

One complicating factor is that, for every out-and-proud Tory, there is another who is far more reticent about their political allegiances. The 'shy Tory', telling pollsters one thing and doing the opposite in the voting booth, has become a staple of political analysis. The Wintertons, as you will have gathered by now, are *not* shy Tories. There are twenty-stone town criers in Liverpool who are more bashful than my parents. But the tribe of which they are part has its fair share of supporters for whom Tory-ism is more akin to a private vice than a burning political creed.

The Tories can be a peculiar bunch, in all sorts of ways, and often misunderstood – not to mention underestimated – by members of different tribes. I have been privileged, if that is the word, to attend many a Tory party conference, the annual knees-up at which the tribe can be viewed in all its glory, relaxing by the seaside. Relaxing, my eye! There is something vaguely feral about these occasions, a whiff of sex and power which is not replicated to the same extent at the other parties' conferences: all those ambitious young men in sharp suits, sucking up to Cabinet ministers; 'Tory totties' dressed up to the nines, on the prowl for their prey; all those snake-oil salesmen from the PR and lobbying industry on the fringes of the conference, trying to get a foot in the political door. It is not an altogether pretty sight, and I would not pretend otherwise.

But the party conference is only a few days in the year. It is the rest of the year that matters, when Tories across the land, unnoticed and unrewarded, do the million tiny things – from organising raffles to stuffing envelopes – that keep the tribe together and make it a viable party of government.

The Tories' opponents like to caricature them as grasping capitalists, rabid free-marketeers, out to make as much money as possible and none too scrupulous about how they make it. But that kind of Tory – although common enough in the City of London – would be a rarity in Cheshire, which is not so much a hotbed of capitalism as the northern outpost of Middle England, that mythical land so beloved of the *Daily Mail*.

If the only people who voted Tory were millionaires and root-and-branch capitalists, the party would never win a single seat. It is its genius for holding together a loose coalition of sensible middle-of-the-roaders, from all walks of life, which accounts for its electoral success.

This memoir is not about banging the Conservative drum. In its human essentials – two backbenchers with minds of their own and the determination to speak those minds – the Winterton story would have been no different if they had been a husband-and-wife team of Labour MPs, going in to bat for their constituents.

Character trumps ideology. Every time. One of the lessons my parents learnt during their long years at Westminster was that the views people hold are generally far less important than their characters. They would hear X make a cracking speech in favour of so-and-so but know that when push came to shove, he would prove flaky: he would change his views to fit the prevailing political orthodoxy because his career was more important than his principles. Y would be the complete opposite, never changing his views one iota, even when it was expedient to do so. And it was Y whom my parents naturally preferred, because they shared that same dogged consistency of outlook.

They believed in getting on with things, not analysing issues to death. When Norman Lamont as Chancellor of the Exchequer quoted Edith Piaf, '*Je ne regrette rien*', my parents knew what he meant. They probably wished he had made his point in plain English rather than French, but they identified with a politician who lived in the here and now, and did not rake over the embers of the past and think 'If only I had done so-and-so...' Mum and Dad have made their share of mistakes, but dwelling on what-ifs and might-have-beens is simply not their style.

Being a conservative with a small c as well as a big C has advantages, as they have learnt from personal experience. The tide of political fashion ebbs and flows and, if you hold firmly to the same basic opinions, as my parents have, you can seem hopelessly old-fashioned one minute, positively *avant-garde* the next.

In 1979, to take one obvious example, my father was virtually in a minority of one when he warned that Robert Mugabe would prove a far less effective leader of Rhodesia/Zimbabwe than Ian Smith. That does not seem such a bad call today. In fact, a lot of people would still be alive today if my father's warnings about Mugabe had been heeded. In the same year, he was calling for the basic rate of income tax to be cut to 25p – it is now 20p – at a time when no Chancellor of Exchequer of either party dared reduce it below 30p.

On Europe, my father pressed Tony Blair at his last Prime Minister's Questions in 2007 to hold a referendum on Britain's membership of the EU. The House chortled and Mr Blair added to the merriment by wishing my father goodbye in three different European languages. But on this substantive issue, not for the first time, he was 100 per cent right. Membership of the EU was *not* compulsory, and only the British people could decide if they wanted to renew their subscription to the club. He could hardly have been more clairvoyant about the way the political tide was flowing.

As I have said, this is a book about people, not opinions. But I think it is worth highlighting some of the shared Tory values which first drew Mum and Dad together – and which, for nearly half a century, anchored them in their local communities.

1. Family values. This one took a hammering when John 'Back to Basics' Major was Prime Minister and, every other day, the *News of the World* seemed to feature a married Tory MP with his trousers at half mast, cheating on his wife. But for Mum and Dad, not to mention most of their constituents, it is a moral bedrock, the very essence of the Britain that is worth fighting to conserve. Strong communities are rooted in strong families, not a constantly shifting *mélange* of individuals. Weaken the family and you weaken society as a whole.

Family values, for them, are underpinned by marriage, defined as being a marriage between a man and woman. They have many gay friends and acquaintances, but were opposed to gay marriage and, I suspect, will go to their graves convinced that David Cameron's championship of it was a profound betrayal of Tory values. Naturally, they are also firm believers that the tax system should be used to support the family as the cornerstone of a strong society.

2. Religion. I have already touched on Dad's regular appearances at local churches, belting out the hymns with gusto and reading the lesson occasionally. He is not the sort of person to wear his religion on his sleeve. He would probably find that rather un-British, the sort of thing you would expect from tub-thumping senators from Kansas or Wyoming. But if there are beliefs that keep him going during times of stress or disappointment, they are usually to be found in the Bible.

'I believe very strongly in basic biblical teachings,' he told one interviewer in 1997. 'The Bible is life.' He also, interestingly, seized on what you might call the non-conformist, anti-Establishment, strand in Christian teaching: 'Some of the things Jesus did were not easy. Doing things that people don't necessarily want you to do is not necessarily wrong.'

For Mum, I suspect that religion was even more important than for Dad. Again, she didn't make a song and dance about it, and there is something so wonderfully un-pious about her, a mischievous, anarchic streak. You would not pick her as a devout churchgoer. But the fact that she chaired the All-Party Parliamentary Pro-Life Group is testimony to the strength of her views. She is as opposed to euthanasia as she is to abortion and gay marriage, and for the same reasons. They all fly in the face of core Christian teaching.

3. Challenging injustice. This one may surprise readers who are convinced that all Tories are hard-hearted bastards, grinding the poor into the dust before repairing to their Pall Mall club for a gin and tonic, but it is an essential strand in the Winterton story, which could easily be subtitled *Championing the Underdog*.

I have already touched on Dad's chivalrous instincts, his urge to ride, John Wayne-like, to the rescue of a constituent in trouble. Those little battles, against the slings and arrows of bureaucracy, were what got him out of bed in the morning. And the same instincts stood him and Mum in good stead when they took their seats at Westminster. Economic minutiae, on the whole, bored them. But show them a blatant injustice – like the unfair treatment affecting pre-1973 war widows, which Dad spent years challenging, successfully in the end – and they were different people, fired with righteous zeal.

4. Sound money. Dad's reluctance to fork out for drinks in the pub is a running joke in Macclesfield. (Specimen gag: 'What's the difference between Nicholas Winterton and a coconut? You can get a drink out of a coconut.' A local journalist once joked that Mum had given Dad a wallet for Christmas, but his jacket had rejected it.) If challenged he would probably say he was following sound Tory principles, in which profligacy plays no part. He is a man of his times, raised before credit cards had been invented, taught to regard saving as a virtue and borrowing as something only to be contemplated in exceptional circumstances. He has applied the same basic principles throughout his life, whether running a small business or superintending the family finances. Governments that cheerfully run up vast financial deficits – generally Labour – make him shudder with horror.

5. Hard work and enterprise. When I was at school, Mum and Dad never expected me to get top marks in every subject or fretted over my academic grades. As graduates of the University of Life, they knew that other things were far more important. But anything that smacked of indolence – not trying hard enough, staying in bed till lunchtime – was quickly stamped on.

Mum was a grammar schoolgirl, with the mind-set of the breed. If you worked hard and applied yourself, you would get on in life. If you did not, you would be bringing up the rear with the also-rans. Dad had, if anything, an even more pronounced work ethic. His engagement diary was never empty: it was full to overflowing, and that is how he liked it. As he saw it, his constituents had sent him to Westminster to work on their behalf, so there was no excuse for slacking. Downing tools at six o'clock, with the job half done, would have been anathema to him.

6. Patriotism. For Mum and Dad, Britain is self-evidently the best country in the world, streets ahead of the competition. In fact, they can sometimes get irritated with people who fail to grasp this, to them, obvious truth. France and Spain and Germany are all very well to visit, but who in their right minds would want to *live* there? America? Come off it! With those accents?

Having grown up in a country still basking in the glory of the Second World War, with memories of the British Empire still fresh, they have the same fierce sense of nationhood that inspired Winston Churchill. If they were ardent supporters of Margaret Thatcher, it was because they recognised in her a fellow Tory patriot of the old school.

Dad, in particular, is adamant that Britain is at its best when it feels proudest of its history, not when it is wallowing in post-colonial guilt or bending over backwards to be nice to foreigners. He loves to quote Hugh Gaitskell, the Labour leader in the early '60s, who argued against Britain joining the Common Market and throwing away 'a thousand years of our history'. If he was as happy as a sandboy with the result of the EU referendum, it was because he believed – cliché or no cliché – that he really was getting his country back.

At heart, he is a screaming romantic, hopelessly in love with the land of Nelson and Wellington and Sir Francis Drake, a plucky island race, repelling all boarders. To take his seat in the House of Commons, in the shadow of Big Ben, a beacon of freedom around the world, was a boyhood dream made true.

7. Service. People who glibly assume that all Tories are in it for themselves will never get the measure of people like my parents. While self-sufficiency is a virtue that Tories rightly prize, as they prize free enterprise in general, it should never be confused with selfishness. The true Tory, as far as my parents are concerned, is not selfish, but the servant of his or her community.

I have already referred to Dad's happy memories of his National Service in Germany. It was only a short period in his life, but it instilled in him an ideal of service – doing one's bit for one's country, even if it meant sleeping in a soggy tent, miles from home – which has never left him. As he sees it, and Mum would heartily agree, no human being can lead a full life unless, for substantial parts of that life, he puts himself at the service of others.

If my parents are both ardent Royalists, it is not least because the Queen has offered her people such a shining example of public service. The more privileged your upbringing, they would argue, the greater your responsibility to others. They have little sympathy with people who bang on about human rights, and cry foul when their human rights are infringed, but have no corresponding sense of responsibility.

In Cheshire, it was my parents' commitment to service that

made them such superb constituency MPs. At Westminster, it was that same sense of commitment that made them willing to chair unglamorous committees rather than seek out the political spotlight. They would never have boasted of the unselfish service they gave, but perhaps, as their daughter, I can be allowed to salute and admire it.

8. The best education for all, according to their needs. For Mum and Dad, if not necessarily for all Tories, grammar schools remain the ideal educational model, enabling bright children from modest backgrounds to make the most of their abilities. Mum benefited from a grammar education herself, while Dad, though privately educated, argued consistently from the very outset of his political career that the supplanting of grammar schools by comprehensives would be an unmitigated disaster. As he saw it, the comprehensive system was a recipe for mediocrity, stifling aspiration when it should have been encouraging it. More recently, he has been cautiously welcoming of academies because, although not as good a model as grammar schools, they sound the death-knell for the one-size-fits-all conformity that has bedevilled our education system for so long.

9. Private enterprise. Faith in the private sector is central to the whole Tory worldview and, for Mum and Dad, that faith was rooted in personal experience. Unlike half the Tory MPs elected since the turn of the millennium, who seem to have spent most of their adult lives as policy wonks or party hacks, Dad had a solid background in business, and had helped to run his father-in-law's firm before he was elected to Parliament. He later turned that experience to good advantage, chairing the influential Manufacturing and Construction Industries Alliance for more than twenty years. He was never happy with the way Ted Heath flirted with essentially socialist ideas such as prices and income controls, and revered Margaret Thatcher for her passionate advocacy of free-market principles.

10. Maintaining the Union. If you think it is only pedants who still refer to the Tory party as the Conservative and Unionist Party, you have not met my father, who includes the 'Unionist' at every opportunity. He was already active in local politics in 1965, the year in which the Conservative Party joined forces with the former Scottish-based Unionist Party, and it has coloured his thinking ever since. (In 1912, believe it or not, the Conservatives briefly marched under the banner of the National Unionist Association of Conservative and Liberal Unionist Organisations, which would have been too much of a mouthful even for my father.)

From his earliest days at Westminster, he found common cause with the Northern Ireland Unionists, regarded concessions to Sinn Féin as tantamount to appeasing terrorism and was delighted when Enoch Powell, one of his political heroes, became a Unionist MP for a Northern Ireland seat.

He has been equally uncompromising in his attitude to the Scottish Nationalist Party, even when the political tide has been flowing in its favour. Devolution? He was against devolution. A Scottish Assembly? The thin end of the wedge. As for offering the Scots a referendum on independence, as David Cameron did in 2014… His thoughts on the subject were largely unprintable. Lovely people, Scots – after all, his wife is half Scottish – but they belonged in the United Kingdom of Great Britain and Northern Ireland. That was better for them. It was better for all of us.

As for Nicola Sturgeon… Let's just say Dad doesn't keep a photo of her under his pillow, perfumed with lavender. In fact, if he had his druthers, he would probably place her under house arrest on a remote Hebridean island, with only sheep for company, before she does any more harm to the Union.

11. Low taxation and minimum regulation. In common with 99.9 per cent of the population, the Wintertons do not enjoy paying taxes. Dad would rather have raging toothache or be stuck in a lift with Nick Clegg than receive an unexpected bill from the Inland

Revenue. He subscribes to the view, so memorably articulated by Margaret Thatcher, that individuals should, so far as possible, be trusted to spend the money they have earned, not have it spent for them by civil servants hundreds of miles away. He is suspicious of big government, the bureaucratic compulsion to interfere, and all the red tape that goes with it.

Mum and Dad are certainly not ideological or fundamentalist tax-cutters, determined to reduce taxation to levels where essential public services such as the NHS can no longer be maintained. They are just imbued with that most Tory of instincts: a horror of taxation for the sake of taxation, regulation for the sake of regulation.

12. Law and order. In popular folklore, the right wing of the Tory party is synonymous with hangers and floggers, and I guess Mum and Dad put a big tick in that box. I am not sure either of them are floggers, although Dad still has his bring-back-the-birch moments, but they are certainly both hangers, and consistently voted for the retention of capital punishment whenever the Commons debated the issue. Needless to say, their stance received the hearty endorsement of their constituents.

The importance Dad attaches to law and order is reflected in the fact that he devoted his maiden speech to the subject. During his time as a county councillor, he had seen the creeping effect of yobbishness and vandalism on the Britain he loved and, in the best of Tory traditions, felt that such behaviour should be challenged.

Whether these various beliefs, gut instincts, attitudes and prejudices add up to anything one could call a philosophy is very doubtful. As I have done my best to explain, Tory-ism is more a way of life, a state of mind, than a set of precisely calibrated beliefs. The Conservative Party has always been a broad church, generally tolerant of dissent, occasionally riven by sectarian in-fighting. I have not even attempted to formulate a 'Tory' attitude to Europe, there being no such animal (although Mum and Dad, ardent Eurosceptics both, would probably disagree). Europe has been a long-festering wound in the party – a wound not fully cauterised by the vote for Brexit – and I will be picking at the scabs in a later chapter.

There have been seven Tory leaders since Dad was first elected to Parliament in 1971 and, as far as he is concerned, some have been more Tory than others. He has generally backed the winning horse in leadership contests – William Hague and Iain Duncan Smith, for example – and had no truck with Michael Heseltine or Kenneth Clarke or other challengers for the leadership from the left wing of the party, whom he regarded as closet socialists with an unhealthy fetish for the EU. He also found it hard to forgive Heseltine for his puerile stunt in the chamber in 1976, when he picked up the Mace – the ancient symbol of the authority of the House of Commons – and brandished it at the Labour benches. Dad, who had a ringside seat, was appalled that a fellow Tory should treat Parliament like a student debating chamber. The Oxford Union had a lot to answer for – and still does.

Top of his personal Tory pantheon, inevitably, is Margaret Thatcher ('a modern Boadicea'). He revered her and, unlike many of his fellow Tory MPs, who behaved like rats on a sinking ship, was loyal to her to the end. He is rightly proud of the fact that, after she had been ousted by her party in 1990, the first constituency function she attended – not least to show my father her gratitude for his unstinting loyalty – was a fundraising dinner in Macclesfield, at which the ever-loyal Denis was also present.

They had been political soulmates since 1975, when Dad had supported her enthusiastically in her bid to topple Ted Heath. 'I shall need all the help I can find from friends in the difficult months ahead,' she wrote to him, days after she had been elected as party leader. 'But we must not fail the people. It may be the last chance to conserve the British way of life.' Post-Brexit, the letter seems eerily prescient, a foretaste of the battles for national sovereignty that would dominate my parents' careers – as well as the career of their leader and flag-bearer.

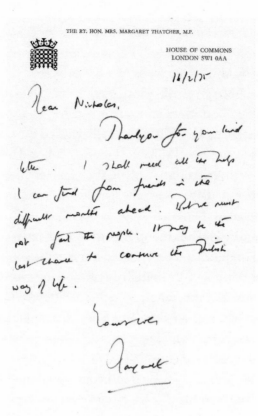

'One of the sad things about Margaret,' my father once told me,

> was that she was a much warmer person than her public image. People saw her as cold and aloof, but she wasn't like that at all, just rather shy. I remember the time she and I had lunch at a primary school in Prestbury where she had just opened a new nursery class. She made a point of going to thank all the kitchen staff afterwards. How many of our male Prime Ministers would have done the same?

Dad's two least favourite Tory leaders were probably Ted Heath, the bounder who took Britain into Europe, and David Cameron ('very able, but not enough gravitas'). I find it telling that, in both cases, strong differences of opinion did not lead to bad blood.

One of my father's most treasured mementoes from his time at Westminster is a handwritten note from Ted Heath – whom he had voted to replace with Margaret Thatcher – thanking him for the fact that, unlike some other Tory MPs, he had acted 'openly and honourably'. There must be more two-faced back-stabbers in London SW1 than any other postcode in England, but Dad was not one of them. His style of politics owed more to the boxing ring than the dark arts of Machiavelli.

'Heath was an enigma,' my father remembers. 'Sexually, he was AC/DC, as I saw it. An unhappy misfit. But he was so lacking in basic communication skills, for such a bright man, that he was his own worst enemy.' Stories about Heath's gracelessness were already legion by the time my father was elected in 1971. At one point, having been urged to spend more time in the House of Commons smoking room, talking to more back-bench MPs, he did just that – only to tell one of his backbenchers, by way of small-talk, 'That was a bloody awful speech you made today.' My father never warmed to Heath. Very few people did. But he certainly respected him.

With David Cameron, too, he remained on reasonable terms despite their ideological differences and despite their, at times, fractious relationship, which reached its nadir during the expenses scandal. Did he think David Cameron's Big Society was so much hot air? Is the Pope a Catholic? Do bears shit in the woods? There were times when he despaired of David Cameron's Tory party and its liberalising tendencies: its priorities were light years away from the priorities of ordinary families in Cheshire. But, although he was glad to see the back of Cameron in the summer of 2016, he acknowledged his courage in allowing the EU referendum to be held in the first place. And he was certainly not among the people queuing up to wish him good riddance. He has never sunk to personal attacks. They are not his style.

The emergence of UKIP on the right of British politics only muddied the waters further. Mum came within a whisker of voting UKIP in 2015, believing that, in its robust brand of patriotism, the party was more truly Tory than the modern Conservative Party. Dad loyally put his cross against the name of the Conservative candidate – and worked tirelessly to help the Tory candidate in Hazel Grove reclaim the seat from the Liberal Democrats – but not without some nagging doubts that, on some issues, Mum might be right. The goalposts are moving the whole time, which is what makes politics so fascinating.

But – and it is a big but, intrinsic to any understanding of the Winterton story – the goalposts don't move nearly as quickly, or nearly as often, in Cheshire as they do in the south of England.

When David Cameron was first elected Leader of the Opposition, the epicentre of the Conservative Party – though not necessarily of Tory-ism – moved to Notting Hill. It later spread to the provinces and encompassed the Chipping Norton set, residing fully seventy miles from London, even if only at the weekends. But the so-called Cameroons were quintessentially metropolitan types, with a metropolitan outlook on life: nervous trend-chasers, creatures of the moment, easily scared by unhelpful newspaper headlines. Cheshire Tory-ism is a sturdier plant altogether.

Go into a pub or shop in Macclesfield or Congleton – communities that seem light years from the plush stockbroker-belt towns in the Tories' southern heartlands – and you will be able to glimpse the bedrock of decency and common sense on which Mum and Dad built their careers. Economically, the area has known good times and less good times, like everywhere else. Multinationals have slowly superseded the traditional textile industries. Farmers' sons who would once have stayed on the land now commute into offices in Manchester. Unemployment is generally below the national average, but you don't see many people chucking money about.

The two constituencies are slightly different in character. Congleton – a riverside town with a population of around 25,000, ringed by farms and villages – has quite a rural feel. It is only twenty miles south of Manchester, but seems much further. It is probably best known for its biannual carnival, once the biggest in Europe.

How apt for my fun-loving mother, who tried to bring a touch of the carnival to Westminster!

Macclesfield is more industrial in character. It is one of those old Victorian canal towns that have seen better days, but are still holding their own, bloodied but unbowed, in the twenty-first century. At one time, it was best known for its silk: Macclesfield produced more finished silk than anywhere else in the world – the silk, I must add, that I used for my wedding dress. The biggest employer there today is the pharmaceutical giant AstraZeneca: a very different industry for a very different age. The town has had to re-invent itself again and again, but thanks to the hard work and resourcefulness of its inhabitants, it has.

Like Congletonians, Maxonians have no illusions that the world owes them a living. They just get on with their lives as best they can. They have kept their feet on the ground – and if they gravitate towards the Tory party, it is because it is the political tribe that best embodies that down-to-earth, safety-first approach to life.

And having joined the tribe, of course, they think and behave *tribally*. Anyone who has never been a member of a political party, i.e. most of the population, finds that tribalism unfathomable. At its worst, it can be pretty moronic: people who cannot be bothered to think for themselves, clinging to each other through thick and thin, like street gangs. But it is a fact of political life. You join a political tribe and, like an Everton or Liverpool supporter, you stay with that tribe for ever. Defect to another tribe and your old tribe will never trust you again. Loyalty to the tribe matters far, far more than loyalty to values or abstract ideas.

You could say that that is a fault-line in British politics, but it is the same the world over. In 2016, there were Republicans who were totally appalled by Donald Trump's brand of politics, but who voted for him anyway. Half of them would have voted for a baboon with a Republican rosette rather than transfer their allegiance to a different tribe and vote for Hillary Clinton. That, as they say, is politics.

When political tribes splinter or break up, the repercussions can rumble on for years. If you go back to the 1980s, when the Labour Party split down the middle over issues such as Europe and uni-lateral disarmament, MPs who joined the breakaway SDP were denounced as traitors by the likes of Roy Hattersley and Denis Healey, party moderates who had chosen to remain within the Labour fold. SDP *policies* were a good deal more Healey-ite than the official Labour Party policies at the time. But that did not matter. The SDP had deserted the tribe and, unforgivably, formed a new tribe. They had to be destroyed!

In recent years, the emergence of UKIP has exposed similarly tribal attitudes in the Tory party. Scratch a Tory and the chances are that he or she is a devout Brexiteer. What was UKIP's main purpose in life? To get Britain out of the EU! So the Tories and UKippers are soulmates, right, singing from the same hymn sheet? Wrong. They may be *ideological* soulmates, but they are certainly not interchangeable. They are rival tribes, competing for the same territory.

At Westminster, tribal political divisions are occasionally susceptible to more nuanced arguments. In the provinces, never. You could travel from Ascot to Aberdeen without finding a more tribally minded group of people than the Tories of East Cheshire. They are like the Winterton family writ large: all for one, one for all, and woe betide anyone who messes with them.

If you were to attend the AGM of the Macclesfield or Congleton Conservative Association – or one of the patrons' dinners, attended by the local party donors, chipping in a couple of hundred quid a year – sometimes a lot more – the first thing that would strike you is the relative antiquity of those present. More than half would be over sixty, and some would be nearer ninety. But the second thing you'd notice would be the unity of purpose: the shared loyalty to an organisation, the clannishness, the readiness to close ranks at times of difficulty. Local Conservative associations, in my exper-ience, tend to develop a siege mentality: they know that a lot of non-Tories detest them, so they fight shoulder to shoulder to keep the enemy at bay.

After one of their many election victories, my parents received a message of congratulations from a constituent which illustrates the uncomplicated tribalism I am talking about. 'WHAT A PAIR! ABSOLUTELY DELIGHTED FOR BOTH OF YOU. TEAR THE RED B*****DS APART.' It could be a roar from the football terraces. Blues versus Reds. An ancient blood feud to rival the Capulets and the Montagues. Yes, there were the Liberal Democrats and the Greens and other small fry. But the real battle was a simple Tory–Labour slugfest, a repelling of the socialist forces trying to take over Cheshire, wasting people's hard-earned money on bureaucratic spending programmes that were all very well in theory but missed the point. Society is made up of individuals, and those individuals are most likely to prosper if they are encouraged to take responsibility for their own lives and run their own communities.

I have chatted to literally hundreds of Cheshire Tories over the years, and one thing strikes me very forcibly: how closely their gut instincts and prejudices chime with those of my parents. Seldom can there have been such a snug match between two MPs and their constituencies.

Political analysts in the Westminster village – another weird tribe, if ever there was one – tend to treat people like my parents as somehow ideologically perverse. How can someone be on the far right of their party on some issues (e.g. law and order, Europe, immigration) and on the far left on other issues, such as transport and health care? The answer, and it is hardly rocket science: because most ordinary voters have exactly that same dichotomy of outlook. They are quite right-wing, to use a simplistic label, on some issues. Criminals are a cancer in society, so crime needs to be stamped on. Immigration needs to be rigorously controlled. The European project needed to be treated with scepticism: if it did not work for Britain, why tag along with it? But they are also quite left-wing, in the narrow sense of valuing publicly run institutions such as schools and the

NHS and expecting them to be properly funded and efficiently administered.

Politics, my father would say, is only complicated if you make it complicated. He has seen too many of his contemporaries at Westminster get their knickers in a twist by over-analysing issues and following the latest fashionable theory. Of course running a country the size of Britain – nearly 70 million individuals, all making demands on the public purse – is a Herculean task. You will never be able to please everyone. But if you place your trust in the common sense of the people, rather than political textbooks, you will be halfway there. And if the man and woman in the street is strongly against drugs *and* strongly against cuts in NHS spending *and* strongly against uncontrolled immigration *and* concerned about fracking, you should trust them on each and every issue – not take up some arbitrary point on a left-to-right spectrum and tailor your views accordingly.

I have already had occasion to quote Edmund Burke, perhaps the greatest of all parliamentarians. There are MPs, on both sides of the House, who can quote verbatim his famous words to the electors of Bristol in 1774: 'Your representative owes you, not his industry only, but his judgement; and he betrays, instead of serving you, if he sacrifices it to your opinion.' My father was a Burkean to his fingertips. He used his judgement. He followed his conscience. He would never have changed the way he voted simply because of a sample opinion poll in the *Macclesfield Express* but always sought to listen intently to the views of his constituents.

But he would also have nodded in agreement with a less well-known Burke quotation – used, incidentally, by Enoch Powell in a parliamentary debate on the Common Market in 1971: 'To follow, not to force, the public inclination, to give a direction, a form, a technical dress and a specific sanction to the general sense of the community, is the true end of the legislature.'

The general sense of the community... Isn't that parliamentary democracy in a nutshell? For Burke, politicians who ignored the general sense of community – or were so caught up with their own concerns that they failed to discern what the general sense of the community was – were guilty of blind hubris. And for Enoch Powell, and for my father, a Parliament that legislated without regard to the sentiments of the man and woman in the street was not just extremely unwise, but failing in its constitutional duty.

Which brings me neatly on to the issue that defined Enoch Powell's career and, to a lesser extent, my parents' – nationalism and immigration.

7.

ENGLAND'S GREEN AND PLEASANT LAND

Look out of my parents' kitchen window in Cheshire and you will see a scene that has hardly changed in the last five hundred years. Their house is not particularly grand, but its surroundings have a grandeur painted by Mother Nature herself.

Beyond the garden hedge, there is a small field, where the family ponies used to graze. Beyond the paddock, there is another farm, a row of buildings, weathered by age, and a field of cows, shimmering in the haze. Beyond the cows, the ground rises gently towards the wooded horizon that marks the county border with Staffordshire. The scene is so peaceful, so pristine – particularly in the early morning, with the sun peeping over the trees, or in the twilight, with the shadows lengthening – that it is crying out to be painted by a Constable or a Turner. You could travel the length of the country without finding a more perfect example of England's green and pleasant land, immortalised by William Blake in 'Jerusalem'.

Blake's famous poem divides opinion. Some people swell with pride as it reaches its climax. Others find its patriotic sentiments embarrassing. *The Guardian* once ran a competition inviting readers to come up with good examples of questions to which the answer was 'no'. The winning entry was: 'And did those feet in ancient time/Walk upon England's mountains green?' But whatever your view of 'Jerusalem', it is important to get to grips with some of the poem's underlying sentiments. They hold the key to the brand of quintessentially rural English Tory-ism which my parents tried to articulate. And the potency of that mythic, Arthurian England, the green and pleasant land which ravishes the eye with its uncluttered beauty, goes some way to explaining attitudes to race and immigration in Macclesfield, Congleton and the surrounding villages.

England isn't *better* than France or Ghana or Thailand or Costa Rica. But it is different, and the people who best appreciate that difference are those whose families have lived there for hundreds of years. Urbanites have roots that go no deeper than the buildings they live in. But when you live close to the land, you are conscious of a vague but nonetheless precious sense of continuity.

My parents, with their rural roots, feel that very strongly. If I had to pinpoint the single thing that most bothers them about mass migration – millions of people uprooted and relocated to alien environments – it would probably be the way it disrupts that sense of continuity and the emotional reassurance that continuity provides. And if they felt that strongly before the age of the jihadist, they feel it even more strongly now, when the jihadist lurking in the shadows is part of the mental landscape of Britain.

In 2005, in the wake of the 7 July terrorist bombings in London, my mother caused a storm in a teacup with an article in the *Congleton Guardian* which described Britain as 'thankfully predominantly a white Christian country'. The response was predictable: the howls of outrage in Hampstead and Islington could have been heard in Cheshire. And no doubt the point could have been better expressed. But most of her constituents, in differing degrees, would have echoed the underlying sentiments. They were just not comfortable – in fact, they were very uncomfortable – with a Britain in which a suicide bomber, plotting carnage and seething with anti-British hatred, could be living next door to them.

Does that make them racists? Or my mother a racist? Or my father? Absolutely not. One of the great ironies of modern Britain is that, although everyone knows that you must not use the N-word in any circumstances, the equally offensive R-word gets sprayed around like confetti. My parents have suffered as much as anyone, been beaten with the same crude stick a thousand times. Every day of the year, people get condemned out of hand as racists, on the scantiest evidence. A single less-than-well-chosen word – from Margaret Thatcher talking about people's fears of being 'swamped' to David Cameron's reference to a 'swarm' of immigrants trying to board UK-bound lorries in Calais – will provoke a reaction out of all proportion to the original offence. There are plenty of genuine racists out there, and they need to be challenged, and challenged hard, but the knee-jerk tendency to condemn and denounce is no good to anyone.

I have seen my parents in the company of people of all races and creeds and can categorically say that, when it comes to dealing with individuals, they are colour-blind: they just take people as they find them. Like all MPs, they had to deal with constituents of many different races and, on a point of iron principle, treated all of them with equal respect. For one thing, it would have been political suicide not to. For another, it chimed with their most basic instincts as human beings. Treat everyone the same. Don't prejudge people. Don't put them in arbitrary pigeon-holes.

To take a simple, practical example, my mother, like all MPs, regularly had constituents come to her for help because they wanted to marry a non-British citizen and were encountering bureaucratic obstacles. Occasionally, she would entertain private suspicions that something fishy was going on, perhaps an arranged marriage. But she always, on principle, took the constituents' stories at face value. My father was just the same. He never discriminated. In fact, two of his closest personal friends among his constituents were a Dutch Jew and a first-generation Polish immigrant. At one of the lowest ebbs of his career, when it looked as if he might find himself in serious financial difficulties over the DeLorean affair, the Pole was on his doorstep within hours. 'Can I help, Nicholas? When do you want me to put my house on the market?'

And if my parents are not racists, the same is true of the

overwhelming majority of their constituents. One of the most popular and charismatic figures in the area – a legend in his own lifetime – is the Vicar of Gawsworth and assistant Bishop of Chester, William A. Pwaisiho, a Solomon Islander. Some of his parishioners were a bit sceptical when he was appointed, but his warmth and good humour – he used one of his first sermons to joke that he was going to teach people how to kill pigs – have endeared him to all and sundry, and he has become a pillar of his community.

UKIP, interestingly, has never made significant inroads in either Macclesfield or Congleton. It is just not classic UKIP territory. There are not large numbers of migrant workers in either town, stoking resentment among locals whose jobs feel threatened. When my mother talked about 'a predominantly white Christian country', she was not making moral judgements, but simply describing the England she saw on her own doorstep.

In the 2011 census, which provided an ethnic snapshot of contemporary Britain, only 45 per cent of people in London were classified as 'white British'. The figures for Birmingham and Manchester were 63 per cent and 83 per cent, respectively. But in Macclesfield, the figure was 91 per cent, and in Congleton, 94 per cent, one of the highest figures in the country. Those are big, big variations and, inevitably, they shape people's perspectives.

In the south east, where I live, multicultural Britain is an unalterable fact of life. My son Jack, now seven, is a child of his times. With a Dutch father and English mother, he started life as a mongrel, and as his education has progressed, he has been cheerfully surrounded by children from around the world – which was certainly not true of me when I was his age, finding my feet at the local village school in Cheshire.

When I then compare Jack with how I imagine my father as an eight-year-old in 1946, the contrast is even more striking. The eight-year-old Nicholas Raymond Winterton, with pink cheeks and blond, curly locks, would still have been glowing with pride at his country's finest hour, the defeat of Hitler. He would barely have seen a black face or heard a foreign accent in the streets. The England to which he was slowly forming such an attachment was simultaneously a great nation and a simple, homogenous community. He misses that simplicity. He misses it a lot.

'If we had to go to war again, do you think the British people would still fight side by side, the way they did then?' I have heard him ask, in a tone of puzzlement rather than aggression. 'Or would we have lost that cohesion in the rush to embrace multicultural-ism?' There is not a pub in Macclesfield where such sentiments would not be met by murmurs – sometimes more than murmurs – of agreement.

From my conversations with people in Cheshire, I would say it is the *idea* of immigration, not immigrants themselves, which is the problem. It is population numbers, not foreign languages or unfamiliar religions, which play on their minds. They look around them – at that green and pleasant land which my parents can see from their kitchen window – and they worry that it will not be half as green or nearly as pleasant if the population of the UK contin-ues to grow at its present rate. 'Britain is full,' you hear people say, and whether you agree or disagree, it is a very human sentiment.

There is probably no topic in British politics on which it is so difficult to have an honest, grown-up debate as race and immigra-tion. Even as I write this chapter, I am conscious of choosing every word with care, to avoid alienating readers. The slightest suggestion of national stereotyping – teasing Poles for their hard-to-pronounce names, for example, or Germans for plonking their towels on the best sun-loungers – is seized on by the PC brigade as evidence of malicious intent.

Last year, an obviously exasperated Archbishop of Canterbury was forced to point out that there was nothing wrong or un-Christian in a fear of mass immigration. Xenophobia, he might have added, means a *fear* of foreigners, not a hatred of foreigners, although the word regularly gets misused. And to castigate someone simply for having a fear of the unknown is as idiotic as to castigate them for having a fear of spiders or flying. Fear is an emotion, not an opinion.

In the 2005 general election, the last one my parents fought, Michael Howard's Conservatives came up with the slogan 'It's not racist to impose limits on immigration'. The slogan could have been pithier but, for my parents, as for most people, the sentiment is not just unobjectionable, but a statement of the obvious. And should one shrink from stating the obvious just because other people are afraid to? Not if one is a Winterton!

As my parents saw it, and still see it, to have pooh-poohed their constituents' concerns about immigration – concerns they had heard on the doorstep a thousand times – would have been not just arrogant, but undemocratic. They had no easy answers to offer. But they were not afraid to acknowledge that there was a problem which needed to be addressed. And if the price was being called racists by people whose views they did not respect, that was a price they were more than happy to pay. Their constituents – not to mention their own self-respect – deserved no less.

I have already described the influence Enoch Powell had on my father at the start of his career. 'The Rivers of Blood speech may have been inflammatory, but Powell was only saying what many ordinary people thought,' he remembers. 'And it was not only Tory voters who approved. I remember trade unionists marching through Dudley in support of Powell. He had touched a raw nerve.' In 1968, when Powell made the speech, fears about the effects of immigration were probably not as pronounced in Macclesfield as in the West Midlands, but the issue was inching up the political agenda all over the country.

By the time my father had been elected to the House of Commons, the politics of race, for want of a better expression, were bedevilling another red-hot topical issue: British foreign policy in southern Africa. The apartheid regime in Pretoria was fast becoming a pariah on the world stage. In the summer of 1970, a scheduled tour of England by the South African cricket team had been cancelled in the face of public opposition. Southern Rhodesia, following the Unilateral Declaration of Independence (UDI) in 1965, was tarred with the same brush, denounced as a bastion of white supremacism. Or denounced by *some* people as a bastion of white supremacism. My father – partly because he had taken the trouble to look at the facts on the ground and not just pontificate from an armchair in London – took a rather different view of the situation.

One of his political heroes, whom he got to know personally, and once described as 'an African Winston Churchill', was Ian Smith, the Rhodesian Prime Minister who had declared UDI. He recognised in Smith someone like himself: a stubborn, bloody-minded maverick, distrusted by the Establishment. The mandarins in the Foreign Office consistently underestimated Smith, regarding him as an uncouth colonial. But he was a man of real substance, as even Nelson Mandela acknowledged.

Smith's great tragedy, in terms of his legacy, was to be remembered for five explosive words – 'never in a thousand years'. The words were off-the-cuff and ill-chosen and seized on by his opponents as evidence of a refusal ever to countenance black majority rule – which was not his real position at all. The words would merit a chapter to themselves in a book entitled *Things Politicians Regret Saying*, but as there would be plenty of quotations from Nicholas and Ann Winterton in such a book, my father never held them against Smith.

Politically, it was a brave, even reckless, friendship for him to form, given Smith's low standing in Britain as a whole, plus the fact that his breakaway Rhodesia had been condemned by virtually the entire international community. He had quite a few fellow Tory MPs on his side – particularly when it came to the issue of economic sanctions against Rhodesia – but was never in a majority in his party. But my father, as ever, was not trying to win a popularity contest. He regarded Smith as a great African, and a true patriot, and was proud to be asked to give the address at his memorial service in London in 2008.

It was a sombre occasion, but no time for diplomatic language, and my father, who is allergic to diplomatic language at the best of times, did not mince his words. He praised Smith as 'a man of courage and principle' who knew and loved his country, and attacked the many politicians – including the British government, which he believed had betrayed Smith at the Lancaster House talks in 1979 – whose manoeuvrings had helped destroy 'the most stable, peaceful and prosperous country in Africa'. He also drew on his own experiences of visiting the continent – including a meeting with the elderly Ian Smith in Cape Town, at which Mum was also present – and his meetings with black Zimbabweans who had told him, sickened by the Mugabe regime: 'It was better under Smith.' There was prolonged applause at the end of his eulogy, and my father felt proud to have celebrated the life of a man whom others, for shabby reasons, had shunned.

The modern history of southern Africa has been so tortuous, and my father has taken such a close interest in the region – he was chairman of the All-Party Parliamentary Group on Zimbabwe, and has made regular visits to Africa – that a book like this can barely skim the surface of the subject. But I hope that, without too much difficulty, I can clear my father of some of the wilder charges that have been levelled against him.

Everyone familiar with politics will be familiar with the process by which moderate views are mysteriously inflated into extreme views by the opponents of the people expressing the moderate views. Criticise Israeli policies in the West Bank and in no time you will be accused of being anti-Semitic. From there to being accused of being 'worse than Hitler' is only a matter of time. It is the same with apartheid. In the 1970s and 1980s, anyone who did anything other than denounce apartheid at the top of his voice was accused of being 'an apologist for apartheid', 'no better than the Ku Klux Klan' etc. etc. Don't get my father started on *this* one!

In one particularly crazy episode, which I will describe in a later chapter, he had to take the BBC to court to clear his name

– successfully – of the most lurid accusations of extreme right-wing sympathies. The Beeb was too dense to see that it was perfectly possible to be neither a liberal nor a fascist, but a pragmatic middle-of-the-roader.

One of my father's closest friends in southern Africa, still going strong in his late eighties, is Dirk Mudge, one of the leading Namibian politicians of the 1970s and 1980s. A white farmer in South West Africa, as Namibia used to be called, in the era when it was governed by South Africa, Mudge was the ultimate pragmatic politician, adapting to changing circumstances rather than clinging to outdated dogmas. He was originally a member of the National Party, the architects of the apartheid system. But long before apartheid had started to crumble in South Africa, Mudge was campaigning – successfully – for a multi-party political system and multi-ethnic elections in Namibia.

My father, like Mudge, took a pragmatic approach to African politics. A transition from colonial rule to black majority rule was both inevitable and desirable. Only nutters doubted that. But there had been too many countries where the process had been rushed, with unfortunate consequences. Evolution was preferable to revolution – a favourite maxim of my father's. Every country had its own distinct problems, which called for local, workable solutions.

One of the very few occasions when my father agreed wholeheartedly with the European Economic Community, the precursor of the European Union, was in 1986, when that organisation decided to apply economic sanctions to South Africa but *not* to Namibia, despite being under considerable political pressure to do so. Recognising in this way that genuine progress had been made in Namibia would 'send a clear message to the people of South Africa that we support peaceful change ... and that we support the interests of the majority and not those of supremacist elites', he wrote in the *Namibia Digest*. He could hardly have made his opposition to apartheid more clear – not, of course, that his critics noticed.

Ignorance is at the root of prejudice, whatever form that

prejudice takes. Nothing irritated my father more than returning from visits to Namibia or Zimbabwe – having taken the political temperature, and talked to people of all races and parties – and being told what was wrong with those countries by people who had never been further than Folkestone.

If the same people then had the cheek to call him a racist, you could see the steam coming out of his ears. He never minded people disagreeing with his *views* – it was a free country, and he liked a good, vigorous debate. But when the debate was rendered meaningless by cheap name-calling, it *really* got the Winterton goat – a stroppy animal at the best of times.

*　*　*

My mother, of course, has also had the R-word thrown at her, although in very different circumstances and for very different reasons. In the supreme irony of her career, what did for her was what, at other times, had been her greatest strength – her love of laughter. It was like a two-act pantomime in which the scenery fell down and Mother Goose had to be carted off in an ambulance. A pantomime with a hint of tragedy, as Mother Goose had been the life and soul of the show. That is certainly how it felt in the Winterton household. 'I was stupid,' my mother now concedes. But worse than stupid? I will leave others to judge.

Act I of the pantomime took place in May 2002, when Mum, then the shadow rural affairs minister, was invited to make an after-dinner speech at the annual dinner of the Congleton Rugby Union Club. Rugby was normally Dad's bag rather than hers, but she had been to enough rugby club dinners to know what was expected of the guest speaker. If she started talking about the state of the economy, or Europe, or Tory education policies, she would be booed off the stage. A few simple jokes were called for, preferably of the kind that would never get printed in a family newspaper. Rugby players don't believe in good clean fun. They believe in good dirty fun. They leave the good clean fun to vicars. And they certainly don't want to be on their best behaviour at their annual dinner. They want to have too much to drink, let their hair down, and swap the kind of wildly non-PC banter that would not be tolerated in a normal social environment. That is not a crime. It is human nature. We all need to escape the prison of politeness and conformity on occasion. We would go mad if we didn't.

Unfortunately, one of my mother's chosen jokes on this occasion, having found its way from an employee at Tory HQ to her email inbox, was a shocker. It was the kind of lame gag that had been standard fare in northern clubs thirty years earlier, and concluded with a punch-line about 'ten-a-penny' Pakistanis – *not* the sort of material a senior Tory politician should have been using in public in the twenty-first century. News of the joke leaked, and my mother – kicking herself for naively assuming that what went on in the Congleton Rugby Union Club would stay in the Congleton Rugby Union Club – issued a prompt, and unconditional, apology. Which should have been the end of the matter.

It normally *would* have been the end of the matter. But after two thrashings at the polls by Tony Blair's Labour Party, the Tories, under the leadership of Iain Duncan Smith, were having the political equivalent of a midlife crisis. The year 2002 was when Theresa May famously challenged her party to reflect that, in the eyes of many voters, the Tories had become the Nasty Party. It was a time of nervous introspection, when image was all-important and the party leadership was bending over backwards to appeal to a new, younger, constituency.

My parents had actually supported IDS when he stood for party leader the previous year. He was a bit wooden, and not the sharpest tool in the box, but he was sound on Europe, and a man who was sound on Europe could be forgiven his other shortcomings. So my mother was not prepared for IDS to telephone her in the aftermath of her ill-chosen joke in Congleton and demand that she resign as a shadow minister.

'I bloody well won't,' she retorted. 'I was a fool, but I have apologised for any offence caused, and it is time to move on.' IDS disagreed and continued to press for her resignation. 'Then you will have to sack me,' said Mum. IDS then mumbled something about refusing to support my father's nomination for a knighthood if she did not resign. Puerile, puerile stuff. In the end, after more dithering, he sacked her. End of Act I of the pantomime.

My parents' feelings at the turn of events can be readily imagined. If IDS really thought my mother had committed a sackable offence, why had he not sacked her in the first place – as Ted Heath, rightly or wrongly, had sacked Enoch Powell after his Rivers of Blood speech in 1968? Why try to manipulate her into resigning – and then, no doubt, come up with some hypocritical guff about how sad he was to lose such a valued colleague? The whole thing stank to high heaven.

Act II of the pantomime took place two years later and followed a depressingly similar script. My mother was attending a private dinner party in a private flat in London, held to further Anglo-Danish relations. She was not the guest speaker but, in the course of a conversation about how fast jokes could travel, mentioned a joke which again had come from Tory HQ and featured a shark and the Chinese cockle-pickers who had recently drowned in Morecambe Bay. It was not a joke she would have dreamed of retelling in a speech, even at the most drunken rugby club dinner. But her political antennae, normally so dependable, had let her down again. Mistakenly assuming that honourable Members were honourable Members, and that private conversations would remain private, she failed to spot the obvious danger lurking in the fact that there was a Labour MP present at the same dinner...

Her goose was cooked. At gas mark 9! The story of the joke leaked, there were demands for her head, and the new Tory leader, Michael Howard, who had replaced IDS, was incandescent. He wanted her to eat humble pie, but she refused to eat humble pie, so he withdrew the Tory whip from her until she had – which she eventually did a few weeks later.

It was one of the low points in her career, and it was months, if not years, before she regained her accustomed good humour. 'I found out who my real friends were,' she remembers. 'Everyone rallied around, and the people criticising me were not people whose opinions I respected in the least, but it was still a grim time. I felt defiant, but also vaguely embarrassed, as if I had let myself down.' Her husband, needless to say, was absolutely tiger-like in his support. So were her children.

At least there was light at the end of the tunnel. The episode had not one, but two sequels – both of which, for very different reasons, put a smile back on her face.

One was an entertaining sub-plot which only reached its climax years later. During Joke-gate, or whatever you want to call it, the fellow Tory who had denounced my mother most vociferously was John Taylor, Baron Taylor of Warwick. The son of Jamaican immigrants, and the only black peer when he was first ennobled, Taylor was supposed to embody a new-look, more inclusive, Conservative Party. But he had been too hasty in leaping on his high horse. Judge not lest ye be judged… Taylor met his nemesis in 2011, when he was jailed for twelve months after fiddling his parliamentary expenses. No tears were shed in the Winterton household. His fall from grace only confirmed what my parents had learnt from long experience: that a politician foolish enough to pitch his tent on the high moral ground is asking to get a kick up the backside.

The other sequel unfolded in the polling stations of Congleton in May 2005, at the general election which followed Joke-gate. As a rule, MPs who have had their names dragged through the mud can expect scant sympathy from their electors. They dread a voter backlash almost as much as they dread getting a phone call from the editor of the *News of the World*. Two of my mother's Tory contemporaries in the 1983 intake – Neil Hamilton, who held the neighbouring seat of Tatton, and Tim Yeo, the MP for South Suffolk – had already experienced just such a backlash.

In Tatton, of the 31,658 voters who put a tick in the Conservative box in 1992, only 18,277 could be persuaded to do the same in 1997. They were unamused by Hamilton's part in the cash-for-questions scandal of the mid-1990s. In South Suffolk, a similar fate befell Yeo, who had resigned from the government in 1994 after being caught out in an extramarital affair. He got 34,793 votes in 1992, but only 19,402 in 1997.

As polling day loomed in 2005, my mother was more than usually anxious. She *hoped* her constituents would forgive her, but nothing is certain in politics. Even in the safest seats, MPs standing for re-election can never relax until the last vote has been counted.

She needn't have worried. There was no voter backlash at all. In fact, to her relief and delight, her vote had *risen* slightly. She had got 20,872 votes in 2001, and, in 2005, got 21,189. It felt like what it was – acquittal in the court of public opinion, the most important court of all.

Some of those voters – I know, because I went canvassing with my mother – were meek, well-mannered, churchgoing types, who would not have dreamed of telling dodgy jokes about Pakistanis at rugby club dinners. They had probably tut-tutted privately about what she had done. But they could also see what the headline-writers in Fleet Street had missed: that she was not a monster, but a warm, decent, fun-loving human being.

I will never forget their support that year. Nor will my parents. It felt like a vindication of the kind of two-way grassroots politics – loyal constituents backing Members of Parliament who had been loyal to them – in which they believed so passionately.

8.

THE WINTERTONS GO
TO WESTMINSTER

Up to this point, I have tried to anchor the Winterton story in its Cheshire heartland, and to capture something of my parents' political roots. But, of course, it had another heartland, the most remarkable, exciting, vibrant workplace in the country. That may sound like an extravagant claim, but I stand by it 100 per cent.

Just try to imagine an office canteen – or, for that matter, a pub or café – at which Alex Salmond, Diane Abbott, Jacob Rees-Mogg, Andrea Leadsom, Dennis Skinner, Sir Bill Cash and Sajid Javid were sitting at adjacent tables. It is quite impossible. What set of circumstances, short of a nuclear catastrophe, could conceivably bring such a broad cross-section of humanity under the same roof? Only in the House of Commons do you get such delicious personality clashes, and in such teeming profusion. All human life is here, from all corners of the United Kingdom. It is like one of those shaggy dog stories that begins, 'An Englishman, a Scotsman, an Irishman and a Welshman', and just gets better and better.

There is no point in pretending that the House of Commons is the object of great public affection, or that, when people think about the place, they feel proud to be British. Centre Court at Wimbledon – which is roughly the same size as the chamber of the House of Commons – has become synonymous with English summer at its best, a place of golden memories, loved by sports fans the world over. Compared with those perfectly manicured lawns of SW19, the bear-pit by the river in SW1 can seem squalid, chaotic, a magnet for louts and charlatans. But the bear-pit is also, lest we forget, the only Parliament we have.

For my parents, with their natural boisterousness, that little bear-pit was very heaven. And I wish I could convey just a fraction of the love they felt for the bear-pit, because it is only by loving it that one can come to love parliamentary democracy itself.

As Congleton's first ever Member of Parliament, my mother knew all about bear-pits. The town's nickname is actually Beartown as a result of a famous episode in the seventeenth century – an episode to which Mum referred in her maiden speech in the House of Commons in 1983. The townsfolk were such enthusiasts for bear-baiting that, when their favourite dancing bear died and they had to buy a replacement at short notice, they asked the Alderman for a loan. The Alderman duly lent them the money, dipping into a fund that had been set up to buy a new Bible for the town. The loan was to be repaid by the proceeds of the bear-baiting. Hence the modern folk song which gives a simplified version of the story:

'Congleton rare, Congleton rare,
Sold the Bible to buy a bear.'

It is a great story and, in its juxtaposition of something as exalted as the Bible with something as debased as bear-baiting, makes a great metaphor for the House of Commons: a simultaneously sacred and profane place, where the Bible and the bear-pit meet.

People understandably get irritated when they see their elected representatives behaving like schoolchildren. But would we rather the Commons was one of those dreary continental debating chambers where the speakers plod up to a rostrum and read out plodding, pompous speeches, listened to in polite silence?

When observers of Parliament talk about the House of Commons at its best, they are usually describing some big set-piece debate at a time of national seriousness. When they talk about it at its worst, they are imagining Prime Minister's Questions at its most unremittingly juvenile: Prime Ministers braying like donkeys; their backbenchers cheering at their feeblest jokes; the opposition in a lather of synthetic outrage. But, for me, and for my parents, it is Parliament's capacity for levity that is its true glory. Nobody is *allowed* to be pompous – which is just as well, as pomposity is the state to which politicians naturally gravitate.

To give one simple example, when poor Iain Duncan Smith was struggling to make an impact as Leader of the Opposition, his speech-writers came up with a good line for him to use at the Conservative Party conference. 'Never underestimate the determination of a quiet man.' Delighted applause from the party faithful. As an attempt to rebrand the lacklustre IDS, it could not be faulted. The trouble was that, the next time he stood up in the House of Commons, Labour backbenchers were ready and waiting. 'Shhh!' they chorused, putting their fingers to their lips. Even the Tories fell about.

Love it or hate it, the House of Commons is far more than an institution. It is a melting-pot of humanity. A place of intrigue, of sound and fury, of hot air and high intentions. A place of dreams.

Yes, dreams. The word may raise a few eyebrows among observers of the Westminster village. It does not chime with the grubby reality with which they have become familiar. Old Trafford styles itself the Theatre of Dreams, and football fans get that. But if you were to put up a sign outside the Palace of Westminster saying WELCOME TO THE THEATRE OF DREAMS, passers-by would laugh their heads off.

But isn't that rather a shame? At the end of the day, whether you like it or not, it is the *dreams* of people like my parents, and the thousands of MPs who preceded them, which have kept the old place going for so long.

Go back to the 2015 general election, when Mhairi Black, a twenty-year-old student at Glasgow University, became the young-est MP since the seventeenth century, swept to power on a tidal wave of Scottish nationalism. It was the most surreal moment of a surreal election, reminiscent of the episode of *Blackadder* in which Pitt the Younger was portrayed as a pubescent boy, worried about his pimples. What was a student doing standing for election in the first place? Shouldn't she have been getting pissed, sleeping till lunchtime and toddling along to the odd philosophy lecture?

But if some scoffed, there was also real excitement in the air. We have got so used to politics being dominated by the cynical and the middle-aged that we have forgotten that the young, too, have visions for the future. The youthful outsider storming the citadels of power, armed with nothing but the passion of their convictions, cuts a heroic figure, and Black fitted the description like a glove. People were on her side, whatever they thought of her politics. Even the sceptics, like my father, whom I heard muttering, 'What is *she* going to be able to contribute?', experienced a feel-good glow.

As Black flew down to London to take her seat, who could fail to warm to this fresh-faced girl – too young to be called a woman – saying she had only been to the capital twice before, and staring excitedly around her like a Japanese tourist on her first visit to Europe? It was as if the fog of cynicism that normally envelops Westminster had lifted. Here was a story that everybody could relate to, even people who had not bothered to vote: a parable of high endeavour to inspire young people across the country.

On one of her previous visits to London, Black said, she had taken a tour of the Houses of Parliament. That gave her an advantage over my father, who had never been inside the building *at all*, extraordinary as it seems, prior to his election as an MP in 1971. He was thirty-three, a veteran compared to Black, at the time he was elected, but in some respects, was even more of a political virgin, journeying boldly into the unknown. Another dreamer in another, very different, age.

Thanks to television, everyone now has a nodding familiarity with the House of Commons and what goes on in the chamber. The thickest contestant on the most moronic TV quiz show would have no trouble deciding if the benches in the House of Commons were (a) green (b) red or (c) orange. Familiarity has bred a certain contempt, and the antics of MPs at Prime Minister's Questions have soured voters' attitudes to an entire political class. But back in the 1970s, Parliament was a remote, mysterious institution. Like a prim dowager duchess, it kept its secrets to itself. It was suspicious of strangers. It rarely, if ever, seemed to smile.

During the war, the clock-face of Big Ben had been familiar around the world, a beacon of liberty and free speech. The very sight of the Houses of Parliament lifted people's spirits. But what went on inside the building was almost as mysterious as what went on inside a Masonic lodge. To dare to penetrate its inner recesses took a certain chutzpah.

My father and Mhairi Black are so physically different, not to mention so different in their political views, that to insist that they are cut from the same cloth might seem like a quixotic enterprise. But I think it is worth labouring the point. Politics is far more than a career: it is an adventure; a challenge; a fairy story.

Like Black, my father in 1971 cut a romantic figure, and for the same reason: he was an outsider, brimming with the confidence of youth, daring to mix with the big boys. How many of his contemporaries at school would have had the audacity to do the same? And I want to keep that youthful Nicholas Winterton, the newly elected MP for Macclesfield, in readers' minds alongside the veteran backbencher and committee chairman.

I like to think of my father driving up to that famous old building one crisp October morning in 1971, his heart pounding and his hands clammy on the steering-wheel. Mum was with him, and so was his mother, but he had only the sketchiest idea what was expected of him when he arrived. Suppose he fluffed his lines? Made a fool of himself? Macclesfield suddenly seemed a long way away.

He gave his name to the policeman at the gate, parked in the shadow of Big Ben and, for the next couple of hours, was treated like a new boy on his first day at school, shepherded around by prefects, fed and watered, pointed in the direction of the lavatories and deluged with information that went in one ear and out the other. Then came the moment he had been looking forward to with nervous anticipation since the by-election: his formal introduction as a new Member of Parliament.

For MPs returned at a general election, there is safety in numbers. They know that they are not the only new boys: there are dozens of others. But winners of by-elections have the parliamentary stage to themselves, with all the attendant stress. Before they can utter a word, they have to be inducted into the holy of holies, under the beady eye of their peers, a bit like new pupils at Hogwarts. It is a rite of passage to test the steadiest nerves.

As with so much else that goes on in the House of Commons, everything happens in accordance with time-honoured rituals that seem to pre-date the brontosaurus. The newly elected MP takes his position at the bar of the House – just a line on the carpet, not a parliamentary watering-hole – and on cue from the Speaker, is shepherded forward by his supporters, Walter Clegg MP and Spencer Le Marchant MP, bowing at regular intervals. He clutches a piece of paper – the official record of his return to Parliament by the Clerk of the Crown – which he hands to the Clerk of the House, a Victorian relic in wig and gown, who then administers the Oath ('I swear by Almighty God etc...') and gets the new MP to sign his name in the parliamentary roll before shaking hands with the Speaker. After that, there are a few desultory shouts of 'Hear! Hear!' and everyone repairs to the bar. The real bar.

The whole business takes less than a minute, but because it takes place immediately after parliamentary questions, in a packed chamber, it is rich in parliamentary theatre. It is the sort of hocus-pocus that, for some people, epitomises everything that is wrong about the House of Commons: its arcane procedures, so remote from the lives of ordinary voters. But to my father, ever the traditionalist, it is *serious* hocus-pocus, steeped in history. I imagine he played his part to perfection, holding himself stiffly, like a keen young soldier on the parade ground.

His first impression of the famous debating chamber – and remember, he had not even seen it on television – was how tiny it was, not much longer than a cricket pitch and about as wide. Was this really the cockpit of the nation from which Winston Churchill had made his great wartime speeches? It seemed cramped, even parochial.

He knew, of course, that the House of Commons had been bombed during the war and rebuilt afterwards, maintaining its Victorian proportions. But it was only when he found himself physically present in the chamber, surrounded by men in suits sitting cheek-by-jowl on the green benches – or standing because there were not enough seats to go round – that he started to appreciate its intimacy and the electrically charged atmosphere which the intimacy can create.

He was not to know it then, but this cramped little room, with its cast of exotic minor characters, was to be his principal place of work for nearly forty years. A place of magic and mystery, hallowed by the centuries. A place of theatre, of high drama and low farce. A place where he would make good friends and bitter enemies. A place where he would find his feet, sometimes shine, sometimes trip on a parliamentary banana-skin, but always *relish*, day in, day out, with a passion that the years did nothing to dim.

He had enjoyed the cut-and-thrust of local politics: the arguments, the banter, the earnest little committee meetings in draughty rooms. Now, like a footballer seeing Wembley for the first time, he could glimpse a bigger stage for his talents. He was still a political tyro, but he had achieved a lifelong dream simply by taking his seat.

But what a strange, strange world he was entering. I have tried to imagine what it must have felt like to be my father in 1971, entering the hallowed portals of the House of Commons for the first time, bursting with pride, trembling with nervous anticipation. But it is very hard to travel that far back in time without losing your bearings. 'The past is a foreign country,' wrote L. P. Hartley in *The Go-Between*. 'They do things differently there.' The aphorism might have been framed with the House of Commons of the early 1970s in mind.

The chamber around which my father squinted as he took his seat, trying not to look like a schoolboy autograph-hunter, was such a male-dominated space that the few women MPs stood out like birds of paradise. He recognised Margaret Thatcher, the Education Secretary. There was that old battle-axe Barbara Castle on the Labour benches. Shirley Williams he was vaguely familiar with. And nobody could miss dear Dame Irene Ward, the redoubtable Tory MP for Tynemouth. But everywhere else he looked, there was just row upon row of middle-aged white males – middle-aged being a kindness to some of them, who would never see seventy again and looked as if they had been on first name terms with Gladstone. It was all a bit sobering, like pitching up at a convention of Welsh Druids.

With no representative of racial minorities, and gay MPs such as Jeremy Thorpe still firmly in the closet, you could hardly have found a less diverse assembly. It would never pass muster today, in our more egalitarian age. But, knowing Dad and his conservative outlook on life, that would not have bothered him.

He liked the whole ambience of the place, redolent of an officers' mess or a gentlemen's club in Pall Mall. He had always enjoyed masculine company, masculine gossip, masculine jokes. In fact, he probably felt more at home in that House of Commons than he would ever have felt in the one elected in 2015, with its record numbers of women, openly gay or lesbian MPs and MPs from ethnic minorities.

Male-dominated though it was, the House my father entered in 1971 was still a generally respected institution. In fact, it stood so much higher in public esteem than the present House that today's MPs can only look back in envy and wonder what went wrong. The age of deference might have passed. A newly elected MP could no longer expect to be treated as a feudal lord in his constituency. The Swinging Sixties had put paid to all that with the Profumo affair, which rocked the entire British Establishment, followed by *That Was The Week That Was*, a satirical TV show that lampooned politicians in a way that would have been unimaginable ten years earlier. But the Commons, with its rich history, was still the object of some reverence, both at home and abroad.

Perhaps it was a bit fuddy-duddy, but it was fit for purpose. Its laws were obeyed. Its proceedings were taken seriously. Its debates – even on minor topics – were reported in all the national broadsheets.

Its big beasts excited the same awe as their counterparts in the jungle. They were not objects of derision.

For my father, with his Army experience behind him, one of the things that gave the House of Commons of that era its authority – an authority it signally lacks today – was the fact that so many MPs, on both sides of the House, had fought in the war. They never talked about it. That generation never did. But unquestionably it had shaped their attitude to life and politics. An accident of history had given them a role in their country's finest hour and, even a quarter of a century later, long past their physical prime, they still had the air of serious men who had done serious things at times of gravest danger.

Ted Heath, the Prime Minister, has served in the Royal Artillery. Willie Whitelaw, the Leader of the House, had been a tank commander at the Normandy landings and had an MC to his name. So did Francis Pym, the Chief Whip, who had fought in north Africa. On the opposition benches, Denis Healey had been a beach-master at Anzio. One could go on and on.

War does not necessarily make someone a better person, but it does give them a sense of perspective. A single bad headline can give modern politicians a fit of the vapours in a way their predecessors would have found laughable. Denis Healey, who endured a torrid five years as Chancellor of the Exchequer, used to say that, when you have been under *real* fire, the brickbats of the political life pale into insignificance. Dad – ex-Army, even if he had not seen active service – understood that perfectly.

He was tickled pink when, in token of his Army background, some of his fellow MPs started referring to him as 'the honourable and gallant gentleman', one of those little parliamentary courtesies – if he had been a lawyer, he would have been called 'the honourable and learned gentleman' – that make the wheels of Westminster go round. And as he settled in at his new workplace and started to make new friends, and learnt a bit more about them, it was often their wartime service that captured his imagination and made him proud to belong to the same club.

Probably no MP embodied the 'old' House of Commons better than Airey Neave, the Conservative MP for Abingdon, who would later become one of Dad's political soulmates. It was Neave who masterminded the campaign to replace Ted Heath with Margaret Thatcher – a campaign in which my father was proud to be a foot-soldier. (Dad was actually the first Tory MP to break cover after the defeat at the October 1974 election and, despite getting a rebuke from Willie Whitelaw, call for Thatcher to replace Heath. Not for the first time, despite being viewed as an ultra-traditionalist in some quarters, he was in the vanguard of change.)

Neave was an Old Etonian, which generally merits a black mark in the Winterton household, but he was an Old Etonian with *bottom* – Conservative code for gravitas. He had been to Oxford and scraped a third-class degree in jurisprudence, but his great claim to fame, making him a legend in his own lifetime, was to have been the first officer to escape from Colditz and make it home to Britain. He later played a prominent part in the Nuremberg war trials.

If he had been born fifty years later, he would probably have got a first-class degree, written brilliant research papers about housing, but escaped from nothing more demanding than a stuck lavatory at Paddington station. But I know which Airey Neave my father would have preferred. And if he still feels a fierce loyalty to the crusty male-dominated House of Commons which he joined in 1971, it is because so many of its members had achieved so much – in tough, rigorous environments – before they took their seats.

My father was still a boy, politically, but he felt as if he was entering a land of giants.

*　　*　　*

It is easy to romanticise the past – nobody has a more selective memory than the political classes – but I hope I can avoid that trap. For my father, fresh from his by-election triumph, the House of Commons was a kind of earthly paradise: an arena in which he

TOP LEFT Dad and Raymond, the infamous but lovely dog

TOP RIGHT Dad playing rugby against Oxford Greyhounds at his school, Rugby, in 1956

LEFT Young and glamorous: my parents with my maternal grandparents at the Hunt Ball, 1959

LEFT Nick (standing in the middle) with Sergeant Wallace and Sergeant Tasker during his National Service

Mum on Volant at the Meynell Hunter Trials, 1964

A young Ann with her horse, Robin

Mum with her parents and two sisters at a meet of the South Staffordshire Hunt

Win with Winterton. The Wintertons out campaigning for the Newcastle-under-Lyme by-election, 1969

We have a winner – Nicholas Winterton – at the Macclesfield by-election, 1971

Being an MP doesn't always go smoothly – at the Congleton Carnival and Tattoo

Dad being interviewed following the declaration of the result for the Macclesfield by-election with constituency agent Frank Horsfield, 1971

Photo of family Winterton by Brian Ollier, 1974

Celebrating Ann's win as the new MP for Congleton, general election 1983

LEFT Mum and Dad with Margaret and Denis Thatcher in the House of Commons, late 1970s

BELOW Dad always wanted to join in – perhaps unwise on occasions, but at least he's not in a leotard!

At the Macclesfield sheepdog trials of which Dad was patron for over forty years

Park Ranger Winterton in South Africa. He is used to swimming with crocodiles

Dad in California with a statue of his hero, John Wayne

Outside No. 10 – it happened once, but only once, and at the Granada studios

TOP Dad standing rather reluctantly next to the *Back to the Future* DeLorean at Universal Studios, Florida

ABOVE With Mum and Dad at Mum's election count in Congleton, 1992

Slipping seamlessly from MPs to models – modelling British brands with Labour MP Janet Anderson

Dad with the Rt Hon. Ian Smith, former Prime Minister of Southern Rhodesia

Dad receives his knighthood for services to Parliament, 2002

The things you have to do as an MP! Mum at the Congleton Carnival and Tattoo

My parents celebrating sixty years of combined service with Lady Thatcher and Speaker Michael Martin, 2008

Lady Thatcher and me, celebrating Mum and Dad's combined service of sixty years in the Speaker's Apartments, 2008

'The great and the good' of the 1922 Committee with the then Prime Minister, Margaret Thatcher

I WAS INSPIRED BY NICHOLAS WINTERTON !

could test himself as a politician, in the highest of company. Simply getting into a lift with a junior Cabinet minister gave him a *frisson*.

He had joined the Westminster club at a particularly exciting time. Barely three weeks into his new career, he was on the edge of his seat on the back benches, glued to one of the most momentous debates in post-war British history. The motion was on whether to join the Common Market on the terms which the then Prime Minister, Ted Heath, had negotiated. The list of speakers on 28 October 1971 reads like a Who's Who of modern British politics. Heath, Harold Wilson, Reginald Maudling, Denis Healey, Jeremy Thorpe, Michael Foot, Enoch Powell, Norman St John-Stevas, Willie Hamilton, Jim Callaghan… Even my father, never backward in coming forward, was content to sit meekly listening to his elders and betters, rather than trying to catch the Speaker's eye.

How did he vote at the end of the debate? With his party and pro-Europe? Or against his party and anti-Europe? Have a guess! All I want to convey here is my father's sheer, knee-trembling excitement at finding himself, at a comparatively young age, at the top table of British politics. He couldn't *wait* to get stuck in. He threw himself heart, body and soul into his new duties. For someone who believed so passionately in politics and in parliament, and who was lucky enough to live in England, the Mother of Parliaments, life could not get any better than this.

Within a few weeks of the Common Market debate, he was on his feet in the chamber, making his maiden speech on the second reading of the Criminal Justice Bill. Was he nervous? You bet he was nervous. Who wouldn't have been nervous? But he gave a good account of himself, speaking on one of his pet subjects, law and order, and rounding off with a nice self-deprecating quote from Pitt the Elder: 'The atrocious crime of being a young man … I shall attempt neither to palliate nor deny.'

His fellow MPs were certainly prepared to forgive the new boy from Macclesfield his atrocious crime. Tory and Labour alike, they queued up to shower bouquets on him. A 'stirring maiden speech,' declared Labour's Renée Short. 'Forceful, forthright and courageous,' said another Labour MP, Edward Lyons. 'I wish with all my heart that I had had the courage to make a maiden speech like that when I made mine,' said Bill Deedes, the Tory MP for Ashford, later editor of the *Daily Telegraph*. Mark Carlisle, the government minister replying to the debate, made a similar point: 'I did not deliver my maiden speech with anything like the confidence and clarity with which he addressed the House.'

What an incredibly heart-warming debut. It must have been like a batsman getting a century in his first innings at Lord's: never to be forgotten, never to be repeated. If my father had doubted it before, he did not doubt it now. This *was* the best club in London.

Or was it? Today, anyone peering back through the mists of time, and looking at the House of Commons of that era through modern eyes, would regard it as, at best, a flawed Eden. That was certainly my mother's first impression when she joined my father in Parliament after the 1983 election. She was, after all, and through no fault of her own, a woman. And the House of Commons in those days must have been one of the least family-friendly workplaces in the country. It was almost as if the elders of the tribe (male) had set about constructing a working environment (male) in which they could deliberate undisturbed and reach conclusions (male), which the rest of the tribe would have to accept.

The few women who were elected as MPs had to get their heads around a working day that began at half-past two in the afternoon and regularly ended at half-two in the morning, or even later. They had to make do with the bare minimum of ladies' loos. If one of them had tried breast-feeding a baby in one of the committee rooms, or in a corridor, she would have incurred the wrath of the Sergeant-at-Arms and been given a stern lecture on the time and place for breasts. Parliamentary sessions bore only a passing resemblance to school terms.

Toddlers? Members of Parliament did not have toddlers. Some of their *wives* had toddlers, but that was different. The wives and toddlers were hundreds of miles away, watching *Blue Peter*. The idea of a crèche in the Palace of Westminster would have been greeted with hoots of derision. The only concession to modernity was a small family room, where I grew up, tucked away off one of the lobbies.

It was an odd place, even by the hide-bound standards of the time. It just didn't feel welcoming. It was if democracy came to a grinding halt at the gates of the Palace of Westminster. Nowadays there is an extensive programme of school visits to the Houses of Parliament; the presence of children is encouraged, not discouraged. There is a decent crèche and the sitting hours are far more family-friendly. It is not yet a model workplace for the twenty-first century, but it is getting there.

In the 1970s and 1980s – my childhood, in other words – the House of Commons was still stuck in the Stone Age. As a child, you don't register that kind of thing. You just deal with the world as you find it. You don't look at institutions with a critical eye. But as I look back, the evidence of an organisation living in the past, reluctant to make necessary changes, is damning.

I don't remember exactly how old I was when I was first allowed into 'the place where Dad works'. It must have been on the occasion of the State Opening of Parliament, which fell on my birthday – always one of the high spots of the Westminster year – in 1978 or 1979. I caught my first glimpse of the Queen, which was excitement enough, and then we had lunch in the Churchill Room, one of the grand dining rooms beside the Thames. It was like a scene in a fairy tale. The pomp and pageantry were overwhelming. But I also remember feeling in awe. After the safety of the village school, the Houses of Parliament seemed dark and forbidding, like a monastery or prison. Big Ben loomed above me, like a one-eyed monster. Even the policemen at the gate, though they smiled, made me uneasy. Why were there policemen at all? Was someone about to be arrested?

It was only when I was in my early teens, and Mum and Dad

were both MPs, that I really started to enjoy my visits to Westminster. It became like an exotic second home, a place of adventure and intrigue. I remember hanging about in the family room, reading Dick Francis novel after Dick Francis novel or doodling on the House of Commons letterhead as I waited for Mum to get back from committee meetings. Odd family members of other MPs would wander in and out and flash me a smile and I would venture out to the cafeteria for a bar of chocolate or speak to the policemen, who were so friendly and who I knew by name.

It all felt relatively normal at one level – though, at other levels, it was not normal at all. The House of Commons *isn't* normal. It's special. A unique workplace with its own unique way of doing things. I remember one particularly surreal night in the family room when I found myself at three o'clock in the morning curled up in an armchair, dozing, surrounded by eight or nine male MPs, also dozing. Some of them were smelling so strongly of drink it could have been a Salvation Army hostel on a Saturday night. But there was nothing untoward in the set-up. There was an all-night sitting on the Abortion Bill and the MPs had nowhere else to kip.

Some days, Mum and I would pop down to the Strangers' Cafeteria for tea or an early supper – the macaroni cheese was great there. The room was packed, and there was a buzz of conversation. It was a time for gawping, eavesdropping, celebrity-spotting. I was starting to take an interest in politics, so there a sporting chance of seeing a familiar face and getting a little rush of excitement.

So *that's* Michael Heseltine! Gosh, he doesn't look much like Tarzan when he's sitting at the next table. More like a bank manager in Macclesfield. Talking of bank managers, how many sugars does John Major have in his tea? Neil Kinnock's *tiny*! Not much taller than me. Who's that interesting-looking woman talking to Douglas Hurd? And what *does* Edwina Currie think she is doing in that dress?

I would stare bug-eyed around me, so greedy for the sight of a familiar face that, more than once, Mum had to tell me off for being nosy. But then I was a political child, and had been for as long as I could remember. Not for me fantasies about bumping into David Bowie or Gary Lineker. Queuing for a cup of tea next to the Lord Privy Seal was excitement enough.

Seeing Margaret Thatcher in the flesh – the dominant political figure of my childhood – was a particular thrill, and even better was getting her signature in my autograph book. Tory MPs and their families were regularly invited to garden parties at Buckingham Palace, after which there would be a reception in Downing Street. I went to several of these as a teenager and remember being introduced to Mrs Thatcher, feeling slightly in awe of her, but also feeling vaguely reassured. She was friendly, approachable, relatively normal – light years from the handbag-wielding harridan of *Spitting Image*.

I may have been only nine when she was first elected, but she was to become one of my greatest heroes, a politician who somehow managed to be more than a politician. One of my proudest possessions is a photograph taken of the two us together at a reception held in 2007 to mark my parents' combined sixty years of service as Members of Parliament. The Iron Lady was beginning to slip into dementia by then, but it meant a lot to my parents – and even more to me – that she took the trouble to attend the party.

There were other brushes with the great and the good during my childhood visits to the House of Commons: some exciting, some a bit scary. One of the most embarrassing involved Denis Healey, one of the big political beasts of the day. Thanks to Mike Yarwood and other TV impressionists, Healey had become a figure of affectionate fun, with his bushy eyebrows and sing-song Yorkshire accent. One of the catch-phrases with which he had been saddled was 'Who's a silly-billy?', which always made me giggle. I had even learnt to deploy the phrase in a passable imitation of the great man. So imagine my shock when, after doing my Denis Healey impersonation in one of the corridors in the Commons, I heard a familiar voice behind me say, 'Who's a silly-billy?' When

I spun round to see who it was, I found Healey beaming like Father Christmas at my embarrassment.

Another great treat was being taken to visit Speaker's House. Like the House of Lords – but unlike the more functional-looking chamber of the House of Commons, which was rebuilt after the war – the Speaker's Pugin-designed State Apartments, in the shadow of Big Ben, are so stunning that the first-time visitor feels slightly awed. I know I was. I just could not stop staring at the soaring ceilings and rich wallpaper. Imagine *working* in this sort of environment! Mum's and Dad's offices at Westminster were nothing special. In fact, they were quite cramped. But elsewhere the Palace of Westminster lives up to its name.

One of the privileges enjoyed by Members of Parliament and their families is the opportunity to get married in the Crypt Chapel or, to give it its full name, the Chapel of St Mary Undercroft, just off Westminster Hall. The beautiful gilded chapel was once the setting for a scene dear to feminists and parliamentarians alike. It was here, in April 1911, that the suffragette Emily Davison – the woman who later died after throwing herself under the King's horse at the 1913 Epsom Derby – hid herself in a cupboard during the night of the national census. By so doing, she could claim, with a symbolism that rang out like a gunshot, that the House of Commons was her normal place of residence.

My parents loved the little chapel so much that Robert, Andrew and I all had our weddings or services of blessing there, followed by receptions in one of the House dining rooms or the Pugin Room. All their grandchildren have been christened there. Apart from being a treat for us, it gave my parents the chance to show their friends from Cheshire the Palace of Westminster at its incomparable best and gave us simply the best wedding albums.

Looking back, being able to get behind the scenes at the House of Commons and glimpse a world that the general public never gets to see, was a tremendous privilege, and one I wish I had appreciated more at the time. When I hear people slagging off Members of

Parliament, I wish more people had had the same opportunities as me and my brothers to view rank-and-file back-bench MPs at first hand. If they had, they would probably view them in a kindlier light.

I have made this point before, but as it is so central to an understanding of politics, I will make it again. Members of Parliament are *individuals*. As soon as you start subdividing them into categories – Tory MPs, Labour MPs, right-wing Tory MPs, left-wing Labour MPs, and so on – you are in danger of losing sight of that individuality and misjudging individual MPs as a result. My parents, after getting up close and personal with their fellow MPs, never made that mistake. They relished every moment of the human comedy around them, incomparable in its variety. They always relished the kindness they were shown, times without number, by their peers.

When my mother is waxing lyrical about the House of Commons she loved, which she regularly does, she likes to tell a story about the Rev. Ian Paisley, the booming-voiced Ulster Unionist MP. In the days before the House of Commons was televised, the only way Members who were not in the chamber at a given time could tell who was speaking was to look at one of the annunciator screens dotted around the Palace of Westminster. If the name Enoch Powell or Michael Foot or Ted Heath came up on the screen, MPs would flock to the chamber. If the name Nicholas Winterton came up, they would stay in the bar. Only joking, Dad.

In late 1983, when the name Ann Winterton came up on the screen for the first time, on the occasion of her maiden speech, Paisley, who was having dinner at the time, interrupted his meal to go into the chamber to listen to what she had to say. He barely knew her, but often sat beside her in the House, wished her well and wanted to show his support. Afterwards, typically, he sent a short note congratulating her.

Many of the fellow MPs my parents most admired were not household names, just ordinary human beings trying, like themselves, to stick up for their constituents and make a contribution to the national debate. Frank Field, the Labour MP for Birkenhead, was a man my father held in particularly high regard: he was almost as big a thorn in the side of the Labour leadership as Dad was of the Tory leadership. He had a lot of time for Renée Short, the feisty, husky-voiced redhead who held Wolverhampton North East for Labour for nearly a quarter of a century. Kate Hoey, the Northern Ireland-born MP for Vauxhall, fiercely Eurosceptic, was another political opponent who did not really feel like an opponent.

Among my parents' fellow Tory MPs, there were very many whom they respected and treasured, for their foibles as much as for the soundness of their opinions: Richard Shepherd, the ever-vigilant parliamentarian, a latter-day Edmund Burke. Peter Lilley, decent, soft-spoken and principled. Geoffrey Dickens, with his bulbous nose and schoolboy humour, who could have stepped straight out of a novel by his namesake. Dr Rhodes Boyson, another Dickensian figure, with side-burns that just went on and on. Philip Hollobone, the loosest cannon in the House, a serial rebel to make my parents' hearts dance. John Biggs-Davison, stalwart of the right-wing Monday Club, who had been a member of the Communist Party at Oxford before learning the error of his ways. Peter Bone, appropriately bone-headed, but with his heart in the right place. Michael Spicer, charming and urbane, rock-solid chairman of the 1922 committee. Peter Fry, God's gift to Wellingborough, a large, lumbering man with a wicked sense of humour and a passion for animal welfare. Michael Brown, the MP for Brigg and Scunthorpe, who had worked for Dad as researcher before being elected. Little Angela Browning, with her bright, breezy laugh. Philip Davies, the puckish MP for Shipley, with a wisecrack for every occasion. Dear old Patrick Wall, scourge of the IRA, possessor of probably the worst toupee in the history of the House of Commons, slithering about on his head like a palsied ferret...

Just names to most people, but names that concealed real human beings, indelibly three-dimensional. And once you had listened to their back stories, and listened to them talk about their lives before they became MPs, they became even more fascinating. I have already mentioned Bill Cash, the celebrated Eurosceptic. It is only when you realise that his father was killed in Normandy during the Second World War that, like pieces of a jigsaw falling into place, the man and his politics start to make sense.

I have only got to know a small fraction of the MPs my parents got to know, but I have met enough of them to form not a rose-tinted, but a *generous* view of them. Their faults become more explicable once you get to know them, while their strengths start to peep through their sometimes unappealing personas. Honestly.

When people talk about the Westminster village, they tend to have a sneer in their voices. There is an insinuation that it is a village of self-important fools who have cut themselves off from the outside world, and that there is unusually stiff competition for the title of village idiot. Maybe so. But as a community of 5,000-odd souls, in the heart of the nation's capital, Westminster is also a reasonably normal, healthy village. By that, I mean that it has a village feel, with everyone knowing everyone else, people looking out for each other and good neighbourliness prized. It is a place of gossip and intrigue, like villages the world over, but it is also a place brimming with the milk of human kindness: people nodding to each other across the street, or asking after each other's families, or having a good grumble about the weather. Westminster might seem light years away from the little Cheshire villages where my parents' constituents lived, but scratch beneath the surface and you find the same human ingredients.

Some of my parents' happiest memories of their days at Westminster are not of their fellow MPs, but of the small army of staff – from policemen to waitresses, from clerks to messengers, from secretaries to librarians – who keep the show on the road. A newly elected Member of Parliament who thought he was too grand to give the policeman at the front gate a friendly smile, or thank the woman in the cafeteria who served him a cup of tea, would quickly come unstuck. He might have an IQ of 200 and a parliamentary majority of 20,000, but his snobbery would find him out. My parents – and not all MPs could say the same, if they were being honest – never failed that test. They showed the staff at Westminster the same courtesy and respect as they showed their constituents.

Parliament is such an iconic institution that those lucky enough to get a job there tend to stay as long as they possibly can. MPs are at the mercy of their constituents, who have this annoying tendency to kick them out when have had enough of them. But the permanent staff of the House of Commons are luckier in that respect. Some of them stay there for forty years or more, happy to be working in such a unique, vibrant place. Their continuing presence in the building, whichever party is in power, creates an extraordinary sense of camaraderie, which extends to everyone in the Westminster village, great or small. People are on the same side.

There is a nice story illustrating this point in *Towards Tomorrow* (1977), the memoirs of the former Labour MP Fenner Brockway, a veteran pacifist who was still active in the House of Lords when Dad took his seat in 1971. Over dinner, while the House was sitting, Brockway started chatting to a waitress in the cafeteria who was worried that the last debate of the day was scheduled to end at 11.45 p.m. For her and other late-night staff, she explained, the timing was critical. If the debate did indeed finish at 11.45, they would be entitled to taxis home, because that was the agreed cut-off point under their conditions of service. But if it finished slightly early – at 11.40, say – they would have to travel home by public transport.

Brockway got the message. He went upstairs to the chamber, thinly attended, and when the debate fizzled out at 11.43 and the Speaker was about to adjourn the House, rose to his feet and spoke for two minutes, without irrelevance or repetition, about a minor administrative problem in a constituency in Wales. It was, in context, one of the most gallant of all parliamentary filibusters, and I am sure Mum or Dad would have done the same in Brockway's position. It would have appealed, like so much else at Westminster, to their sense of fun and duty.

9.

THE WORK HORSES OF SW1

When Dad finally stood down as an MP in 2010, fulsome tributes were paid to him by fellow MPs, constituency workers and many others. Some of the tributes are so generous and heart-felt that they bring a lump to my throat as I read them. I know they meant the world to him. But my favourite, by Sir George Young, aka the Bicycling Baronet, who served in David Cameron's first Cabinet, is probably the one that sheds most light on my father's parliamentary career.

Sir George recalls wandering in to a debate in Westminster Hall. Dad was on his feet talking about maternity services, a subject on which he had become extremely knowledgeable during his time as chairman of the Health Committee. He probably knew a lot more about maternity services than most women of child-bearing age. It was one of his specialised subjects, like Namibia, the textile industry and real ale. Sir George, curious, stopped to hear what Mr Maternity Services, as Mr Macclesfield had temporarily become, had to say:

'The home birth rate is 3.7 per cent. The rate for non-pharmocological analgesia is 65 per cent. The rate for spontaneous vaginal delivery is very high, at 78.9 per cent. The rate for intact perineum is 63.5 per cent – that is very important to women…'

Pole-axed by too much information, Sir George beat a hasty retreat. 'That was enough for me. I felt the colour draining from my face and had to leave.' And who could blame him? But the profusion of detail is important to any understanding of my father – and, for that matter, of any conscientious back-bench MP.

The job is hard work. Bloody hard work. Some backbenchers get elected to safe seats, keep their constituency associations sweet, then loaf about in the best club in London for twenty years or more, keeping their interventions to a minimum. But my father didn't want to be one of the Westminster drones: he was a worker bee, from the moment he entered the House. He brought the same ferocious work ethic to his duties in London as he brought to his duties in his constituency.

I can vouch for that from personal experience, having watched him running around like a blue-arsed fly, year after year after year, long after the rest of the population had downed tools for the day. He may have had a love affair with the sound of his own voice, but he took pride in ensuring that what came out his mouth was well-informed and rooted in hard facts – facts he had checked personally.

A lot of politicians make the mistake of thinking that they can get their point across by rhetoric alone. Whatever the case they are trying to make – whether it is in favour of capital punishment, or against fox-hunting, or in favour of euthanasia, or against proportional representation – they just dig up two or three facts that support their case and try to bluster their way through. They fool themselves that, if they repeat the same basic tune, a bit louder each time, they will sweep their audience along on a tidal wave of emotion. My father was better than that. He could be quite a simple politician, in some ways: he had straightforward views, to which the man in the street could relate. But he also liked to marshal enough facts to give his arguments real ballast.

I have already mentioned his maiden speech in the House of Commons, on the theme of law and order, and the favourable comments it attracted from his fellow MPs. Re-reading that speech today, what strikes me is the wealth of well-chosen statistics used to support his basic theme: that crime rates in Britain were spiralling out of control, and that the problem needed to be addressed as a matter of urgency. He also, as he often did, drew on his personal experiences at local level – in this case, as chairman of a county youth services sub-committee – to buttress his case.

In the opening chapter, I compared Dad to Dennis the Menace: a natural trouble-maker, inclined to be contemptuous of school rules. But unlike Dennis the Menace, he was also the school swat: the boy staying on after class to mug up on his Latin and chemistry. It made for an intriguing combination, which wrong-footed some of his fellow MPs.

Those comically detailed statistics about maternity services were not about showing off: they were about achieving change in the face of heel-dragging in Whitehall. I have already mentioned the fact that my father is an Honorary Vice-President of the Royal College of Midwives. Perhaps I should also elaborate on why he was offered the position. Before the 1992 Winterton Report on Maternity Services – produced by the House of Commons Health Select Committee under my father's chairmanship – the role of midwives had been scandalously neglected, as many mothers who gave birth in that era will testify. There was simply no continuity of care: women in labour in hospital were passed from hand to hand like sacks of potatoes; one nurse would go off duty at nine o'clock sharp, to be replaced by another, whom the mother-to-be had never met. It was my father's mulish determination to shame the Department of Health into finding a better way, with dedicated midwives offering continuity of care, which shifted attitudes. Remember that next time you are giving birth at three in the morning.

As he beavered away, at all hours of the day and night, in his cramped little office in the House of Commons, he had a touch of the guerrilla fighter about him: the lone wolf, holed up in the forest, planning his next assault on the citadels of power. He knew that he was heavily outnumbered by government forces. He also knew that, if he retained the element of surprise, and made meticulous preparations, he could inflict significant damage. But those preparations did need to be meticulous. He could not just loll about under a tree, smoking a cigar, waiting for the revolution to happen. He had to *make* it happen.

Perhaps I am guilty of romanticising him again, giving John Wayne a dash of Che Guevara. But I think there is a germ of truth in the guerrilla analogy. To use a term which has been popularised by analysts of the war on global terrorism, Westminster v. Whitehall is a textbook example of 'asymmetrical warfare': a trial of strength between forces of unequal size using fundamentally different weapons.

Being an effective backbencher is not just about coming up with airy soundbites and asking ministers the odd probing question: it involves getting down and dirty with the nuts and bolts of government policy. If you do not do your homework, the mandarins of Whitehall will have you for breakfast. And Dad – more than he ever did at school – did his homework. If that meant staying up till one in the morning, mugging up statistics on spontaneous vaginal delivery, he would stay up till one in the morning. Let other backbenchers hang around in bars, flirting with Canadian research assistants. He had a job to do.

He was not heavily armed, any more than the guerrilla in the jungle is heavily armed. Like my mother – and unlike the Oxbridge-educated types who predominate in Whitehall – he had not been to university or acquired any formal qualifications. But he was diligent, naturally curious and, in terms of his interests, a genuine all-rounder. He became chairman of the Health Select Committee, but could equally have been chairman of the Defence Committee, Trade and Industry Committee, Education Committee or Home Affairs Committee. The subject matter would have been very different – weapons systems or GCSE statistics, not vaginal deliveries – but you can be sure he would have toiled just at hard at his homework, burning the midnight oil to master his brief, pecking away at the subject, looking for ways to get past Whitehall's defences.

And like the guerrilla, he knew he had to play a long game. The enemy's fortifications were not going to be dismantled by a single devastating assault, but by a series of smaller assaults, lasting for years, if necessary. Patience and tenacity were his trump cards.

One of his most rewarding parliamentary campaigns – to secure justice for the so-called 'pre-1973 war widows' – dragged on for longer than the ten-year siege of Troy. It began under one government, continued under successive governments and had to be waged against a backdrop of bureaucratic apathy and inertia that would have broken a lesser man. It would have made a splendid episode of *Yes Minister* – except that it would have required twenty episodes to do it justice and half the characters would have died off before the saga reached its conclusion.

The issues of principle were quite straightforward. Due to a legislative anomaly, the widows of servicemen killed in action before 1973 – many in Northern Ireland – received less generous treatment than the widows of those who had lost their spouses after 1973. In particular, if they remarried, they lost their widow's pensions – which was not the case with the later tranche of widows. Irene Wills, of the War Widows' Association, and Iris Strange, of the British War Widows and Associates, set out to achieve justice for their fellow widows – a fight in which my father and several other back-bench MPs were happy to be their allies. (One of them was Alec Woodall, the Labour MP for Hemsworth, a no-nonsense ex-miner whom my father held in the very highest regard, and also Geoffrey Dickens, a Conservative MP who was outspoken and controversial.) They won the fight in the end, but not until they had subjected ministers to an unrelenting bombardment of questions, amendments to Bills and all the other weapons of the parliamentary guerrilla. 'We basically shamed them into doing the decent thing,' Dad remembers. 'If you can make ministers feel embarrassed, that is half the battle.'

Another of his great parliamentary battles – still remembered with gratitude, three decades later, by some of the people he helped – was his campaign to secure justice for victims of the infamous Barlow Clowes collapse in the 1980s. The villain of the piece, Peter Clowes, was a buccaneering fraudster in the John DeLorean mould.

He was actually a constituent of my father's for a time, operating out of an office block in Poynton and residing in a lavish six-bedroom property with a swimming pool in the village of Whiteley Green. Arrogant and unscrupulous, he was riding for a fall, subsidising his extravagant lifestyle by fleecing others.

Some 18,000 customers – many of them elderly pensioners – had sunk their life savings into a complex 'bond-washing' operation devised by Barlow Clowes. They had been told it was a risk-free investment, only to receive a nasty shock in 1988, when Barlow Clowes was wound up by the High Court with debts of £190 million. Clowes himself was later convicted of fraud and theft and sentenced to ten years in prison.

What chance did the swindled investors have of recouping some of their money? Not much, if the Department and Trade and Industry had had anything to do with it. The Department – headed at that time by Lord Young of Graffham – faced accusations that it had known as early as 1984 that Barlow Clowes was trading without a licence and should have kept closer tabs on the company. Young hastily commissioned a report which concluded that the Department had acted reasonably and therefore had no liability to the investors. 'Not good enough!' howled my father and other MPs who had taken an interest in the case. 'Whitewash!'

Breathing fire, as he tends to when he sniffs an injustice, my father led calls for the matter be referred to Anthony Barrowclough, the Parliamentary and Health Service Ombudsman, who conducted a root-and-branch examination of the whole Barlow Clowes affair. Barrowclough's 170-page report, published in December 1989, identified a string of acts of maladministration by departmental officials. The government, humiliated, reversed its decision not to compensate investors and quickly cobbled together a package under which those who had invested £50,000 or less would receive 90 per cent of their money back. There is nothing to beat a good U-turn, and nothing gives a backbencher like my father more satisfaction than forcing a government into such a U-turn.

But it all took time, like everything else he did at Westminster. When the House was sitting – around thirty-five weeks a year – he worked such long hours that he was probably breaking some obscure EU directive designed to protect white-collar workers from being exploited. Just keeping on top of his correspondence, even with the help of a full-time secretary, was a logistical struggle and I was often drafted in to stuff envelopes during school holidays or after work. He had to deal with around 400 letters a week, bewildering in their variety. Some were from crackpots, but it was often the crackpots who needed the most careful handling – particularly if the crackpots happened to be government ministers.

If you write to some MPs, you might get a reply, but not necessarily one signed by the MP – leaving you wondering whether the MP has even bothered to read your original letter. My father was not going to go down *that* route. He would dictate replies to his secretary in the morning then, in the evening, sign each and every letter personally, before putting them in envelopes and posting them himself. It was a routine rooted in the twin principles of courtesy and accountability. It also took a lot longer than the leave-it-to-the-secretary approach.

Asked by one interviewer how many hours he worked a week, my father did his sums and came up with the figure eighty-four. But some weeks it must have risen to well over 100, once you took into account all his constituency engagements at the weekend – not to mention the fact that he often travelled abroad to parliamentary conferences and such, and had to catch up with the backlog of work when he got home.

People will probably look at those figures and conclude that he must have been a workaholic in the same way that he was a compulsive talker. But I am not sure that is true. He was just very, very conscientious. He did not want to be one of those dilettante MPs who dabble in politics the way they might have dabbled in banking or the law, but have no real sense of mission. He *did* have a mission: to serve the people of Macclesfield. And just as he found it very hard to say no to a constituent who needed help, he found it very hard to say no to the requests – many and various, some almost comical in their prolixity – that get made of a jobbing back-bench MP.

The parliamentary committees of which the general public gets to hear – departmental committees such as the Treasury Committee and the Public Accounts Committee – are only the tip of the Westminster iceberg. There are literally hundreds of other committees and sub-committees and action groups – some carrying real political weight, others just excuses for a get-together over a beer, or a junket abroad – trying to conscript backbenchers like my father to their cause. In forty years, hardly a month went by without him being asked to take on new responsibilities.

Would he like to chair the All-Party Parliamentary West Coast Main Line Group? Could he do his bit to help the Conservative Friends of Gibraltar? Was he prepared to serve as a treasurer of the UK branch of the Commonwealth Parliamentary Association? Any chance he could do a stint on the All-Party Parliamentary Group for the Chemical Industry? Did he know anything about Sri Lanka? Could he give a ten-minute talk to the All-Party Parliamentary Group for Rural Affairs? How about being the token male on the All-Party Maternity Group? Did he fancy meeting some visiting MPs from Copenhagen in his capacity as chairman of the British–Danish All-Party Parliamentary Group? Did he know anything about municipal swimming pools in Cheshire? There was a new back-bench sub-committee...

Some of the committees he joined, he now admits, were a waste of time. The venerable 1922 Committee, comprising Tory back-benchers, of which he was treasurer and vice-chairman, was an important sounding-board for ministers. But many of the other Tory back-bench committees – on agriculture or health, say – carried far less weight than the all-party departmental select committees, which could summon witnesses and hold public evidence sessions.

The most influential of his many committee positions – to which I will be returning in more detail later in the book – was his chairmanship of the Health Committee in the early 1990s. But there were umpteen more low-key committees – for example, the Procedure Committee, which he chaired from 1997 to 2005 – on which he served, and which did good, solid work.

He may have been an ultra-traditionalist, but where his beloved House of Commons was concerned, he was adamant that the institution could not stand still, that it had to adapt and evolve if it was to continue to work effectively. As well as chairing the Procedure Committee, he was, for many years, a member of the Select Committee on the Modernisation of the House of Commons. How could the House organise its time better? What more could be done to keep ministers on the ball? What tweaks were needed in the scrutiny of government legislation? Detailed, fiddly stuff, generating yet more paperwork to read and digest.

As for those 84-hour weeks, don't forget that, back in the 1970s, when his parliamentary career began, very late sittings, even all-night sittings, were a good deal more common than they are today. A typical working day would involve a committee in the morning, parliamentary questions in the chamber at two-thirty, any ministerial statements, then the main debate of the day, culminating in a vote at ten o'clock. But if legislation was being debated, line by line, amendment by amendment, ten o'clock quickly became midnight, became two in the morning, became four in the morning. The use of guillotines – a parliamentary device to ration debating time on legislation – was generally frowned upon, so the opposition basically stalled for time. They knew they would be outnumbered in the division lobbies, but if they moved amendment after amendment, and talked, and talked, and talked, at least they could deprive the other lot of their sleep. Childish game-playing? Or parliamentary democracy at its best? I leave you to decide. (Clue: the party whips *adore* guillotines, which strikes me as an excellent reason for being suspicious of them.)

Dad never really minded the late-night sittings. He thought government legislation *should* be fought tooth-and-nail – or certainly subjected to detailed scrutiny – and that was part of his job as a back-bench MP. If he was tired, he could always get forty winks in an armchair in the Tea Room before being woken by the division bells and staggering to the lobbies to vote, bleary-eyed. But the punishing working hours took their toll.

I once asked him how many times he and Mum went out for the evening when they were staying in London: took in a show, went to the cinema, met friends at a restaurant for dinner, strolled along the Thames in the moonlight – all the things any other couple from Cheshire would do if they spent their working weeks together in a flat in London. He seemed taken back by the question, then said, 'At very most, fifty.' Fifty outings! In more than a quarter of a century in Parliament together! Do the maths.

The House of Commons, not the various flats he rented, *was* his London home. At one point, he lived in a flat in Dolphin Square in Pimlico, which has attracted so much bad publicity over the years that it has been called the 'most notorious address in London'. The upmarket residential development has been popular with MPs for the best part of a century and has witnessed umpteen unsavoury dramas, from peers snorting cocaine with prostitutes to a Tory MP being found dead of alcohol poisoning. Winston Churchill's daughter Sarah was once evicted from her Dolphin Square flat for throwing gin bottles out of her window. More recently, it has been at the centre of investigations into an alleged paedophile ring in the 1980s. But my father simply never noticed anything fishy, salacious or untoward. He just treated Dolphin Square as a crash-pad.

Apart from the need to hang around the House for hours in case there was a vote, he had committee meetings to prepare for, constituency paperwork to catch up with – all the small beer of an MP's life which goes largely unreported.

Talking of beer, one of the causes he took up with particular gusto – a bit frivolous, some would say, but not without its symbolic importance – was to campaign for the bars in the Palace of Westminster to serve real ale, not keg bitter. For years, the Commons authorities had made excuses for not introducing real ale. There was not enough demand, they said. The beer would go off at the weekends, when the MPs were in their constituencies. But Dad kept banging on about it, and he got his way in the end. It did not escape his attention that his main allies in the campaign were Labour MPs who shared his passion for real ale. Half his fellow Tories barely knew what real ale was: they were too busy quaffing fine wines in the Members' dining room.

As a legislator by profession, one of his ambitions, naturally, was to get one of his own Bills on the statute book – an ambition which he finally achieved in 1995. The vast majority of legislation at Westminster is government legislation, but some private members' Bills, as they are known, do get debated, and a few end up being passed into law, having negotiated a gruelling parliamentary obstacle course.

The Winterton Act – as we call it in Cheshire, although it is more generally known as the Olympic Symbol etc. (Protection) Act 1995 – does exactly what it says on the tin. As the Olympic movement had grown from modest origins to a global brand, my father, like others, had seen the obvious danger of the brand being exploited for commercial gain. If every Tom, Dick and Harry could use the famous five Olympic rings to advertise any product they wanted, it could only tarnish the amateur ethos which lay at the heart of the games. They had to be stopped, if they were not to deprive the Olympic movement of a vital revenue stream.

Protecting the Olympics from commercial exploitation has been an uphill struggle, as sports fans will know, and there have been some defeats as well as victories in the battle to maintain the purity of the brand. But it was a battle in which my father, with his many amateur sporting interests, was happy to fight, winning enough cross-party support to get his Bill through both Houses of Parliament.

So next time you see a British medal-winner on the podium at the Olympics, and are glad that, unlike Chelsea footballers, they are not wearing sponsored shirts, raise a glass – real ale, preferably – to the hard-working back-bench Member of Parliament who, back in the 1990s, helped keep the Olympics special.

*   *   *

While my father was beavering away in one part of the Palace of Westminster, my mother was beavering away in another. Sometimes their paths would cross. They might find themselves side by side at Prime Minister's Questions. Or they might pass, with a cheery grin, in a corridor, Dad heading off to a meeting of the All-Party Parliamentary Clothing and Textiles Group, Mum to a meeting of the National Drug Strategy Committee. They might even meet by prior arrangement for a quick cuppa in the Tea Room, before heading off in different directions again.

By the end of their parliamentary careers, there was a third Winterton beaver in the Palace of Westminster – me! My public affairs work often took me to the House of Commons, and many was the social function at which all three of us were present, prompting good-natured banter about the Wintertons from Labour MPs. 'You're the dangerous type of Tory,' one of them once joked – by which he meant, I think, that we were too good company to be treated as political enemies.

My father, naturally, was delighted that our working lives overlapped, and demonstrated his delight with his customary gusto. On more than one occasion, I was meeting a client in the Central Lobby when there was a yodelled 'Coo-ee!' in the distance and I had to explain, crimson-faced, that the balding yodeller was a blood relation.

My mother, thankfully, was not the yodelling type. As a parliamentarian, she was not quite as driven as my father, but she had the same work ethic. She wanted to *use* her time. That was what her constituents expected of her. So, when she was not attending debates in the chamber or dealing with constituency correspondence, she threw herself into the same kind of useful, unglamorous committee work as my father: everything from the Social Security Committee to pro-life groups to the Unopposed Bills Panel, whatever that is.

Like my father, she had a wide range of interests which steadily expanded the longer she was a Member of Parliament. And like any good constituent MP, she listened to the concerns of local people before sounding off in the House of Commons. Her maiden speech, in November 1983, was about small businesses. She was on her home turf: her father had run a small business. But she had also spent the 1983 summer recess touring small businesses in her constituency and gaining fresh perspectives on things like business rates and employment protection legislation. 'Think British and buy British,' she concluded her speech, wrapping herself up in the Union Jack, not for the first time. Paddy Ashdown, who spoke next, congratulated her on a fine maiden speech and noted that he had just been through the same hurdle himself. '*Over* the same hurdle,' shouted another MP, from a sedentary position. My mother, who was probably the best equestrian in the House, loved that.

In her last Parliament, Mum found herself with a bit less on her plate, in terms of committees, than she had before. 'I needed to find something to keep me out of mischief,' she told me. What a lovely thought, particularly from such a known mischief-maker. But I know what she meant. Plenty of back-bench MPs (no names) find themselves with time on their side and *do* get into mischief. They spend horizontal time with their Portuguese researchers. Or they prop up the bar for hours on end in one of the many parliamentary watering-holes. My mother was not going to fall into that trap. She hunted around for something useful she could do, some new cause into which she could channel her energies. And she duly found one: not some quirky side issue, but a matter of life and death. Literally.

With British troops deployed in both Afghanistan and Iraq, one of the burning issues of the day was their equipment. Too many of the troops on patrol had been killed or maimed by roadside bombs, so it was vital that the vehicles in which they were patrolling were the very best available – whether or not they were British-made. Defence experts were in broad agreement that the best option would be to buy American Mastiff tanks, then modify them to suit the needs of British forces. But the Army was dragging its heels, reluctant to commit the necessary funds from the already over-stretched defence budget. Couldn't the money come out of general public expenditure?

The issue was batted to and fro between the Treasury and the Ministry of Defence in the time-honoured way. Soldiers were dying in Iraq while civil servants went around in circles in London. It needed a small group of MPs, with my mother in the vanguard, to bang heads together and see that what needed to be done to protect our troops *was* done. And quickly.

Here she is in the House of Commons on 8 October 2007, pressing the Prime Minister, Gordon Brown:

> I very much welcome the Prime Minister's announcement about the extra 140 Mastiff vehicles. Will he ensure that any necessary medium-protected patrol vehicles – and they are greatly needed, particularly in Iraq – will be provided, and that modern doctrine will be overturned so that the vehicles that are procured will be designed to ensure maximum protection for our troops? I am talking about V-shaped hull vehicles.

Mum's homework paid dividends. The Mastiffs were a great suc-cess. The Army got their V-shaped hull vehicles, and fewer British soldiers were killed by roadside bombs as a result. If that does not represent a good day's work by the Member of Parliament for Congleton, I would like to know what does.

Mum's extensive knowledge of Mastiff tanks makes a nice counterpoint to the detailed knowledge of female anatomy which my father acquired while chairman of the Health Committee.

If this were a Hollywood movie script, the producer would throw up his hands at this point and say, 'But this is *ridiculous*! You've got your hero and heroine mixed up! It's the woman who should know all about vaginal deliveries and the man who should know all about tanks. I thought you told me that she had had three children and that he was a tank commander in Berlin? I don't get these Wintertons. They're *crazy*! They keep pinching each other's lines.'

A fair point, I suppose. But then if my mother had been a bog-standard female MP, confining herself to traditional women's issues, and my father had been a bog-standard male MP, banging on about nuclear weapons and interest rates, they would not have been half such good MPs – or half such interesting parents.

In the weird, weird world of Westminster, where no two days are the same and nobody ever seems to keep to the script, the weird, weird Wintertons blended into the background perfectly.

10.

THE WINTERTONS IN THE FIRING LINE

Anyone who has watched MPs horsing about at Prime Minister's Questions will take a lot of persuading that politics is a grown-up profession, let alone one that comes with serious risks attached. That cynical view of politics took a nasty jolt during the 2016 EU referendum campaign, when the Labour MP Jo Cox was gunned down and killed outside her constituency surgery in Yorkshire. In the national outpouring of grief that followed her death, a simple thought could be seen taking root across the country: 'We *shouldn't* just be sneering indiscriminately at our elected Members of Parliament. Their willingness to put their heads above the parapet is what guarantees our democratic freedoms.' And, as my parents see it, MPs not prepared to put themselves in harm's way from time to time – take the flak, risk the brickbats – are not doing their job properly.

Some MPs get elected, then quietly and ruthlessly plot their path up the Westminster political ladder. As the old political saying goes, they rise without trace, ingratiating themselves with the right people, making a few low-key interventions in the chamber, putting out statements supportive of the party leadership, establishing themselves as good team players. But they rarely, if ever, take *risks*. At heart, they are apparatchiks, not warriors.

My parents were – and are – warriors. They just love a good scrap. Margaret Thatcher was the same. She never minded being called a battle-axe: she took it as compliment. And if she was my parents' favourite among the Tory leaders they served under, it was her pugnacity, her willingness to put her head above the parapet, that they so admired.

Perhaps it all goes back to those black-and-white Westerns my father watched as a boy. Did John Wayne do a runner when the Apaches appeared on the horizon? Of course not. He stood and fought. And to a parliamentary romantic like my father, the need to display courage under fire was an essential part of the job description of a Member of Parliament. Others might flinch at times of danger, but my father almost seemed to *embrace* danger.

Sometimes he could be his own worst enemy, opening his mouth before engaging his brain. But that impetuous, buccaneering streak also won him the admiration of more timid souls – and I include myself here. If he was pig-headed at times, it was the pig-headedness of the soldier who wins a posthumous VC after charging enemy lines in a hail of bullets. I never loved him more than when he was taking the kind of hair-raising risks from which lesser men shrink.

I saluted his work ethic in the previous chapter. But a strong work ethic can only get you so far in life. There are times when you need to stop being the school swot, earnest and methodical, and just go with your gut instincts.

Probably my father's most courageous, even life-threatening, political stance was his implacable support for the Unionist cause in Northern Ireland. It was not a popular stance, even within his own party, but he had strong convictions on the subject and stuck to them through thick and thin, whatever the personal risks – and they were considerable. In the 1970s and 1980s, when the IRA took their campaign to the British mainland, Tory MPs from the Unionist wing of the party, adamantly opposed to deals with Nationalists, were top of their target list.

They claimed their first victim just before the 1979 election, when Airey Neave, another implacable Unionist, who had been shadow Northern Ireland secretary under Margaret Thatcher, was killed by a car-bomb while leaving the underground car park at the

House of Commons. Dad had been talking to him only minutes earlier and nearly accepted a lift from him. He had been a staunch ally to Dad, who took his death very hard.

Five years later, the IRA struck to even more devastating effect, when Brighton's Grand Hotel was bombed during the 1984 Tory party conference. The victims included a back-bench Tory MP, Sir Anthony Berry, who lost his life, and the wife of Norman Tebbit, who was left permanently paralysed. My parents were not at the conference, but they easily could have been.

In 1990, a second IRA car bomb claimed the life of another of Margaret Thatcher's closest allies, the Conservative MP for Eastbourne, Ian Gow. Like Airey Neave, he was not a Tory MP chosen at random, but one from the outspoken Unionist wing of the party. He had resigned as a junior minister in 1985 in protest at the signing of the Anglo-Irish agreement – an agreement which my parents also opposed, joining Gow and around a dozen other Tory rebels in the No lobby. You can bet the IRA's commanders in Belfast made a note of their names. In fact, they were such obvious targets that special security measures were introduced at the family home in Cheshire – measures which are still in place today and which became a way of life.

The world has moved on since then, of course, and the terrorist threat comes from a very different quarter. But when the IRA was at its most murderous, it was not easy being a Winterton. I remember some of my own anxieties as a child when I started to put two and two together and realise that Dad's staunch brand of Unionism came at a price, and that it was not inconceivable that he could come to a grisly end. Being an outspoken MP, even one representing a sleepy rural seat in Cheshire, was no picnic.

*   *   *

If car-bombs were always at the back of Dad's mind, there was no shortage of other threats to his mental health, even to his survival as a Member of Parliament. He was not a man to settle for the quiet life. If there were battles worth fighting, he wanted to be in the thick of them, even if – you could almost say *particularly* if – the odds were stacked against him.

They were certainly stacked against him in 1981, when he found himself at the centre of a political storm – originating in Northern Ireland, ironically, although not directly connected with terrorism – which raged with such ferocity that it would have broken a lesser man. It was an extraordinary, nerve-racking episode, putting the entire family under strain, although its origins could hardly have been more banal. This was not a case of my father deciding to champion a cause that had always been close to his heart. The cause fell into his lap, quite by chance, although the fact that it involved a damsel in distress and a particularly dastardly villain naturally excited his interest. Another case for John Wayne!

Dad was doing what he did most weekends, visiting constituents, when a constituent asked him if he would like to meet a friend, Marion Gibson, who had a story she wanted to share. Boy, did Marion Gibson have a story to share! It was pure political dynamite and, as Dad listened to her tale, hardly believing what he was hearing, its implications were obvious. It was more redolent of a Hollywood gangster movie than anything he had come across in leafy Cheshire.

In essence, Marion Gibson, the office private secretary at the De-Lorean car factory in Northern Ireland, wanted to blow the whistle on her boss – the charismatic but flawed American businessman, John Z. DeLorean. The world now knows DeLorean, who died in 2005, as one of the great charlatans of the twentieth century, a larger-than-life entrepreneur who enjoyed a meteoric rise, followed by an equally spectacular fall from grace. He was a colourful chancer, riding for a fall, which finally came in 1999 when he was declared bankrupt. But in 1981, he was still a widely admired figure, an American icon who ticked all the boxes. A brilliant maverick who had first risen to prominence at General Motors in his home town of Detroit, DeLorean was tall and good-looking and married to a fashion model. He had dated Candice Bergen and Ursula Andress. He had appeared on the cover of *Time* magazine. He was extremely wealthy and extremely successful, a risk-taker in the great American tradition. Now, on top of everything, he was offering the people of Northern Ireland a beacon of hope amid their troubles. He had a big, even noble, dream – and, for a time, a lot of people shared it.

The dream was that his iconic new sports car, the DMC-12, would not just be a commercial success – DeLorean talked up its chances so successfully that there was a flood of celebrity investors, including Johnny Carson and Sammy Davis Jr – but bring much needed employment to the Province. The British government was naturally enthusiastic and supported the project with millions of pounds of development grants and loan guarantees. Equal numbers of Protestants and Catholics were employed at the DeLorean plant, which had its own symbolic significance.

The construction of the DeLorean factory in Dunmurry, a suburb of Belfast, began in 1978, and when the first DMC-12 rolled off the production line in January 1981, optimism was in the air. There was something boldly futuristic about the car, with its fibreglass chassis and gull-wing doors – the DMC-12 would later achieve immortality in the movie *Back to the Future* – and the fact that it had been built in Belfast, a by-word for sectarian violence, only made a good story even better.

Tensions were running high in the province. The dominant political story of 1981 was the hunger strikes in the Maze prison, which claimed the lives of Bobby Sands and nine other Republican prisoners, and which dragged on for most of the year. Here, thanks to DeLorean, there was a glimmer of hope, even a hint of cosmopolitan glamour, unimaginable during the darkest days of the Troubles.

The snag was that – as Marion Gibson explained to my father over a cup of tea in Cheshire – the DeLorean dream was built on sand. Despite all the glowing advance publicity about the DMC-12, the car was not everything it was cracked up to be. The claims that it would be able to accelerate from 0 to 60 in 8.5 seconds were not confirmed by tests, nor was its promised top speed of 125 mph. It was still a fine car but, with development costs soaring, it no longer looked like a runaway commercial winner, compared with the Porsche 911 SC and other competitors. Projected sales of 30,000-plus – mainly based on half-baked advance orders from dealers in the States – were beginning to look like pie in the sky.

DeLorean, master of all he surveyed, was pocketing a salary of £276,000 – mega-bucks, by the standards of the time. He entertained visitors to Northern Ireland at a lavishly furnished property, built for the purpose. There were reports of gold taps in the bathrooms, domestic servants put on the company payroll. But, behind the scenes, the company was in deep financial trouble – far deeper than the British government, which had invested so heavily in its success, realised.

The warning signs were certainly there. In 1980, with the company beginning to experience cash flow problems, DeLorean had applied for an extra £14 million as a grant from the British government. When told he could only have the money as a loan, he reacted with fury. There was a lot of buck-passing and brinkmanship. Nerves were getting frayed. But the idea that the company might be on the verge of total collapse was so appalling that nobody dared contemplate it. Now, with Marion Gibson hell-bent on blowing the whistle, the unthinkable suddenly *did* have to be contemplated.

The gist of the allegations she made to my father was that DeLorean was secretly fleecing UK taxpayers: putting in far less of his own money into the project than he had promised, then diverting money earmarked for the Northern Ireland factory to other parts of his business empire. Dad asked whether she could substantiate her allegations. Not a problem, she said. She had solid documentary evidence, in the form of internal company memoranda, which she would be happy to produce. The next week, the two of them met again and Dad studied the documents, wading through two hefty files and copying the more pertinent documents. To his mind, the evidence was pretty damning and, although not 100 per cent watertight, exposed DeLorean as little better than a common thief.

His mind was made up – although he was far from sure what he should do next. There was so much riding on the DMC-12, and the whole political situation in Northern Ireland was so fragile, that it would be a brave man to upset the apple-cart. The situation needed sensitive handling. It called for a rapier, not a blunderbuss. Someone basically needed to dig a bit deeper into the DeLorean finances and try to get to the bottom of the allegations which Marion Gibson had made.

My father's first instinct was to write in confidence to Mrs Thatcher's parliamentary private secretary, Ian Gow, and convey the substance of Marion Gibson's allegations. He also spoke privately to the Solicitor General, Sir Ian Percival. Soon afterwards, two policemen came to interview him in Cheshire and took away the files which Marion Gibson had given him. Soon after that, with rumours about the affair beginning to surface in the press, No. 10 put out a holding statement to the effect that the Prime Minister had asked the Attorney General to get the police to look into the matter. Two officers from Scotland Yard were despatched to New York to interview Bill Haddad, the former DeLorean employee who was key to the inquiry.

The trouble was that, by this stage, events had developed a momentum of their own. Marion Gibson had taken her story to Fleet Street and Dad's name had come out. All Sunday, the phone did not stop ringing and, although he tried to respond to inquiries with a straight bat, the media interest was insatiable. The next morning, a small army of reporters and cameramen was camped outside the family home in Cheshire, clambering up trees, completely blocking the lane outside the house. I was away at school at time, but Mum tells me it was a pretty scary experience, almost as if Dad, not DeLorean, was the villain of the piece. Who was this jumped-up back-bench MP daring to impugn the integrity of the charismatic American who had brought such hope to Northern Ireland?

A more cautious man in my father's shoes would have stalled for time and hidden behind the fact that the matter was under investigation by the police, so it would be wrong for him to comment, etc. But Dad does not do caution. Shooting from the hip, as we have seen, is in the Winterton DNA. And even though there was a small voice in his head whispering, 'Suppose Marion Gibson is *wrong*?', he did what he generally does in such situations and trusted his gut instincts. In the course of the morning, he gave interviews to both the BBC and ITN – interviews that appeared on news bulletins throughout the day – and simply repeated the substance of Marion Gibson's allegations against DeLorean. The die was cast.

With hindsight, it was a brave, even foolhardy, course of action and, by nightfall, turning over the events of the day in his head, Dad was far from sure he had done the right thing. One important legal nuance of the situation was slowly sinking in. If he had repeated Marion Gibson's allegations on the floor of the House of Commons, he would have enjoyed the protection of parliamentary privilege, which gives Members of Parliament immunity from libel actions. Repeating them on a doorstep in Cheshire was not the same thing at all. So he had to be 100 per cent sure of his ground.

But was he? In all honesty, no. How well did he really know Marion Gibson? Perhaps she was just a disgruntled employee with an axe to grind? Perhaps the incriminating documents he thought he had seen with his own eyes were forgeries? He spent a sleepless night, worrying about worst-case scenarios, of which there was no shortage.

His basic assumption – naïve, with hindsight – was that, now that the matter had been placed in the hands of the British police, fabled for their bulldog determination, the truth was bound to come out, and his stance would be vindicated. Alas, and to his horror, the police in this case acted more like poodles than bulldogs – and pretty toothless poodles at that.

The two Scotland Yard officers sent to New York to interview Bill Haddad spent so little time in the Big Apple that they hardly had time to get over their jet lag. They were supposed to be quizzing Haddad about the authenticity of a confidential memorandum which made clear DeLorean's plan to fleece the UK government, but they never actually met the man face to face. They spoke to him on the phone, and made an appointment to meet him, but were then instructed by the Department of Public Prosecutions (DPP) to return home, just three days after they had arrived. Two days after that, on 12 October 1981, the DPP issued a statement in London formally acquitting DeLorean of any criminal offence.

Why? How? On what evidence? The whole statement, and the speed with which it was produced, stank to high heaven. As conspiracy theories swirled around, there were veiled hints that the memorandum at the centre of the investigation – and whose authenticity Haddad would have vouched for, if questioned – had been forged or fabricated. Off-the-record briefings from the DeLorean camp called Marion Gibson's reliability as a witness into question in the most vicious way.

Given the gravity of her allegations – now, of course, known to be true in every particular – that three-day police trip to New York must rank as one of the most cursory investigations in the entire history of Scotland Yard. To say that my father was gobsmacked would be the understatement of the century. He simply could not understand – and still does not understand – how such damning *prima facie* evidence, with such massive implications, could be swept so unceremoniously under the carpet.

One explanation, clearly, was political. If DeLorean were to be exposed as a knave, then the British government, by extension, would be exposed as fools for having trusted him in the first place. They had sunk a lot of taxpayers' money into his Belfast car factory – over £80 million, when the smoke had finally cleared – and they were desperate to convince themselves, and others, that it had been a punt worth taking.

The ministers responsible scrambled to cover their backs. Soon after the DPP statement clearing DeLorean of wrongdoing, Roy Mason, the Labour Secretary of State for Northern Ireland who had first approved the loans to DeLorean, leapt to his defence in a trenchant article in *The Times*. The headline was DELOREAN IS A WINNER, DAMN IT!, and the article struck a strong chord, particularly in Belfast, where DeLorean was a household name and where people, understandably, wanted to cling on to the dream rather than confront the increasingly unsavoury reality.

The fact that the article appeared in the Murdoch-owned *Times* was also significant. It is often overlooked that, although newspapers have a track record of exposing scandals, they also have a track record of suppressing scandals for their own ends. As the freelance journalist John Lisners documents in his book *The Rise and Fall of the Murdoch Empire*, the Australian media mogul was a good friend of DeLorean and, as the vultures circled, mounted a ferocious defence of him.

For most of that autumn, Lisners had been hunting the same fox as my father. He had also been approached by Marion Gibson, was also convinced that her allegations were credible and had travelled to New York to conduct his own investigations into the DeLorean finances. The evidence stacked up, and he was on the brink of selling the story to the Murdoch-owned *News of the World* when Murdoch, in typically high-handed fashion, killed the story stone dead. Lisners took it to the *Mirror* instead, which so incensed Murdoch that he banned the journalist from working for any of his titles ever again. Then things got *really* nasty.

DeLorean, formally cleared of wrongdoing by the DPP's statement of 12 October, now occupied the moral high ground, if only temporarily, and took full advantage. The following day, my father, BBC, ITN and others were served a libel writ and demands for damages to the tune of $250 million – big bucks indeed to a back-bench Member of Parliament who paid his wife a weekly housekeeping allowance of £32.50. One can smile now, but there were not too many smiles in Cheshire when the writ was served.

As Dad knew only too well, there are very few grounds on which a Member of Parliament can be formally disqualified, but one of them is bankruptcy. Suppose he fought the libel case and lost? Or was forced to shell out thousands on ruinous litigation? The prospect hardly bore thinking about.

Further pressure was piled on him by the fact that DeLorean had been advised by his friend Rupert Murdoch to get the legendary Lord Goodman to act for him. Wily and well-connected, Goodman was the Establishment lawyer *par excellence*, a formidable legal operator who took no prisoners. Luckily, Dad had a first-class lawyer of his own, Richard Sykes, a personal friend as well as a man of intelligence and principle. There are literally scores of letters from Richard Sykes in my father's files, and his sharp mind and dry humour leap from every page.

In cases of this type, Richard Sykes explained to my father, Lord Goodman's tactic was invariably the same: 'to come out with all guns blazing and try to frighten the opposition into submission'. DeLorean was not seriously after the Winterton millions; he didn't think the Wintertons had millions. He just wanted Dad to retract his allegations. As soon as he did, the libel suit would be dropped.

Dad, typically, refused to buckle. It seems the obvious choice now, given what we know about DeLorean, but it was by no means the obvious choice at the time. Luckily, Mum, who can be as obstinate as Dad when she thinks she is in the right, supported him throughout the ordeal. Luckily, too, the other defendants in the libel suit stood firm. In fact, in the best traditions of the law, they were soon filing counterclaims of their own against DeLorean – claims that would drag on for years and years.

Dad's file on the case is nearly six inches thick, stuffed with affidavits and legal depositions. He has forgotten a lot of the details now, but he has never forgotten the ugly, nit-picking atmosphere surrounding the case, or his terror of coming out on the losing side. Going to the law is always risky. The only certainty is that it is going to cost you money – money you may or may not recoup.

In a highly publicised case like this, there is also the collateral damage inflicted by inaccurate or misleading newspaper reports. Amid the welter of legal claims and counterclaims, Dad had to put up with a drip-drip of insinuation against his own character, put about by the DeLorean camp. He had been dim-witted to trust Marion Gibson. Or he was giving material assistance to the IRA. (A blatant slur, if ever there was one. In fact, there were some who believed that DeLorean himself had been giving the IRA kickbacks in exchange for leaving his factory alone.) Each slur was nastier and more ridiculous than the last. Dad took it on the chin, as best he could, but he felt horribly exposed. His instincts told him he was right about DeLorean and that the man was a cynical con man. But he was also painfully aware that he was a David taking on a Goliath backed up by vast wealth and powerful friends.

Could he trust the Tory party to rally round him in his hour of need? Sadly not. In fact, for Dad, one of the most depressing aspects of the episode was the way colleagues gave him a wide berth, as if he was a loose cannon, damaging the party.

At one point, he was approached in the division lobby by Winston Churchill MP, the grandson of the wartime leader and a personal friend of Lord Goodman. Churchill told Dad he was making a fool of himself and begged him to withdraw the allegations against DeLorean and apologise – in which case DeLorean would withdraw his writ. Dad, spitting tacks, told him to get stuffed. Young Winston retired, hurt. But Dad was feeling increasingly isolated. In 1982, he requested, and got, a meeting with Margaret Thatcher to discuss the DeLorean situation. But it was a one-sided affair: the Prime Minister was flanked by the Attorney General while his own request to bring his lawyer with him was refused. At times, he remembers, he was made to feel like a naughty schoolboy who had spoken out of turn.

At least the tide was slowly turning in his direction. The legal evidence against John DeLorean was starting to stack up. Richard Sykes, Dad's lawyer, took a trip to New York and made the hard-nosed inquiries which the Scotland Yard police had failed to make. It meant yet another legal bill for Dad, who was struggling to cope financially and at one point had to rely on a £1,000 contribution from his old friend and constituent, Eddie Koopman. But the net was slowly closing around DeLorean. Some of the legal and financial minutiae remained murky, but the game was clearly up for the car plant in Belfast. It was continuing to turn out cars, but there was no market for them and the company was spiralling into the red.

In January 1982, James Prior, the Northern Ireland secretary, decided that enough was enough and that public money could no longer be used to prop up such an obviously doomed enterprise. On 19 February, the company was forced into receivership, with Sir Kenneth Cork, a former chairman of the Northern Ireland Development Authority, appointed the official receiver. The work force at Dunmurry was cut back to the bone and, although DeLorean spent the spring and summer trying to cobble together a rescue package, Sir Kenneth remained properly sceptical.

After much toing and froing, he gave the American until 20 October to complete the rescue package – at which point Fate intervened with such an improbable twist that the story really did start to resemble a Hollywood film script.

On 19 October, with Sir Kenneth still waiting by the phone in Belfast, and Dad still lying awake at night in Cheshire, worried he would be bankrupt by the libel case, John DeLorean was arrested in a Las Vegas hotel room – he had been caught on camera in an FBI sting operation – and charged with conspiracy to distribute more than $24 million worth of cocaine. When the case eventually came to court in 1984, he got off, successfully claiming entrapment, but his arrest and imprisonment were the last nail in the coffin for the DeLorean plant in Belfast, which shut down, never to be reopened.

The dream was dead and, like a character in Greek tragedy, the once-mighty DeLorean had met his nemesis. 'Would you buy a used car off me?' he joked bitterly, surveying the ruins of his business empire. His mind turned to other projects, including a movie of his life – never filmed, alas – starring James Coburn. Whoever would have been cast as my father? Richard Attenborough? Edward Fox?

Back in Britain, the wheels of the law ground slowly on. And on. It was 17 February 1983 before Dad finally got what he had been praying for – a letter from his lawyer to tell him that the DeLorean libel action against him had been struck out. Up to that point, and for nearly eighteen months, it had hung over him like the sword of Damocles. Now he could finally sleep easy again and, although subsidiary legal actions involving DeLorean would drag on for years, the main battle had been won.

And what a battle it had been! Wasn't this why he had gone into politics in the first place? To fight the good fight, take on vested interests and speak truth to power, without fear or favour? Fate had presented him with a mighty challenge, and he had not flinched. He was not a man to rest on his laurels – there were far too many other challenges ahead – but as the dust of the DeLorean affair settled, he felt a sense of quiet satisfaction. He had faced financial ruin and come through unscathed. He had stood up to bullies on both sides of the Atlantic. He had backed his instincts and been triumphantly vindicated. Against all the odds – and with scandalously little support from his own party – he had won his bloodiest battle yet.

Incidentally, there was an amusing postscript to the DeLorean affair, involving my mother. In May 1983, on the day the libel action against my father was formally struck out in court, she had been at his side at the Old Bailey, and she had also been summoned to a meeting of new Tory MPs with the Prime Minister, Margaret Thatcher. Her taxi back to Westminster from the Old Bailey was stuck in traffic and she was five minutes late.

She wanted to say: 'I'm sorry I'm late, Prime Minister. I have been held up at the Old Bailey because of a court action which has been giving me and my family sleepless nights for the last two years. And one of the people I blame for those sleepless nights is *you*! If you had given my husband the backing he deserved, instead of taking the soft option and siding with John bloody DeLorean, you would have saved my family a lot of grief.'

Instead she bit and tongue and said: 'I'm sorry I'm late, Prime Minister.'

*　　*　　*

The DeLorean affair kicked off exactly ten years after my father was first elected to Parliament. It brought him more public exposure than all his previous parliamentary exertions combined. It also taught him a brutal lesson. In politics, you can never be too wrong. But you can be too right.

By rights, he should have been the hero of the hour, exposing wrongdoing in high places when everyone else was turning a blind eye. To some people, he *was* the hero of the hour. But the people who had turned a blind eye – sadly, from Mrs Thatcher downwards – were not exactly queuing up to thank him. He had made them look naïve, gullible, incompetent. He had committed the Eighth Deadly Sin of party politics. He had rocked the boat.

After the Conservatives won a landslide election victory in May 1983, Richard Sykes wrote to Dad joking that he was looking forward to his appointment as Home Secretary. No such luck. In fact, not even the most junior ministerial portfolio could be found for the man whose courageous stance had helped bring DeLorean to book. He remained on the back benches – only partly consoled by the fact that Mum, the newly elected Member of Parliament, was sitting beside him.

The DeLorean affair had also given Dad a new wariness of the media. He had got some good headlines out of the affair, but he had also garnered some thoroughly nasty ones, full of snide innuendo about his character and motives. When powerful people are briefing against an MP, he is a sitting duck. It can be hell for him and hell for his family. The truth goes out of the window completely – which, to an emotional volcano like my father, is totally infuriating.

He is certainly not one of those politicians who regard the press as a sworn enemy and come out in a rash every time they see a journalist. He knows that, while politicians are at the mercy of the wrong sort of headlines, they also need the oxygen of publicity which newspapers can provide. In fact, one of his many initiatives in the House of Commons was to co-found an All-Party Parliamentary Media Group, whose aim was to build bridges between Members of Parliament and the media and help the two, often warring, parties understand each other a little better.

Every MP who has ever been elected has had to budget for his views being misrepresented and distorted by others. It goes with the territory, and any MP worth his salt will shrug it off with a merry laugh. Journalists will be journalists… But there are times when the misrepresentation is so extreme – and so damaging to an MP's reputation – that it cannot simply be ignored. The MP has to gird up his loins and fight to clear his name.

That was the position in which my father found himself in January 1984, when *Panorama*, the BBC's flagship current affairs programme, ran an edition entitled 'Maggie's Militant Tendency'. The general idea was to demonstrate that, just as the Labour Party had been infiltrated by left-wing extremists, the Conservative Party had problems of its own. A significant number of Tory MPs – or so it was alleged – had links with organisations which were, to different degrees, extreme and racist. Allegations of neo-fascism and anti-Semitism were cheerfully thrown into the mix. It was an inflammatory programme at every level.

My father's feelings at seeing his name included on the list can readily be imagined. It was a cock-and-bull story, if ever there was one, putting two and two together to get seven and tarring several Tory MPs with the same crude brush. The sole grounds for suggesting that he was a racist extremist were the fact that he had once addressed – *addressed*, note, not endorsed the views of – a small anti-immigration lobbying group called WISE, an acronym for Welsh Irish Scots English, whom one might fairly characterise as proto-UKippers. Think flag-waving patriots, not the Ku Klux Klan. There were clearly some small-time racists in their midst, but they were about as dangerous to public order as a knitting circle. To get out the big artillery and level charges of extreme racism at someone who had briefly rubbed shoulders with the organisation was absurd.

Dad promptly consulted his lawyer, Richard Sykes, as to whether libel proceedings should be initiated. It was the start of a legal process that lasted nearly four years. My father was totally vindicated in the end – the BBC apologised, accepted that his name should never have appeared in the programme and paid him £20,000 in damages – but he was left bewildered and exhausted by the whole experience. How could a world-renowned broadcaster get something so wrong? And what did it say about the arrogance of power that it took the BBC so long to admit that it had trashed his reputation without a shred of justification?

At this remove of time, the episode seems more comic than tragic: lawyer's letter after lawyer's letter, going round and round in ever-decreasing circles. Richard Sykes's private views on John Selwyn Gummer, then the party chairman, are priceless. ('I do wish you could persuade him to keep quiet. He is probably the worst Chairman of the Conservative Party it has ever had, and only the present Prime Minister could ever have appointed him.') But it sheds harsh light on the sheer mulishness of supposedly great national institutions. They are not too big to get things wrong, but they sure as hell are too big to *admit* to that when it happens.

'All Mr Winterton wants is a short correction and apology, not involving the BBC in eating humble pie,' Sykes wrote to the Director-General of the BBC on 12 March 1984. The tone of the letter could hardly have been less bellicose or confrontational. But ask any media outlet for an apology, however necessary, and you run into a brick wall. The BBC was forced to apologise in the end, and in open court, but it could have saved everyone a lot of time and money by doing what was right and necessary earlier on, instead of stalling for time with interminable letters asking for clarification of side issues. There is a lesson there, and it is a childishly simple one. Never confuse apologising with moral weakness: it is often a sign of moral strength.

For my father, hung out to dry, the BBC's reluctance to apologise had damaging consequences. In the general scheme of things, four years is not a long time to right an injustice. Think how long it took for the injustices suffered by the Guildford Four and the Birmingham Six to be remedied. But when you are the victim of an injustice, every day feels like a year.

How many people gave my father a wide berth after he had been branded an extremist racist by the BBC? How many failed to take his views on other subjects seriously? How many transferred their allegiance to another party?

At the May 1987 election, when the *Panorama* smear was still 'live', Dad's majority in Macclesfield, though still substantial, fell slightly. He normally performed better locally than the Conservative Party nationally. In 1987, it was the other way round. Just a coincidence? I wonder. Bad publicity can have an insidious effect. It poisons minds. Were there voters who dithered in the polling booth, worried that if they put their cross against Winterton, they would be giving the thumbs-up to fascism? Give a dog a bad name…

And after the election, when the party whips were considering which back-bench MPs to promote to ministerial posts, did they, too, subconsciously steer clear of Winterton, worried that it would look bad for the government to promote 'known' extremists? Just a hypothetical question, obviously, but I hope one that illustrates the damage that inaccurate or misleading reporting can cause.

My father is generally pretty thick-skinned: he resembles one of those rhinoceroses to whom he routinely gets compared when he is on the warpath about something. He would understand that journalists are working under pressure, just like politicians, and are not going to get every story spot-on. The *Panorama* episode, in its totality, was not nearly as stressful as the DeLorean affair. But it

certainly hurt and angered him. It also undermined his effective-
ness as an MP, a profession where reputation is all-important.

In the course of his long parliamentary career, there must have
been at least half a dozen times when he had to consider taking
out libel proceedings, simply to protect his good name. Some of
them were comparatively small beer – like the time he sued a local
Labour councillor who had impugned his integrity over his conduct
in Northern Ireland, and received £100 in damages. He did better
out of the *Sunday Express*, pocketing £4,000 after they had libelled
him, again on a matter concerning Northern Ireland.

In the great lottery of the law, he did not always find himself on
the winning side. In 1985, he was successfully sued by two Namibian
bishops, about whom he had repeated damaging – and, in the event,
untrue – allegations in the *Macclesfield Express Advertiser*. Did a single
soul in Namibia read the *Macclesfield Express Advertiser*? Irrelevant.
Dad's words were down in black and white and he had to apologise
for them. Luckily, the bishops, being good Christians, did not try to
sting him for damages.

Win or lose, he was paying the price for being in the public eye:
always under scrutiny; always at risk of being misreported; an easy
target in a world of cynicism and not a little malice.

One of the paradoxes of a free society is that, although it is much
harder to suppress the truth in a democracy than in a totalitarian
regime, it can also be much harder to correct manifest untruths.
In the last few years, a whole string of public figures – some dead,
some still alive – have been tainted with the stain of paedophilia,
one of the most vicious slurs of all. Some of them have been guilty
as charged. Some of them may turn out to be guilty if and when
they are charged. But there are others who are totally innocent, and
who have had to wait long years to clear their names. Even then, suspicions have lingered, not because there are any grounds for them,
but simply because the allegations have been made in the first place.

I have no easy solution to the problem. I don't think anybody
does. My parents, when not tearing their hair out in frustration

and saying unprintable things about journalists, would probably put it down to the rough-and-tumble of politics. But I hope next time people are slagging off MPs, heaping scorn on an entire profession, they will remember the price they have to pay as public figures – there to be shot at, and by heavy artillery, but with paper-thin defences.

*   *   *

If the DeLorean episode was the cause of sleepless nights in Cheshire, and the *Panorama* libel case a long-running irritant, the real kick in the Winterton solar plexus – the wounds not yet fully healed – was the MPs' expenses scandal that dominated the 2005–10 parliament. It was unlike anything they had ever experienced before, like one of those freak storms that only blow in once in a generation and bring 500-year-old trees crashing down. Those rhinoceros-thick Winterton skins were tested as never before.

The scandal raged with a fury that took the most seasoned Westminster observers aback, and came to a head in May 2009, when the *Daily Telegraph* started publishing leaked details of MPs' expenses claims, dating back a number of years. The sums of money involved were not vast. But some of the claims were so mind-boggling that the public was spellbound by the unfolding drama. It normally takes lashings of kinky sex to make a parliamentary scandal into good box-office material. Here it was the accumulation of domestic trivia – from lavatory seats to duck-houses, from moat-cleaning to bath plugs – that made the revelations so compelling. It was like an end-of-the-pier peep-show. One had the sense of looking in on private vice – though how much real vice was involved is a very moot point. The public mood was febrile and, as often happens, there was a discrepancy between the shrill newspaper headlines and the often banal reality behind them.

I lost count of the number of times I had to tell friends that they should not take the stories they read in the newspapers at face value: they had to put them in *context*. But I would be lying if I said that all my friends – even the ones who are generally well-informed about politics – got the message. The truth can never compete with a colourful half-truth or even with an untruth in lurid Technicolor. As so often in politics, perceptions were far more important than facts.

People thought that, compared with economic policy or foreign policy, parliamentary expenses was quite a simple issue. They could not have been more wrong. If you doubt that, just imagine that you were a politics student sitting an exam paper and were confronted with this question:

There are 650 MPs, with constituencies between 100 yards and 700 miles of the House of Commons. They spend roughly half their time in their constituencies and half at Westminster. Some of them own property, some of them do not own property. Devise a regime for remunerating them for their work-related expenses which is:
(a) fair to the taxpayer;
(b) fair to individual MPs.
You have three hours.

Within ten minutes, you would be completely stumped, bewildered by the complexity of the topic, the sheer number of variables that need to be taken into account. Remunerating MPs for their *bona fide* expenses, and in a transparent, accountable way, is a logistical nightmare.

Satirists had a field day with the expenses scandal, gleefully lampooning these supposedly light-fingered legislators, but you did not need to have a vested interest to see that fair play – that quint-essential British virtue – had gone out of the window. Take the famous duck-house which came to symbolise the whole expenses scandal. Contrary to public perceptions, not a penny of taxpayer's money was actually spent on the duck-house. Sir Peter Viggers, the long-serving Tory MP for Gosport, simply lumped it in with the general gardening costs at his second home, which were legitimately reclaimable. When it was deemed to fall outside the parliamentary rules, he accepted the ruling without demur. He had certainly been foolish and committed an error of judgement. But for an honourable parliamentary career of more than thirty years to end in a cacophony of recriminations felt very harsh.

'The evil that men do lives after them,' says Mark Antony in *Julius Caesar*. 'The good is oft interred with their bones.' Watching the expenses scandal unfold, and from a ringside seat, I found myself thinking along the same lines. The expenses MPs claimed would live after them and, in some cases, come to define their entire careers. The good they did – the causes they lobbied for, the committees they served on, the constituents they helped – would be forgotten. Perhaps there was a kind of very rough justice at work. Certainly some MPs deserved their comeuppance. But there was also rank injustice: crime and punishment totally out of kilter.

With hindsight, it is easy to see that the expenses scandal had been brewing for some years, and that the House of Commons as an institution conspicuously failed to tackle shortcomings in its own accounting procedures – shortcomings which were painfully clear once the searchlight of public scrutiny was trained on them. It is also easy to see that public outrage at the expenses scandal, sedulously fanned by Fleet Street, was wildly, *wildly*, disproportionate. Some good men and women – my parents not least – were painted as monsters of greed and corruption.

The public pillorying of the Wintertons – and that is how it felt at the time: a real throwback to medieval times in its raw ferocity – took place in February 2008, more than a year before the general free-for-all that followed the *Telegraph* revelations in May 2009.

What my parents had done, in a nutshell, was claim rent on a London flat, close to the House of Commons, which was owned by a family trust. The flat had previously been owned by my parents, and mortgaged, but my father had paid off the mortgage with some inheritance money and the proceeds of a life insurance policy. There was nothing wrong with the flat being owned by a trust – plenty of families put properties in trust as a legitimate way of reducing their inheritance tax liabilities. And there was nothing wrong, initially, with them reclaiming rent paid to the trust as part of the London living allowance to which they were entitled.

Crucially, the arrangement had been cleared with the House of Commons authorities in 2002. I will repeat that because it is so important. The arrangement had been *cleared with the House of Commons authorities*. Would someone who had cleared their tax return with the Inland Revenue before submitting it be subsequently charged with falsifying their tax return? Think about it!

The other key point – though missed in the general hullaballoo – was that the arrangement which they had agreed with the House authorities in 2002 had no adverse implications for the taxpayer. They were paying an approved commercial rent and, if they had rented a different flat in the same area – perhaps while I lived in the flat owned by the family trust – they would have had to pay, and be reimbursed for, the same amount of money. So far, so straightforward.

What skewered them was a tightening of the parliamentary rules in 2006. To avoid any appearance of impropriety, the House decided that MPs would not henceforth be allowed to reclaim rent on properties owned by family members. If an MP from Nottinghamshire, say, wanted to stay in a flat owned by his sister while he was in London, then pay her rent, how could people be sure that the rent had been fixed at a proper commercial rate? The system was clearly open to abuse. Stricter new rules would ensure that MPs' living arrangements were above reproach, and *seen* to be above reproach. But the ramifications for my parents were unclear.

Did the new rule change mean they would need to move to different accommodation immediately? Or did the fact that their living arrangements had received prior approval by the Commons authorities mean that those earlier arrangements could remain in place? It was, as they say, a reasonable debating point. So my parents entered into correspondence with the Commons authorities to clarify their position. Letters were exchanged.

At which point – and subscribers to the cock-up theory of politics will find plenty of ammunition here – the correspondence simply fizzled out. A letter was drafted by Commons officials – telling my parents, basically, that they would need to change their living arrangements – but *never sent*. It was like one of those hapless accidents that have tragic repercussions in a Victorian melodrama. My parents, none the wiser, carried on as usual. There was a banana-skin ten yards down the pavement, but they never saw it. And a few months later, with a ferocity that still sends a shiver down my spine, the Westminster air went blue with the sound of excrement hitting the fan. Confidential details of my parents' living arrangements were leaked to the press – they still have no idea who was responsible – and my parents were painted in such a lurid light that were made to look like a cross between Bonnie and Clyde and the Addams family. A parliamentary committee was charged with looking into the matter.

Full details of the whole sorry saga can be found in the committee's subsequent report (Select Committee on Standards and Privileges, Twelfth Report, Session 2007–08). I have included the report's conclusions as an appendix, as I think they go to the heart of the issue, and the report in its entirety is available online. I would advise anyone still convinced the Wintertons are Cheshire's answer to the Lehman Brothers to read it. It is not exactly a gripping read – parliamentary reports never are. Page for page, the Congleton telephone directory is far more entertaining. But it does (a) drive home the point that stories which look black-and-white in the press are invariably more complicated than they seem on the surface and (b) substantially exonerate my parents from blame.

I say 'substantially' advisedly. The committee concluded that, notwithstanding the unsent letter, my parents should have acted earlier to change their living arrangements, in order to conform to the new rules. My parents argued the toss at the time, but now accept that they were dilatory in adapting to the new regime. But the committee also concluded that they had never at any stage tried to conceal what they were doing, and that, as soon as their position had been fully clarified, they took prompt steps to change their arrangements. Significantly, they were *not* required to repay any money they had received in expenses – as many other MPs were – and they were *not* required to apologise to the House. In layman's terms, it was a light rap on the knuckles. Ten minutes on the naughty step.

Lady Luck, as she often does in politics, played a critical role – in this case, to my parents' disadvantage. If the story about their living arrangements had broken a year later, at the same time as the *Telegraph* was publishing details of all 650 MPs' expenses, it would have been swallowed up in the general brouhaha. Their 'crimes' would have paled into insignificance compared with the excesses of many other MPs – some of whom eventually ended up in jail. In news terms, my parents' living arrangements would have been pretty much a non-story. As it was, they had to take the flak, and the hysterical headlines, alone.

Would they have done things differently if they could turn the clock back to the time before the shit the fan? Of course. If they could have looked into a crystal ball and foreseen the merciless spotlight of public scrutiny on what they had assumed were confidential arrangements – private correspondence between themselves and the Commons authorities – they would have made damn sure those arrangements were totally above reproach, conforming to every last comma of every last regulation and sub-regulation. Alas, nobody had given them a crystal ball.

Incidentally, there was a nasty sting in the tail for them, although it was not reported in the press at the time. Following the investigation into their living arrangements in 2008, they moved out of the flat owned by the family trust into a different flat in the same area. Soon afterwards, a sub-committee chaired by the Speaker, Michael Martin, ruled that, where two MPs were sharing the same accommodation, only one of them – not both, as had previously been the case – could claim an accommodation allowance. This eventually left my parents some £17,000 out of pocket, which really was rubbing salt in the wound.

The trouble is that, as they say in Cheshire, shit sticks. As had happened with the *Panorama* libel case, a false impression had been given which was difficult, if not impossible, to erase. By the time the committee report appeared, the damage caused by the original lurid newspaper headlines had been done. And, as anyone who has ever been mauled by what Tony Blair called the 'feral beast' of Fleet Street will tell you, the wounds of such a mauling never fully heal.

David Cameron, who might have come to my parents' defence, did the opposite, hinting that they had been guilty of an impropriety and were *personae non gratae* as far as the Tory party was concerned. Mum and Dad felt badly let down, and with good reason. If their own party leader was not prepared to look at the issues dispassionately and come to a balanced judgement, what chance of ordinary voters doing the same? One way and another, it was a low point – perhaps *the* low point – in their long parliamentary careers.

What made the whole episode so galling for my father was that, just a year before, he had come third in a *Daily Telegraph* league table of MPs offering their constituents the best value for money. In a rough-and-ready accounting exercise, the newspaper had put on one side of the ledger the expenses claimed by individual MPs and, on the other, the volume of work which the MPs did at Westminster, in terms of voting, attending debates, sitting on committees etc. The only two MPs above my father on the list were Philip Hollobone, the Tory MP for Kettering, a famously thrifty former paratrooper who does all his own paperwork, and Dennis Skinner, the legendary Beast of Bolsover, a Labour stalwart who is such a sedulous attender of debates in the chamber that his buttocks sometimes seem to be glued to the famous green benches.

Frugality is in my father's DNA, so he was proud, but not surprised, to come near the top of the value-for-money list. He worked his butt off in the House of Commons and he did not expect the taxpayer to pay for him to live in the lap of luxury while he was at Westminster. There was no nonsense about claiming for plasma TVs or ludicrously expensive sofas. And he probably gave a wry smile when he saw the identity of the two MPs at the bottom of the list – Clare Short and George Galloway, high-profile Labour firebrands who had trenchant political views but enjoyed an increasingly semi-detached relationship with the House of Commons itself. Not for the first time, the Tories had trumped Labour when it came to offering value for money.

In another unofficial league table published at around the same time, my father was one of only fourteen MPs whose 'total additional expenditure' on items such as staff costs, living allowance and stationery etc. was below £100,000. He had always run a tight ship, and taken pride in not chucking public money around. He hated waste, whatever form it took. When MPs, for example, awarded themselves a 'communications allowance' – basically to undertake personal promotion under the guise of reporting to their constituents – he called for it to be scrapped. So when the expenses scandal broke and he found himself portrayed in the media as someone cynically milking the system, it was particularly infuriating.

The collateral damage of the expenses saga – not just to Brand Winterton, but to the House of Commons as a whole – was extensive and long-lasting. As a communications practitioner, what I found astonishing about the whole expenses episode was the complete lack of a crisis communications plan – of the kind that would be standard in any major organisation. As more and more details of MPs' expenses were leaked, nobody was primed to defend the reputation of Parliament, front up to the media, give explanatory interviews, put allegations in context, stem the tide of adverse publicity before it did irreparable reputational damage. Individual MPs were left to the mercy of Fleet Street and picked off one by one. The institution they served was powerless to protect them – or its own good name.

It is no exaggeration to say that the episode marked a watershed in post-war British politics. The House has since put its affairs in order, up to a point, and public confidence in Parliament has been restored, up to a point. But at the time of writing, the situation is still far from satisfactory. Every time there is the faintest whiff, even the faintest *imaginary* whiff, of politicians lining their own pockets at taxpayers' expense, there is a public outcry: not just the kind of synthetic anger whipped up by newspapers, but real disgust, real exasperation.

You often hear it said that cynicism about politics has become so endemic that public expectations of politicians have reached rock-bottom. In my own experience, the reverse is the case. People want very much to be led by men and women they can respect. It genuinely disconcerts them when they learn that MPs are fallible, just as it disconcerts them when they discover that teachers or doctors are fallible. They hunger for a national parliament of which they can be proud, not one which is bloated and dysfunctional. And they have surprisingly strong views about how such a parliament should function and what kind of people should sit in it. There is a lot of idealism lurking beneath the surface cynicism with which politics tends to be discussed – an idealism which regularly stubs its toe against harsh and depressing realities.

Take that long-running sore, MPs' salaries. How much should an MP earn in a modern democracy? More than their constituents? And, if so, how much more? Pay them silly money and they will lose touch with the real world. Pay them peanuts and only monkeys will apply. We all know the arguments. You would have thought that the oldest major Parliament in the world would have cracked the riddle by now, and come up with some reasonably robust formula for fixing MPs' remuneration – a formula which would make sense to the man and woman in the street – but there is not even the glimmer of a solution on the horizon.

In the nearly fifty years since my father was first elected, MPs' pay has increased twenty-fold – his starting salary was just £3,250

– but in such erratic fashion that it has been like watching a drunk staggering from lamp-post to lamp-post. Periods of monkish abstinence, when MPs' pay has been frozen for years at a time to set a good example, have been followed by periods of playing catch-up, with MPs awarding themselves pay rises which, taken out of context, look excessive. Government after government has fudged the issue. And while fudging issues is not always to be deplored – you could say the British have a great knack for it – the way this issue has been fudged has been catastrophic for the reputation of Parliament.

It now seems to be common ground among political observers that the expenses scandal that erupted in the 2005–10 parliament had its origins many years earlier, when Margaret Thatcher was in power. 'She was out of touch,' remembers my father. Again and again, the independent Senior Salaries Review Board would recommend a substantial rise in MPs' pay, only for Mrs Thatcher, nervous of a public backlash, to veto the idea. 'It was all right for *her*,' says Dad darkly. 'Thanks to Denis, she was very well off, and had no understanding of the financial pressures which ordinary back-bench MPs sometime faced.'

What followed was rank hypocrisy, a piece of financial jiggery-pokery which may have fooled voters, but was rooted in a kind of confidence trick. Backbenchers were asked to show re-straint over their basic pay but, as a *quid pro quo*, tipped the wink that the expenses regime would err on the side of generosity. MPs had always grumbled that they had not been properly reimbursed for the *real* costs of being an MP. First, they had to maintain two different domestic establishments, one in London and one in their constituency. Secondly, they had to meet all kinds of incidental expenses not likely to be incurred by people in other professions. 'Every village fete I went to set me back about £50,' Mum remem-bers. 'As the local MP, you could not be seen refusing to buy raffle tickets or supporting good causes.' Now, suddenly, relief was at hand, with the party whips giving MPs the green light – not to fiddle their expenses, but to put in expenses claims that would not be subjected to line-by-line scrutiny by nit-picking officials.

It was a pretty lax regime and open to abuse. One urban myth at Westminster – or perhaps it was not an urban myth, my mother certainly subscribes to it – was that four Labour MPs from Glasgow shared a car down from Scotland every week and put in four separate mileage claims. And officials in the House of Commons Fees Office played along, to some extent, helpfully finding MPs ingenious ways to maximise their allowable expenses. This was particularly true of the so-called 'flippers' – MPs who reversed the designation of their 'main' and 'second' home to qualify for additional allowances.

The name of the game was not keeping costs to a minimum, but helping back-bench MPs supplement their income by all reasonable means, subject to oversight by the parliamentary authorities. And that game, begun under Mrs Thatcher, continued under her successors. The Prime Minister of the day would try to keep a lid on MPs' salaries, to set a good example to the rest of the country. And backbenchers would grumble, bite the bullet, but make sure their generous expenses regime remained intact.

As late as 2008, just a year before the expenses scandal broke, MPs voted for a modest pay increase, at Gordon Brown's behest, but defeated a motion to tighten up the expenses regime – by, for example, requiring receipts to be produced for items costing under £25. Rank-and-file backbenchers, my parents included, resented being made to jump through ever more hoops just to keep the bean-counters happy. They liked things the way they were, warts and all. They did not foresee how bad some of the warts would look once exposed to the public gaze.

One cannot possibly defend some of the abuses that took place, and I would not attempt to, but I find it hard to be too censorious of the MPs who claimed for X, having explicitly asked the Commons authorities beforehand, 'Can I claim for X?' and got an unequivocal yes. They played by the rules and, if the rules were unclear, they asked for a ruling and accepted it. My parents, as should be clear by now, were rule-keepers, not rule-breakers. They never did anything dishonest or underhand, and are naturally mortified when there is any suggestion to the contrary.

Among their fellow MPs – many of whom also saw their reputations trashed during the expenses scandal – what still rankles is the sense that things they had done in good faith were being judged retrospectively, by new and different standards. A cardinal principle of all legislation is that, if you ban smoking on buses, say, by a 2010 Act of Parliament, you cannot prosecute someone for smoking on a bus in 2004. With parliamentary expenses, the pendulum swung so suddenly and so violently that expenses claims that were above board in 2007 – nodded through by the Fees Office without a murmur of protest – became the object of hysterical opprobrium and name-calling just two years later. That just didn't feel fair. It still doesn't feel fair.

In every workplace on the planet, from Siberia to New Zealand, new employees will inquire what expenses, if any, they are able to reclaim in relation to their duties. Travel costs? Uniform allowances? Anything else? Then they will just go through any bureaucratic hoops required of them, in terms of form-filling, keeping receipts etc. What they will not expect, or deserve – unless they have deliberately lied or tried to cheat the system – is to have their integrity called into question. I would hope that reasonable people would grasp that point, and understand my parents' frustration at the turn of events in their case.

On the general issue of MPs' pay and remuneration, they have consistently taken the view – and voted accordingly whenever they had the opportunity – that MPs' salaries need to be rather higher than they are at present. Not massively higher, but high enough to attract parliamentary candidates of sufficient calibre.

My father, for what it is worth, believes the basic MP's salary should be closer to £95,000 than the present £75,000. He accepts that any plans to pay MPs the higher figure would go down like a lead balloon in Macclesfield – it was one of the very few issues on which he was out of step with his constituents – but has his answer ready. How can people simultaneously insist that MPs are overpaid and that they are incompetent and a waste of space? Is paying them *less* going to remedy the problem? What happened to the trusty old law of supply and demand?

This is a tricky one and, as a taxpayer, I feel conflicted. There are Members of Parliament – no names, they know who they are – to whom I resent paying a single penny. There are others whose salary I would double tomorrow, if I could. How does one begin to set remuneration rates for such a mixed-ability workforce?

Twenty years ago, if you had stopped someone in the street in Macclesfield, and asked them, 'Do you think your local MP should be paid the same as your local doctor?', they would probably have pondered the question, then said, 'Yes, that sounds about right.' You would have got the same answer if you had asked whether the local MP should be paid the same as the head of the local comprehensive school. Nowadays, of course, many GPs earn in excess of £100,000 a year, as do the heads of high-achieving state schools. MPs, rightly or wrongly, have been left behind. Quite a long way behind. But has the relative importance of the three professions changed in that period? Not to my way of thinking.

In my father's case, his £3,250 starting salary as an MP in 1971 was certainly enough to get by on – the national average wage at the time was around £2,000 – but hardly a strong inducement to go into politics. It was roughly what he was earning as a senior manager at Stevens and Hodgson, but not enough to cover all his outgoings at that time, which included school fees. Luckily, Stevens and Hodgson continued paying him after he had been elected – it was seen as quite a coup to have an MP on their payroll – and in time, like many MPs, he would take on various paid consultancies – for example, with the Paper and Board Industry Federation – to supplement his parliamentary income.

He got by, financially, with a bit to spare, but that was it. At times – such as when he was involved in potentially costly lawsuits – he would have given his eye-teeth to be paid the same as a banker or professional footballer. It was a slightly hand-to-mouth existence – particularly when you take into account the fact that an MP's employment can be terminated by his employers, the electorate, at short notice, and with no right of appeal.

Among Tory MPs of his generation to whom I have talked, it was common to hear the refrain, 'You can't live on a Member of Parliament's salary.' By 'live', of course, they did not mean keeping body and soul together, but enjoying the kind of middle-class comforts – owning a nice house in a nice area, taking foreign holidays, perhaps sending their children to private school – which people in other professions would take for granted. Were they being greedy? Or were others being unrealistic in expecting them to do such responsible jobs for such modest remuneration? I will leave others to judge.

Election to the House of Commons certainly did not catapult my father into a dramatically higher earning bracket or protect him from the kind of financial worries with which his constituents were all too familiar. If he had not caught the political bug in a big way, he would probably have thought twice about standing for Parliament – as many gifted men and women have, for that very reason.

Fat-cat MPs? There is no such animal. In February 2016, it was reported that the Tory MP William Wragg – whom my father helped win the Hazel Grove constituency from the Liberal Democrats at the 2015 general election – had had to move back in with his parents because he could not afford to buy his own home. Even on his parliamentary salary of £74,000, he explained during a TV debate, he could not afford to live in rented accommodation while, at the same time, saving enough money to put down a deposit on a house. At twenty-eight, he was stuck in exactly the same bind as others of the so-called 'boomerang generation'.

At this point, some of his less well-paid constituents probably started screaming at the television. And quite right, too. As a pitch for the Hazel Grove sympathy vote, it was a disaster. 'I'm sure he'll learn his lesson,' says my father. 'In fact, he is shaping up as an excellent MP, hard-working and talented.' But the story did underscore something that often gets overlooked. Many Members of Parliament, particularly at the outset of their careers, have a lifestyle closer to that of a student living out of a suitcase than to that of an established professional. In the ten years after he was elected, my father lived in a series of pretty modest digs in London: not quite rat-infested, but certainly not chandelier-infested. It is a career move that involves genuine sacrifices – sacrifices which a lot of people who would otherwise make excellent MPs are not prepared to make. We should be doing more – or so my father would argue – to encourage them to make those sacrifices.

He accepts that selling the idea of better-paid MPs is an uphill struggle. Some of his former constituents might buy into the idea, but most would reject it out of hand. It is such a toxic subject, that rational debate has become impossible. One way or another, the mess will go on, with under-incentivised MPs perceived as overpaid by misinformed voters – their prejudices inflamed, in many cases, by journalists whose own expenses claims would not stand five minutes' scrutiny.

My parents are not given to self-pity. When they were in the House together, they thought of themselves as extraordinarily privileged, and had to pinch themselves that they had been given the opportunity to serve their Cheshire constituents for so long. But of the various crosses they had to bear, this was probably the hardest – the perception, ludicrously wide of the mark, that they and their fellow backbenchers had gone into politics to get rich.

If only.

11.

THE AWKWARD SQUAD
IN THEIR POMP

On 18 July 1990, a man called Timothy Renton – one of those chinless Old Etonians who enjoy successful political careers without ever really putting their heads above the parapet – wrote a letter to my father. (His place of education is not strictly relevant, but as it may help explain my parents' allergy to Etonians, I thought I should mention it in passing.) The letter precipitated what was, in some ways, Dad's finest hour: a bruising battle from which he emerged, not just unscathed, but strengthened. He was having to fight the battle from the back benches, but he fought it with verve and conviction: a politician in his prime.

The villain of the piece, Mr Renton, now Baron Renton of Mount Harry, was then the Conservative Chief Whip under Margaret Thatcher. You could say he had time on his hands. There are years when the Chief Whip is a major player, other years when he is an ornate irrelevance. The year 1990 was one of the latter. The Tories had a majority of over 100, so herding enough back-benchers through the lobbies to defeat opposition amendments to the Agriculture (Miscellaneous Provisions) (Scotland) Bill was not exactly a task calling for consummate political skills. A baboon with a swagger-stick could have performed it. One imagines Mr Renton sitting in his office, twiddling his thumbs, checking his shares in the *Financial Times*, then staring out of the window and brooding.

As he brooded, his thoughts turned to the Member for Macclesfield, one of the more troublesome members of his flock, if not the most troublesome. Dad was then a senior member of the Social Services Committee, forming a strong cross-party axis with Labour's Frank Field, the committee chairman, and chivvying under-performing government ministers on a range of issues. He had voted against the government on twelve separate occasions since the start of the parliamentary session, on issues ranging from water privatisation to the NHS to football spectators.

It was a great time to be a Winterton, and I can remember the pride I felt as a teenager as my father took centre stage, attracting a blizzard of overwhelmingly positive publicity. As one newspaper columnist put it: 'Mr Winterton has excelled himself, garnering more column inches than Madonna and Paul Gascoigne put together.' Not bad for a balding, middle-aged backbencher! As the battle raged, he was suddenly the toast, not just of Tory voters in Macclesfield, but of people across the country who cared about free speech, fair play and all those other ingredients that make Britain the country it is.

Politics is a tribal business. If your party wins a landslide – as Labour did in 1945 and 1997, and the Conservatives did under Margaret Thatcher in 1983 and 1987 – it is natural to feel like a football team that has won 5–0. But there is a time for celebrating and a time for sober reflection. Governments with huge majorities can be a bad thing – as Francis Pym, Foreign Secretary under Mrs Thatcher, had the temerity to point out, much to his boss's irritation. And my father, Thatcherite or no Thatcherite, could see enough of the big picture to know that, however much his party was in the political ascendancy, the need to subject its decisions to proper parliamentary scrutiny remained paramount. If he disagreed with something it was doing, he would cheerfully troop through the No lobby with the opposition. What was the point of being a Member of Parliament otherwise? He was a man, not a sheep.

To the party whips, of course, a single act of rebellion is anathema.

They *want* backbenchers to behave like sheep, preferably neutered and with their horns and tongues surgically removed. And to poor Mr Renton, totting up the score in his little black book, and wincing as it reached double figures, a dozen such rebellions must have seemed like the vilest perfidy. What the hell was Nick Winterton playing at? Whose side was he on? It was not as if the man just voted the wrong way occasionally. He was giving government ministers a piece of his mind in public, and on a regular basis. Some of the language he had directed at senior colleagues was blunt to the point of rudeness. And that ghastly wife of his! She was rebelling almost as often as her husband. The pair of them had completely lost the plot. Trouble-makers. Loose cannons. Bad eggs. If this voting-with-the-opposition malarkey wasn't nipped in the bud…

His brooding concluded, the Chief Whip dictated a stiff letter to the Member for Macclesfield, drawing attention to his erratic voting record and complaining that he had twice shown 'exceptional rudeness' to a senior member of the government, not named. Mr Renton concluded his letter with a veiled threat to report Dad to his constituency association in Macclesfield, who might like to consider de-selecting him if he didn't toe the party line…

Oh, to have been a fly on the wall when this little *billet-doux* landed on Dad's desk. I have already referred to his penchant for returning insults with interest, a natural pugnacity that had silenced many a heckler at the hustings. At Westminster, his abrasive style of politics earned him the grudging nickname 'the Macclesfield Boot Boy'. Temperamentally, he was like an Angry Young Man who had never grown up. But never, in twenty years in Parliament, had such a red rag been waved at the raging bull that was Nicholas Raymond Winterton. He took pen to paper and, burning with righteous indignation, wrote Mr Renton a stinker of a letter that ran to seven pages. There is a photocopy of it among the family papers and, even a quarter of a century later, you can still feel the raw emotion in the writing. It is a wonder his pen didn't burn a hole in the paper.

Page 1 is icy and controlled, the calm before the storm. ('I am surprised and disappointed at the impertinent and discourteous tone of your letter...') By page 3, he is fast warming to his theme. ('Your reference to my commitment and loyalty is beyond contempt...') But by page 4, he has completely lost it, pouring out his heart in a torrent of sarcasm. ('I have served in public life for nearly a quarter of a century – no, not in the cushy south east [Tim Renton was MP for Mid Sussex, about as cushy as a constituency gets], but in the West Midlands and the north west, where consistency, principle and honour still mean something...') Best of all is the magnificent rant that occupies almost the whole of page 6. ('I would advise you that I treat with contempt the colleagues who you allege have complained to your office about my attitude and behaviour. If they were genuine colleagues and gentlemen, they would complain to me personally and not behind my back – we are not at prep school...')

At this point, of course, the 'normal' back-bench MP – by which I mean one primarily concerned with staying out of trouble and keeping his nose clean – would have re-read the letter and had second thoughts about sending it. Or he would have redrafted it, taking out some of the more inflammatory phrases. That 'cushy' had better go. Was 'beyond contempt' too strong? And perhaps the line about prep school was a bit childish? Not Dad. Still seething, like a man who had been stung by a hornet, he just bunged the letter in an envelope and, not wanting to spoil the ship for a ha'porth of tar, made sure a copy of it found its way into the hands of the press.

All hell, predictably, broke loose. And Dad – perhaps not quite so predictably – became an overnight hero, lionised across the political spectrum. People who had never heard of him thrilled to his full-blooded rhetoric.

The timing of the letter could hardly have been better. By the summer of 1990, the Tories might have had a thumping majority in Parliament but, in the country at large, a lot of people had become heartily sick of them. There was a whiff of decay, of power grown arrogant. And Dad's fierce anti-government tirade ('If I am given bland, irrelevant and incompetent answers to questions, I will react accordingly') struck a far more powerful chord than if he had been Leader of the Opposition. People sat up and took notice as one of the bit-party players suddenly took centre stage. Winterton? Winterton? Wasn't he one of the Tory right-wingers who had propelled Margaret Thatcher to power? And if *he* was cheesed off...

Mum, naturally, leapt to his defence, taking a side-swipe at her least favourite school. 'There seems to be a touch of July madness in the air,' she told an interviewer. 'But it will take more than an Old Etonian to beat an Old Wintertonian.' Then others started piling in.

In Macclesfield, it goes without saying, the man in the street backed my father to the hilt. 'He seems to be the only Tory these days capable of telling the truth about certain matters,' said one Maxonian interviewed by *The Guardian*. 'If he stood as an independent, he would increase his majority massively.' Others agreed wholeheartedly. 'The best thing that's ever happened to Macclesfield.' 'He has fought long and hard for this town.' 'I'd rather have him than a lot of other Conservatives who talk a lot but don't do half as much.' He had stood up for them. Now they were standing up for him. But what was noticeable on this occasion was how the chattering classes in London – who were normally inclined to be sniffy about 'Mr Macclesfield' and probably assumed his constituents were Cheshire hillbillies with straw in their hair – took up the same refrain.

The late, great Bernard Levin, at his sarcastic polemical best, devoted an entire article in *The Times* to the Renton letter. It was entitled *Whips and the Insolence of Office* and, while teasing my father for his intemperateness, recognised that his heart was in the right place.

'Whatever the offence given, do not write an angry seven-page letter to anyone on any subject,' Levin cautioned, tongue-in-cheek.

There is conclusive evidence, based on years of research, that nobody has ever read a seven-page letter, whoever sent it and whatever it was about, with the single exception of the one St Paul sent to the Hebrews… Some of the more colourful passages in Mr Winterton's letter suggest that, if he does get thrown out of Parliament, he could make a new career by chalking rude words on walls… He clearly believes that the best form of defence is a swift kick to his opponent's left temple followed by another to the right. But since I hold the same precept myself… I believe he is on admirable ground.

What Dad had demonstrated – and with a panache that Levin could only applaud – was that he was his own man, willing to speak his mind even when it ran contrary to the party line.

The glory of democracy is that it is capable of tolerating dissent … but because whips are men of limited understanding, they cannot see that Mr Winterton and his like should be cherished, bloody nuisances though they are… Who but a poltroon would stifle dissidents like that rather than put them forward as proof of their party's breadth of mind? Only a whip, of course… Mr Winterton, though he is noisy, difficult, obstinate, disobedient, bad-tempered, touchy and prolix, is worth more to his party than the entire contents of the whips' office.

What made this bouquet particularly pleasing to Dad was that it came from a commentator who would have disagreed with his views on just about everything – *apart* from his right to hold views and express them without fear or favour. Another article published on the same day – this one by Hugo Young in *The Guardian* – gave him even greater pleasure.

Young and Dad had form, as the saying goes. A few years before, Young, who was just starting out as a lobby correspondent, had described Dad as the biggest buffoon in the House of Commons – an insane piece of hyperbole in such a buffoon-rich environment. Lawyers' letters were exchanged. (It is a minor tragedy the case never came to court, as Dad's counsel could have had a field day listing MPs who, by any reasonable yardstick, were far bigger buffoons.) Now he was happy to eat humble pie and, in an article entitled *As You Were: For Buffoon Read Hero,* made gracious amends:

> I withdraw the charge and apologise... Mr Winterton is a serious hero of democracy... Compared with the cohorts of junior ministers who have never in their lives offered the Chief Whip anything but quivering acquiescence ... he has settled for the role of constituency MP and independent spirit ... turned truculence to good cause ... and left ministers poised between rage and apprehension at his refusal to toe the party line.

Young seized on a sentence in Dad's letter in which his entire political philosophy is encapsulated: 'My loyalty is to my country, my constituency and a way of life.' No mention of party, note. As he put it later in the letter, although he was proud to be a Conservative and promote Conservative values, he was 'sent to the House by the electors of Macclesfield and not exclusively by the Conservative Party'. It was a pet maxim of his and, if this book has an overarching theme, it is to be found in this sentence.

People who get involved in politics can be as tribal in their allegiances as football fans – not to mention as noisy. They see politics as a game of Them and Us, in which their own team is always right and the other team are in league with the Devil. I have tried to describe the mind-set and shared values of the Tory tribe in which Mum and Dad grew up: the small army of patriots and upright citizens joining their local Conservative associations. But tribalism has its limits – and Mum and Dad had a far better understanding of those limits than most of the MPs sitting on the Tory benches in the House of Commons.

Suppose your own team, in a fit of collective madness, suddenly decides to sup with the Devil? It can happen. It does happen. You can't just blind yourself to what is going on and say nothing. You need to step back from the parliamentary fray, think for yourself and listen to the good sense of the men and women who matter most – the ones whose votes sent you to Westminster.

In the same month as he crossed swords so memorably with Mr Renton, Dad gave a magazine interview in which he again spelled out his philosophy:

> The constituency is every MP's power base. If you are doing a good job there, your electorate will sustain you against any party pressure... In the House, I have never conformed as people expect me to conform... Throughout my career, I have voted against Tory legislation I disagreed with. But I have never regretted any stand I have taken... I have been a thorn in the whips' side for years, and been summoned into the whips' office many times. I am always happy to talk to them, but they won't make me change my mind.

There have been other independent-minded MPs, of course, and a backbencher rebelling against his party is hardly front page news. But what strikes me about my father, looking back on his parliamentary record, is the consistency with which he ploughed his own, sometimes lonely, furrow at Westminster. Other Members of Parliament get elected, try to ingratiate themselves with senior members of their parties, put convenient friendships before inconvenient principles. My father, though an excellent mixer socially, was more of a loner by temperament.

He was not one of those weather-vane MPs who only start rebelling once their hopes of promotion have been thwarted and whose interventions have an inevitable whiff of sour grapes. He knew what he thought. He knew what his constituents expected of him. And that was enough to dictate which way he voted. Trying to make him change his mind was not just futile, but counterproductive: it only hardened his resolve to do what he thought was right.

In his very first parliament, when he had barely had time to find the lavatories, Dad found himself in total disagreement with his party leadership on the vexed question of Northern Ireland. When

Ted Heath decided to prorogue the Stormont parliament, Dad did not mince his words. 'I never thought I would hear a Conservative Prime Minister announce a policy which I consider to be the most insidious surrender to terrorism.' Bang went any chance of promotion while Heath was in Downing Street.

When Margaret Thatcher became Prime Minister in 1979, Dad might reasonably have entertained hopes of promotion – he had been one of her strongest supporters when she had challenged Heath, and been unwaveringly loyal to her. Not a bit of it. The early years of the Thatcher administration saw massive job losses across the country and, when textile workers in Macclesfield joined the ranks of the unemployed, Dad let the government have it with both barrels. In 1981, to audible gasps in the chamber, he launched a savage attack on his own front bench, accusing it of throwing thousands out of work through their 'insensitive and inflexible' policies. Bang went any chances of promotion under Mrs Thatcher, too.

A Tory accusing a Tory government of being insensitive? Whatever next? The man must be what Denis Thatcher would have called a four-letter fellow and a dangerous pinko.

His last realistic chance of getting a frontbench job came when Margaret Thatcher was replaced by John Major in late 1990. Did my father grovel to the new leader? The hell he did! When the Major government announced significant pit closures, he complained publicly that it had 'gone quite doolally' – *not* the kind of comment that gets a backbencher invited to be the next Foreign Secretary.

Dad has hinted in interviews that, if he had been offered the right job at the right time, he would have relished the opportunity to hold ministerial office. There were moments when the carrot seemed to dangle tantalisingly in front of his nose. 'We need to use your talents,' Cecil Parkinson, party chairman at the time, told my father, when they found themselves in the Bahamas at the same time just before the 1983 election. My father, who was an officer of the All-Party Bahamas Group, still smiles ruefully when he recalls that conversation. If Parkinson had remained what he was at his political zenith – Margaret Thatcher's favoured successor – he would surely have seen to it that Dad was offered a ministerial position. Instead, of course, following Parkinson's affair with his secretary and subsequent resignation, he was no longer the friend at court my father had hoped for. The law of unintended consequences, the one every politician understands, had kicked in with a vengeance.

And Parkinson was quite right – in my admittedly biased view – in recognising that my father had talents which needed to be put to better use. Then as now, MPs who could spread the Tory gospel with verve and conviction were thin on the ground. Dad would have made a superb deputy party chairman – a key figure in the Conservative Party hierarchy – touring the country, rallying the party faithful.

But I doubt if he would have lasted very long on the front benches. I just cannot see him sitting in Cabinet listening to his colleagues talking bollocks and not *telling* them they were talking bollocks. There would have been a blazing row about the NHS, or the EU, and he would have blown his top and flounced out of the room, like Michael Heseltine. He was far too outspoken to be a good team man.

Mum *was* promoted to the front bench – twice – when the Tories were in opposition between 1997 and 2010. I suspect that reflects the fact that she was more naturally diplomatic than Dad – something not too difficult to achieve, to be honest. There was probably a small part of Dad that, if not resentful of her promotion, thought, 'Why not *me*?' But it certainly should not be taken to demonstrate that Mum was less independent-minded than him. In fact, if you examine their respective voting records, you will find umpteen times when they both rebelled, as well as times – which must *really* have had the whips scratching their heads – when Dad rebelled and Mum abstained or Mum rebelled or Dad abstained. They were never in perfect harmony – not always trotting through the same division lobby hand in hand – nor should they have been, as independent thinkers.

I could write a whole book about their run-ins with the Tory whips which most would find shocking – it would contain so many expletives it would be like a Quentin Tarantino film script.

Even the most casual observer of Westminster has worked out by now that party whips are, by and large, a Bad Thing. They never speak in the House, or voice opinions of their own, if they can possibly help it. They just try to browbeat as many backbenchers as possible to follow the party line. Not surprisingly, the job appeals to serial bullies with a penchant for strong-arm tactics.

There is an interesting letter in my father's files from Tristan Garel-Jones, a leading Tory whip under both Margaret Thatcher and John Major. A *bête noire* of the Eurosceptics, and known as the Member for Madrid Central, having once taught at a language school in the Spanish capital, Garel-Jones was such a celebrated and ruthless schemer that he is sometimes said to have been one of the models for Francis Urquhart in *House of Cards*. But there is an almost disarming candour in his letter, written after he had moved on from whipping to higher things:

> ...I have always regarded myself as a first-class, second-rank politician. That is why I have been a ruthless loyalist. I was a hired gun for Thatcher and a hired gun for Major and make no apology for either. What matters to me is the Conservative Party. Not because I think it is perfect, but because I think it *is* England. And, as a hired gun, I killed ruthlessly – even if it brought me into conflict with more active politicians.

Cynics will not be surprised to learn that the ruthless killer now sits in the House of Lords, as Baron Garel-Jones of Watford, flanked by other ruthless killers from the Tory whips office. I love the Conservative Party. I really do. But there are times when I could kick it to Madrid and back.

* * *

Dad's run-in with Tim Renton was the start of an extraordinary two-year period in which he never seemed to be out of the headlines – and for the right reasons. The Tories were still in power but, with the ineffectual Neil Kinnock as Leader of the Opposition, it could hardly be said that they were being put under constant pressure by their opponents. If anyone was going to keep them honest, it had to be someone within their own ranks – and Dad, as much by accident as design, got the part. If he had walked physically across the floor of the House of Commons, he could not have made his intentions more clear. A right-wing Tory on many issues he remained. But as the Member of Parliament for Macclesfield, he meant to carry on doing what he always done – holding the government to account.

To the casual observer, it was a surreal period in British politics. In the blue corner, steam coming out of his nostrils, the Member for Macclesfield. In the red corner, steam coming out of *their* nostrils, the rest of the parliamentary Conservative Party. That was the way the two teams lined up, with the vast majority of neutrals, so far as one could see, on my father's side. It was a bit like one of those infamous Cabinet meetings in the early 1980s when Margaret Thatcher found herself comprehensively outnumbered, but laid about her with her handbag until she had won over the doubters.

Never had Dad's determination to be his own man, and sod the Conservative Party, been put to a sterner test. There is an old Westminster saying that the people on the benches opposite are your opponents: your *enemies* are the ones sitting behind you. It sounds cynical, but there is a grain of truth in it. Certainly, if you were to ask Mum and Dad who were the fellow MPs towards whom they felt the greatest animosity, the names at the top of their respective lists would be Tories.

Dad was no stranger to being outspoken or finding himself in a minority. Now it sometimes felt as if he was a minority of one within his own party. Did it rattle him? Not a bit of it. In fact, it spurred him to even greater efforts. I have never known a period when he was more energised, more focussed, more determined to fight the good fight.

He had earned his spurs. He had been in the House for nearly twenty years, which put him in the veteran class. He knew the parliamentary ropes. But, most of all, he trusted his own judgement. He had never been afraid to challenge the conventional wisdom. Now he could challenge it, not just in a spirit of youthful iconoclasm, but with experience on his side. He could smell when something was not quite right, when the government was not being straight with people. And if he got involved getting into the odd punch-up with colleagues, so be it. He had never shrunk from a good punch-up. It was what got him out of bed in the morning.

The next major fracas in his career took place in late 1990, when the dust was still settling after the run-in with Tim Renton. In November of that year, the parliamentary Conservative Party – though not Mum and Dad, who were loyal to the end – dramatically jettisoned Margaret Thatcher as leader. Soon afterwards, reflecting changes in Whitehall, the Social Services Committee, of which Dad had been a prominent member, and a typically spiky thorn in the government's side, was split into two committees: a Social Security Committee and a Health Committee. Dad was put on the latter and, at its first meeting, in January 1991, was elected chairman – though *not* without a fight. Not for the first time in the Winterton story, there were bumps in the road.

There were five other Tory MPs on the committee, but only one of them could be persuaded to vote for him as chairman. The others, no doubt primed behind the scenes by the whips, voted for Sir David Price, a safe pair of hands who could be relied on to toe the party line on health issues. So Dad needed the votes of the four Labour members of the committee, plus the support of the Ulster Unionist member, Rev. Martin Smyth, to get the job. Behind the scenes, there was much skulduggery and tactical manoeuvring, and the *Sunday Express* later alleged that Dad had only secured the Ulsterman's vote by improper means. He had done nothing of the kind, but anti-Winterton feeling in some sections of the party was so strong by this stage that his fellow Tory MPs regularly briefed against him. One way and another, it was a nasty little episode, and left a sour taste.

In terms of knowledge and experience, my father was much the strongest candidate for the chairmanship. But after the Renton business he was a marked man, distrusted on his own side. The whips were particularly anxious to block his bid for the chairmanship because, a couple of years earlier, he had been only one of two Tory rebels to vote against the legislation setting up hospital trusts. It was a flagship Conservative reform and they did not want it sabotaged by some loose cannon asking awkward questions. Unfortunately for them, Dad was determined to ask those questions. He had always been a staunch champion of the NHS, and he did not like people tinkering with it, whether they were Tory ministers or Martians from outer space. Defying the whips, and securing the all-important chairmanship, was vital. He had won round one. But the fight was far from over.

Round two, played out in a blaze of publicity, took place in the summer of 1991. The new Health Committee had set to work, under Dad's chairmanship, and among the subjects it inquired into was the hospital trusts, still in their infancy and still controversial. Evidence was taken and, at the conclusion of the evidence, it fell to Dad, as chairman, to put a draft report before the committee. He duly did so, and did not pull his punches, incorporating some passages strongly critical of the trusts in his draft report. The draft was circulated to the other members of the committee, who submitted draft amendments for the committee's consideration. Up to this point, the whole process had been entirely normal and above board.

It was only when my father studied a raft of amendments submitted by Jerry Hayes, the Tory MP for Harlow, that he got suspicious. Hayes was a bit of an oddball, a beard-wearer at a time when, for a Conservative MP, it was political suicide. A barrister by profession, he had a weakness for the kind of political stunts – letting himself be pelted by custard pies while in the stocks – that raised his profile while casting doubt on his seriousness. He was well to the left of the Conservative Party on most issues and, in other circumstances, might have been a useful ally for Dad in his championship of his revered NHS. But Dad had never quite trusted the man – and those draft amendments were the final straw.

In a nutshell, the amendments were far too detailed and polished to have been drafted by the laid-back Jerry Hayes. They had the fingerprints of the Department of Health all over them. And if Hayes was submitting amendments drafted by officials in the Department of Health, it could only mean one thing. The committee's draft report had been leaked to the department – quite improperly, and in blatant breach of parliamentary protocol – before the committee had had time to consider it.

The final showdown came after the meeting at which the committee considered the draft report. With Dad in the chair, and unable to vote except in the case of a tied vote, the Conservative majority on the committee simply voted through most of the Hayes/Department of Health amendments – including one which deleted a large chunk of the report critical of the hospital trusts. In plain English, the committee had been nobbled, like the favourite at a dog-track being fed doped biscuits. Shocker!

The situation obviously called for a leak inquiry which, as fans of *Yes Minister* will know, is normally just a device for kicking something into the long grass. The leaker is never found and the episode is quietly forgotten. Dad was not going to let that happen. Using tactics that owed something to the junior dormitory at Rugby School and something to the late Torquemada, he got to the bottom of the leak in double-quick time, writing personally to every member of the committee and its staff and asking them in so many words: 'Did *you* leak the draft report?' He also reported the leak to the powerful Privileges Committee, the guardian of the rights of the House of Commons in such situations.

The Tories on the committee were aghast. 'He is nothing but a puffed-up bullfrog,' said one of them, off the record. 'He flounces around like Dame Edith Evans with a fit of vapours because his report has been the subject of a democratic vote,' said another, also off the record. But the bullfrog and Dame Edith got their man. The culprit was quickly found: Jerry Hayes's American research assistant who, ignorant of British parliamentary niceties, had passed the draft report to the Department of Health. Hayes himself accepted responsibility and resigned from the committee. The research assistant returned to the States with his tail between his legs. He probably still regales his neighbours in Tulsa or Cincinnati with horror stories about a fire-breathing Englishman called Winterton.

The good guys had won – even if it was a pyrrhic victory. By the time the leaker had been identified and Jerry Hayes had walked the plank, it was far too late to repair the damage the leak had caused: the emasculating of the report by the government-drafted amendments. But a victory it most certainly was. Whitehall officials, who should have known better, had tried to interfere with due parliamentary process at Westminster and been given a bloody nose. Round two to Winterton!

Round three, alas, was a very different matter. If Dad's name had been mud in the Tory whips' office after the Renton episode, one can only imagine the kind of expletives that now flew around the whips' office at the mention of his name. I have not had the privilege of receiving a bollocking from the Tory whips, but I am assured by two impeccable sources, viz. my parents, that their use of un-parliamentary language has to be heard to be believed. They begin where Scottish football managers leave off. So it is fair to assume that a fly on the wall of the whips' office at its Christmas party in 1991 would have picked up angry mutterings along the following lines:

That ******* Winterton is a ****ing disgrace! Who the **** does he think he is, putting the boot into hospital trusts? He's no more a

Tory than Chairman ****ing Mao. He's become a complete pain in the ****ing arse, and he's got to be got off that ****ing Health Committee before he does any more ****ing damage to the party. Anyone got any good ideas for shafting the ****er?

Not very edifying, I am afraid. And the bad news, for lovers of parliamentary democracy, is that the Tory whips *did* finally manage to shaft that ****er Winterton, and in the most shabby way imaginable. They could not win fair and square, and so – always the last refuge of the scoundrel – they changed the rules. My father's blood still boils when he remembers what happened, and who would blame him?

To give a bit of the parliamentary background, departmental select committees as we know them, with each Whitehall department shadowed by an all-party committee at Westminster, are of comparatively recent origin. There were just a handful of select committees when Dad was first elected in 1971. It was only in 1979, when Norman St John-Stevas was Leader of the House, that the House went the whole departmental-committee hog. But there was still a slightly experimental feel to the committees. They seemed like a good idea in theory, beefing up the scrutiny of the Executive by Parliament. But suppose Parliament, in the shape of the new committees, got too big for its boots? The Sir Humphreys of Whitehall were nervous, and so were their political masters. Wouldn't select committees with real teeth, asking tough questions of ministers and badgering under-performing civil servants, be a menace? Wouldn't they be a bit, well, *American*?

On Capitol Hill, congressional committees had been part of the political furniture for years. They were a real power in the land, their public hearings – often highly dramatic and confrontational – televised for public consumption. They subjected legislation to line-by-line scrutiny. They even presumed – unimaginable at Westminster in the 1980s – to hold confirmation hearings to vet Presidential appointments.

Probably the feature of American congressional committees which most exercised constitutional conservatives at Westminster – and which they were determined not to replicate – was the power wielded by committee chairmen. They won the chairmanships, clung on to them like limpets and, the longer they clung on, the more influential they became. Wilbur Mills, the Arkansas Congressman who chaired the House Ways and Means Committee for seventeen years, between 1958 and 1974, was regularly called 'the most power-ful man in Washington'. Carl Hayden from Arizona, who chaired the powerful Senate Appropriations Committee for fourteen years, between 1955 and 1969, was another great survivor. 'No man in Senate history has wielded more power with less oratory,' quipped one rueful colleague.

The limpet-like committee chairmen on Capitol Hill were admired and resented in equal measure. Sometimes there would be mutterings that it was time for them to step aside and give others a chance. But there was also acknowledgement that, with length of service, had come a formidable expertise. The chairmen were potent and, more important, independent figures. They did not kow-tow to Presidents, of whatever political stripe.

At Westminster, at the time the departmental select committees were first established in 1979, the idea of committee chairmen serving for parliament after parliament, growing in power and authority, was not really on anybody's radar. The chairmanships were doled out to long-serving back-bench MPs, as a consolation prize for not achieving ministerial office. Or they were doled out to recently demoted ministers, as a salve to their bruised egos. Most of the doling out was done, behind the scenes, by the party whips. That was how the House of Commons worked.

Dad's bold seizure of the Health Committee chairmanship, with Labour support, had already infuriated the Tory whips. They could now imagine him holding the chairmanship for ten years or more, announcing awkward inquiries, summoning reluctant witnesses, harrying ministers from pillar to post. They could not simply remove him from the chairmanship – it is the prerogative of a select committee to choose its own chairman. But what they *could* do, at a pinch, was ensure that, when Parliament met again after the 1992 general election, he was kept off the committee altogether.

A cunning new rule was duly concocted, debarring MPs from sitting on the same select committee for three successive parliaments. Under the new rule, my father could no longer sit on the Health Committee, having sat on that committee and its predecessor, the Social Services Committee, since 1979. But he could have no grounds for complaint, as the same rules applied to everyone!

It was a squalid little plot, doubtless hatched in the darkest recesses of the whips' office, where Tim Renton had been replaced as Chief Whip by the boyish but equally ruthless Richard Ryder. The body that actually came up with the new rule was the Tory-dominated Committee of Selection, chaired by the ultra-loyalist Sir Marcus Fox, who made a pig's ear of the whole thing.

One look at the nominations for membership of the select committees put forward by the Committee of Selection showed that it had not even applied its own rules consistently. If Dad had to forgo his chairmanship of the Health Committee, then Sir John 'Safe Pair of Hands' Wheeler, the Tory chairman of the Home Affairs Committee, who had also served for three parliaments, should step down, too. Whoops! Sir John gallantly fell on his sword. But then the spotlight fell on *other* Tory MPs who, under the new rule, should not have been nominated to the select committees either. Double whoops!

There is a classic dividing line between those who see conspiracies everywhere and those who subscribe to the cock-up theory of politics. Well, this was a conspiracy *and* a cock-up. Everything people find most objectionable in politicians – the deviousness, the cynicism, the naked abuse of power – conflated into a single inglorious episode. I was in my early twenties at the time and remember the mixture of disgust and anger I felt that the Tory whips – my own party – could stoop so low.

By the time the House debated the matter, on 13 July 1992, nobody had any doubts that the new 'rule' had been anything other than a clumsy *ad hominem* device to oust Dad from the chairmanship of the Health Committee. When he rose to speak, before a packed House, he did not mince his words. 'After nearly fourteen years of Conservative government, I believe that government year after year can create an arrogance that leads to dictatorship... The select committees of this House are the last bastions of the defences of this country against excessive government... And it seems to me that the independent view and freedom of speech is being squeezed out of this House.' He also gave it to Sir Marcus Fox with both barrels, telling him that he 'lacked credibility and integrity' in his role as chairman of the Committee of Selection, and the sooner he was gone, the better.

He was – of course – right. And everyone knew he was right. But Sir Marcus – of course – remained as chairman of the Committee of Selection. And the whips – of course – ensured that efforts to reinstate my father on the Health Committee were defeated in the division lobbies. The big loser, not for the first time, was Parliament.

To this day, my father feels rather sad at the cynical way his days as chairman of the Health Committee were cut short by the party whips. He felt as if he was only just beginning to make his mark: battling for his beloved NHS and, in the process, reminding the world that he was a Conservative with a social conscience, not a right-wing head-banger. He could not stand the sort of Tory who approached the NHS from an ideological, free-market vantage point and let patients go hang.

One of his favourite aphorisms is that select committees at their best are the House of Commons at its best. They operate in a bi-partisan way and try to reach conclusions rooted in hard, empirical evidence – even if those conclusions are anathema to the government of the day. Much as he enjoyed getting up on his hind legs in the chamber and banging on about one of his pet topics, he enjoyed the work of select committees – the little cross-party alliances, the striving for consensus, a totally different type of politics to the one on view at Prime Minister's Questions – even more. They reminded him of his days in local government, where a bi-partisan approach to problems was far more common than at Westminster. The committees were about getting things done, sifting evidence, chiselling money out of the coffers of Whitehall for people who desperately needed it. In a word, grown-up politics, not playground games.

*　*　*

And what was Mum doing while Dad was fighting the good fight on the Health Committee? She was also fighting the good fight, up to a point, on the Agriculture Committee.

I say up to a point, not to pooh-pooh the contributions she made to the committee, but to alert readers to the fact that the Agriculture Committee in the late 1980s and early 1990s was not a *totally* serious body. To the general public, the workings of parliamentary committees are a closed book. One group of middle-aged MPs sitting around a horse-shoe table looks much like another. But to the connoisseur, the fact that each committee is a law unto itself, with its own distinctive way of doing business, is what makes the Palace of Westminster such a uniquely fascinating workplace. And for ripe human comedy – quirky characters, wacky plot-lines, little tales of the unexpected – the Agriculture Committee on which Mum served between 1987 and 1997 took some beating.

If the Health Committee under Dad's chairmanship was like *Question Time* with David Dimbleby, addressing important issues in a reasonably grown-up way, the Agriculture Committee under the chairmanship of the late Sir Jerry Wiggin was more like a touring production of *The Mikado*, touring being the operative word. Some of the best scenes took place thousands of miles from Westminster.

Sir Jerry, a genial, baby-faced Old Etonian – that school again! – had acquired the nickname 'Junket Jerry', and it was well earned. At Westminster, he had a modicum of gravitas, and had been a junior minister in the Thatcher administration for a while. He was a shrewd political operator, and he served his Weston-super-Mare constituents assiduously. He was a fundamentally decent man, and did not take himself over-seriously – always a commendable quality in a politician. But his Achilles heel was his wanderlust. The further the Agriculture Committee found itself from London SW1, on fact-finding missions of varying degrees of credibility, the happier he was.

I don't want to sound as if I am getting on my high horse and being censorious about free-loading Members of Parliament. Joe Public is very naturally indignant when he reads that his MP is on a visit to Hong Kong or the Maldives when he should be speaking up for his constituents in Parliament. But, by and large, a well-travelled MP, to my mind, is preferable to one who has hardly got a stamp in his passport. The world looks different from another country: that gives you fresh perspectives, fresh ideas; it shakes you out of the complacent assumption that the British way of doing things is automatically the best way. The old cliché is true: foreign travel *does* broaden the mind; it is insularity that is the real danger.

Even so, the Agriculture Committee under Sir Jerry tested the theory of travel broadening the mind to its limits. All departmental select committees get the travel itch from time to time. Even the Health Committee under my father's chairmanship was not averse to the odd foreign trip when justified. Its ground-breaking inquiry into maternity services entailed a trip to Sweden, a world leader in the field, and it is betraying no confidences to say that my father relished the chance to cross-examine Swedish nurses in crisp uniforms about matters ante-natal. But there was a brazenness about the Agriculture Committee's methods that raised eyebrows across the Palace of Westminster. When its wanderlust was at its most rampant, it ought really to have been called the Thomas Cook Agriculture Committee and held its meetings in the departure lounge at Heathrow.

At the very first meeting of the committee which Mum attended, in 1987, the committee resolved to hold an inquiry into the forestry sector. It further resolved that, in order to better acquaint itself with the problems facing British foresters, it was necessary to go and look at trees in... New Zealand. Mum, a trifle nervously – how would this play in the Dog and Duck in Congleton? – acquiesced.

A couple of months later, she found herself looking at trees in New Zealand and discovering that, much like trees in Cheshire, they were green and had branches. Further visits, to France and Sweden, confirmed that European trees were also green and had branches. The inquiry was making solid progress. Where next for this definitive parliamentary investigation into forestry? The committee pondered the matter. The answer was obvious... Russia! Unfortunately for the Wintertons – I can just see Mum striding across the steppes in a bearskin hat – Sir Jerry misplayed his hand. Overseas trips by select committees require the prior approval of a body called the Liaison Committee, which comprises the chairmen of all Commons select committees. Sir Jerry duly lobbied the Liaison Committee for funds, pointing out that Britain imported more timber from Russia than any other country. There was a stupefied silence, broken by Michael Mates, chairman of the Defence Committee, muttering: 'Can't you just go and watch the timber being unloaded at Tilbury?'

The trip to Russia was vetoed, and there was no trip to Tilbury either. But, after independent research had confirmed that Russian trees were indeed green and had branches, the committee was finally able to conclude its inquiry and make a report of its findings to Parliament. I am told that students of forestry still occasionally dip into the report for its nuggets of wisdom. But had Sir Jerry and his fellow committee members lost their appetite for globe-trotting? They had not!

Mum has fond memories of a trip to the USA and Canada in 1990, which she *thinks* was connected with wheat but, as it included a visit to a hog farm near Chicago, may have had a porcine theme as well. A trip to Rome, purpose obscure, whizzed by in a happy blur. She also remembers quaffing perfectly chilled white wine at a café on Las Ramblas in Barcelona in the spring of 1992, but cannot for the life of her think what the Agriculture Committee was doing in Spain. Olives? Lemons? The implications for British high streets of the proliferation of tapas bars?

Dipping deeper into the old memory-bank, she remembers a trip to South Africa which she thinks may have had something to do with apples. The committee certainly spent a morning in an orchard, and there was a nice young apple-farmer with a beard who knew his Granny Smiths from his Golden Deliciouses. It was all great fun, and there was probably some compelling reason why taxpayer's money had been found to pay for the trip, but she is hazy about the details.

The one big jaunt she missed out on – and one of Sir Jerry's masterstrokes, a triumph of sheer *chutzpah* – was a trip to Ecuador and St Lucia in the autumn of 1992, just as the English winter was about to close in and a change of climate was called for.

The pretext for the visit was forthcoming legislation by Brussels to harmonise arrangements for the import of bananas into the EU. (Britain and France had previously offered preferential trading terms to their former colonies.) A simple trip to Brussels would have sufficed, but just as a tree in New Zealand makes more sense when you have seen it with your own eyes, so a Caribbean banana needs to be viewed *in context*, not just on a supermarket shelf, next to the apples and peaches.

In the event, the committee's trip was a fiasco from start to finish. After a lightning stop in Ecuador, where there was barely time for a cocktail party at the British embassy and a photo opportunity with a llama, the committee flew on to St Lucia, where the heavens opened as soon as their plane hit the runway. They had to spend most of the next seventy-two hours watching the rain lash down on the disgruntled honeymooners braving the hotel swimming-pool. Between showers, they were able to inspect enough bananas, just, to conclude that they were yellow and sweet-tasting and grew on trees.

I have all this on the authority of the committee's learned clerk, whose specially purchased tropical suit – claimed on expenses, in the best parliamentary tradition – never recovered from its dowsing. The entire visit could have been stage-managed by the Congleton Pantomime Society, and Mum was sorry to miss it.

You may be thinking by now that the Agriculture Committee must have been so busy plotting its next overseas jolly that it had no time to buckle down at Westminster and conduct serious, evidence-based inquiries. Well, you would be wrong. One of the beauties of politics is that nothing, *nothing*, can ever be predicted with confidence. As Harold Macmillan famously said: 'Events, dear boy, events…' Junket Jerry and his troops might have wanted to be thousands of miles from Westminster with the sun on their backs, but events kept dragging them back to SW1.

Who would have thought that an explosion at a nuclear reactor in the Soviet Union would fall under the province of the House of Commons Agriculture Committee? The after-effects of the blast – at Chernobyl in the Ukraine in April 1986 – would be felt right across Europe for years to come. In upland areas in the UK, rainfall containing radioactive caesium-137 led to restrictions on the movement of sheep, for fear of contaminated lamb entering the food chain. The Ministry of Agriculture had to devise a suitable way of keeping the public safe and compensating sheep-farmers affected by the ban. The Agriculture Committee in turn had to monitor the situation and make sure that ministers were on the ball and farmers were not being short-changed. It made for an interesting – and necessary – inquiry.

Mum's close knowledge of rural life suddenly stood her in good stead. She knew how farmers operated. She knew that it could be a hand-to-mouth profession, and that the government could not always be relied on to be on the farmers' side. If nothing else, a committee inquiry would keep the government honest, and she was happy to be part of it.

But the unpredictable event that *really* catapulted the Agriculture

Committee into the limelight, and made its members put away their travel brochures and concentrate on events closer to home, was a TV interview given by Edwina Currie, then a junior health minister, in December 1988. The notoriously brash MP for South Derbyshire had such a keen eye for publicity that, at one point, she was the best-known Conservative politician after Margaret Thatcher herself. But her on-air statement that 'most of the egg production in this country, sadly, is now infected with salmonella' caused panic and consternation. The ambiguity in the statement – what exactly did she mean by 'egg production'? – was never properly clarified, egg sales plummeted and four million squawking hens had to be slaughtered. Currie herself had to resign, making it four million and one.

An urgent parliamentary inquiry was called for, and the obvious body to conduct it – if they could refrain from visiting New Zealand and the Caribbean for a few weeks – was the Agriculture Committee. The committee duly set to work, asked for written evidence and drew up a list of witnesses, in the usual way, at which point Mrs Currie upped the ante by announcing that she refused to appear before the committee. 'But you must!' yelped the committee. 'You're the main witness.' 'I won't!' said Mrs Currie. 'Oh yes, you will!' said the committee. 'Oh no, I won't!' said Mrs C. Once again, the resemblance to a show cobbled together in two days by the Congleton Pantomime Society was uncanny.

Mrs Currie was eventually hauled before the committee, in a highly charged hearing in a committee room off Westminster Hall. She was grilled by the committee and, in the circumstances, gave a pretty good account of herself. 'EGG ON THEIR FACES!' ran the front-page headline in one of the following morning's tabloids. There were enough puns on scrambled eggs, curried eggs and hard-boiled eggs to last a lifetime.

Against expectations, the Agriculture Committee had suddenly become the hottest ticket in town. And its report on the salmonella-in-eggs crisis, when it was eventually published a few weeks later, was as eagerly awaited as a new Elton John single. The report pulled no punches and was critical, not just of Edwina Currie, but of other government ministers, such as Kenneth Clarke, who had also botched the situation. Beyond the theatricals, one could see a back-bench committee doing what a back-bench committee should always do – speak truth to power.

The salmonella crisis had hardly blown over before another, and far more serious, food-related health scare loomed on the horizon. BSE, or 'mad cow disease' as it was colloquially known, had started to manifest itself in British cattle, and there were concerns that people who had eaten infected meat might develop the human equivalent, Creutzfeldt-Jakob disease, or CJD, a rare and fatal condition affecting the brain. We lost a great friend, supporter and colleague, Baroness (Ziki) Wharton, to this terrible disease. In simple terms, was British beef safe? The Ministry of Agriculture, on the basis of expert advice, insisted that it was. Other experts were sceptical. So it fell to the Agriculture Committee to hold public hearings and cross-examine the various expert witnesses. Naturally, given public concern about mad cow disease, the inquiry attracted a good deal of attention. It was right that the issues should be ventilated, and in public, not behind closed doors.

Looking back, though, it is hard to think that the BSE inquiry was Parliament's finest hour. How on earth was a group of back-bench MPs – even ones like my mother, with extensive knowledge of the beef industry – expected to arbitrate between the views of competing scientific experts on such an arcane medical topic, calling for detailed knowledge of the central nervous system?

The committee took evidence, cross-examined scientific witnesses and reached the same conclusion about BSE as the government. Yes, it *was* safe to eat British beef. Panic over. But, with the wisdom of hindsight, that conclusion looks horribly premature, even complacent. A clear causal link between BSE and CJD has since been established – which suggests that, at very least, the committee should have asked some tougher questions of the various expert witnesses.

At least Mum did make one helpful intervention, sparing the committee's blushes. At the start of the BSE crisis, John Gummer, Minister of Agriculture at the time, famously tried to force-feed his daughter a beef-burger to reinforce the message that beef was safe. Gummer Junior, on camera, nearly threw up. It should have been a cautionary tale, but the moral of it had escaped Sir Jerry Wiggin, the chairman of the Agriculture Committee. On the day the committee was due to publish its report, giving beef the all-clear, he proposed that the members of the committee hold a group photocall at the nearest supermarket, scoffing something suitably bovine. My mother quickly applied the presidential veto. She did not mind a bit of knockabout comedy, but there were limits.

She still has fond memories of her time on the Agriculture Committee. She cannot stand pomposity in politics, or in life in general, so a committee where levity was never too far from the surface suited her down to the ground. With her rural background, she was on top of the subject matter and understood the ways of farmers, in particular their disdain for red tape and bureaucracy. She was also learning more about how government functions. There is no better training for a frontbench position than time spent serving on a back-bench committee. And, years later, after the 2001 general election, when Iain Duncan Smith was looking for an opposition agriculture spokesman, she was the natural choice.

The time spent looking at trees in New Zealand and apples in South Africa had not been wasted.

*　　*　　*

After all the ructions of the early 1990s, my parents could have been forgiven for thinking that, after the Tories' unexpected victory in the 1992 general election, life was about to get a bit easier. They could not have been more wrong. The next few years were to be dominated by a period of internecine strife within the Tory party, whose wounds have not yet healed. You just have to whisper the single word 'Maastricht' – the further handover of powers from the UK to Brussels – into the ear of a Conservative supporter who is over fifty, and you will see a wince of pain cross their face. It was an ugly, ugly time. And my parents, never ones to miss a punch-up in the school playground, were in the thick of it.

As a general rule, when a political party wins a general election – particularly one it had not expected to win – a mood of elation sweeps through the party, and the new government enjoys a honeymoon period that lasts several months. The 1992 election was the exception that proved the rule. The honeymoon was over within days, as if the bride had discovered her new husband in bed with the chambermaid, or as if someone had let off a smoke bomb in the matrimonial suite. My parents still look back on the period with bewilderment, wondering where it all went wrong. How did things turn quite so nasty, quite so quickly?

And I do mean nasty. In Gyles Brandreth's diaries, *Breaking the Code*, there is a vignette of Nicholas Soames – a Tory grandee, and a grandson of Winston Churchill – shouting at my parents after they had voted against the government, 'You're *c**ts* – and ugly ones to boot.' To say his choice of words was less than Churchillian is the understatement of the century. Soames, in fairness, had been educated at Eton. He had probably been brought up to talk to women like that. But what possessed a man so pitifully bereft of good looks to call other people *ugly*? In a nutshell, the madness of the times.

Soames is an anthropological oddity at the best of times. My father remembers him, more than once, creeping up behind him, putting his arms around him in a bear hug, then tweaking his nipples, quite hard. What was that about?

Soames was certainly not the only Tory to abjure normal parliamentary courtesies during the Maastricht debates. Seldom in the long history of the House of Commons can so many MPs have lost the plot at the same time. Why? How? My parents were as baffled as anyone.

If their party had not ditched Margaret Thatcher in favour of John Major... If John Major had not signed the Maastricht Treaty in February 1992... If, before the final implementation of the treaty, he had decided to put the matter to the British people in a referendum... So many ifs, all academic now. What was *not* academic, as far as my parents were concerned, was that in May 1992, immediately after the general election, the European Communities (Amendment) Bill, giving effect to the Maastricht Treaty, was awaiting their attention as legislators. And, as legislators – Eurosceptic by inclination, like most of their constituents – they thought the Bill was a shocker, one of the worst pieces of legislation ever brought before Parliament by a Conservative administration. They simply could not support it. Let the whips twist their arms till they snapped. They knew which way they were voting.

At the second reading of the Bill, on 21 May 1992, they joined twenty other Tory MPs in the No lobby. It was not enough to defeat the government, but it was a start. The rebellion grew. And grew. During the committee stage, my parents voted against their party more than forty times. Only Bill Cash and Teddy Taylor out-rebelled them. By the time of the third reading, on 20 May 1993, the original twenty-two Tory rebels had become forty-one: still not enough to defeat the government, with Labour abstaining, but enough to send the Tory whips into a frenzy of indignation – a state, of course, in which my parents were always happy to see them.

What infuriated them was the number of their Tory colleagues who privately agreed with them on the substantive issue of Maastricht, but trooped through the government lobby anyway, out of loyalty to the leadership. One of them was Neil Hamilton, who represented Tatton, the neighbouring constituency. He was Parliamentary Under-Secretary of State for Corporate Affairs – one of those minor government jobs which takes longer to say than to do – and therefore duty-bound to support the party whip or resign. 'You're my conscience, Nicholas,' Dad remembers Hamilton telling him, with a grandiose wave, as they headed off to vote in their respective lobbies. Didn't he have his *own* conscience? There were similar admissions from other Tories. 'We'd love to join the rebellion, but…' Wimps!

It was like a premonition of similar intellectual somersaults performed by a later generation of Conservative MPs a quarter of a century later, during the 2016 EU referendum. How many of the Tories who supported David Cameron's disastrous Remain campaign really *believed* in the cause?

One of my father's favourite maxims, which I would commend to anybody going into politics, is 'Your vote must always match your voice'. Nothing infuriates voters more than MPs who say one thing to get elected, then tack a different course at Westminster.

My parents might not have been able to stop the Maastricht Bill getting on the statute book, but they had – as ever – spoken their minds, despite the whips' bullying attempts to stop them. And, incidentally, the minds of their constituents. Ever closer union with Europe? You would have struggled to find a single voter in Macclesfield or Congleton who wanted *that*. The whole idea was a non-starter, whatever dog-eared piece of paper John Major had signed to keep the Euro-crats in Brussels happy.

The story of the Maastricht rebellion has been told so many times that there is no point in going over the same ground again. There is a full and frank account of the Tory in-fighting by Christopher Gill, the former MP for Ludlow, and a good friend of my parents, in his memoir, *Whips' Nightmare*. It contains a nice vignette of my mother in a Commons cafeteria, her eyes shining with excitement at the prospect of backbenchers finally doing what they *should* be doing – asserting control over the Executive. On the Eurosceptic spectrum, Gill was, and is, even more allergic to the shenanigans in Brussels than Mum and Dad. The son of a butcher and, like my parents, brought up in the Midlands, he actually stood as a UKIP candidate in the 2010 election and is now President of the Freedom Association, a libertarian pressure group. A good man, and a brave one.

But if the parliamentary battles over Maastricht are ancient history, the issue of Europe, like the related issue of immigration, is key to the Winterton story. It taps a surprisingly deep vein of emotion in them: they *care* about the subject, with a passion that would take more detached observers of Europe aback. See them on the ski slopes of Austria and – apart, of course, from the Union Jack hat which my father wears as a style statement – they could almost pass for a German or Swiss couple: they do not behave like Little Englanders, throwing their weight about. They take people as they find them, in whatever country they happen to be in. But get them back to Cheshire, in the heart of the land they love, and a patriotic pride seems to swell within them. *This* is home. Home with a capital H. A great nation, populated by a great people, with a great history.

They have always been British and proud of it. They have never been European and proud of it. They are not ashamed of being European. They just think that Europe is such a huge continent, and Europeanism such a loose, amorphous concept, that it does not really add up to anything – certainly not something they would die in a ditch to defend, as they would defend their own country.

The key word – the one which always provokes a Pavlovian reaction in them – is sovereignty. They have no problem with free-trade areas: they make good economic sense. But the slightest suspicion of things being decided in Brussels or Strasbourg which should be decided in Westminster is like a red rag to the Winterton bull. They might be relatively trivial things: people being forced to change their lightbulbs because of EU regulations; or having to stomach the idea of prisoners being given the vote because of rulings by the European Court of Justice. But to people like my parents, for whom notions of freedom and independence are absolutely central to British history, they are anathema.

As far back as the 1960s, when the Common Market was taking shape, my father was instinctively suspicious of the whole project. Like many of his fellow Tories, he saw the Common Market as a Franco-German alliance that Britain, with her own distinct national interests, should be wary of joining. His very first speech at the Tory party conference – which he addressed in 1969, as the prospective candidate for Newcastle-under-Lyme – developed this theme with gusto, infuriating the young Conservatives in the gallery, but delighting the elder party members in the hall below, who cheered him to the echo. He quickly gained a reputation as an anti-Marketeer, a reputation he still enjoyed when he was adopted as the Tory candidate for Macclesfield in May 1971.

After that, he wobbled a bit. Or perhaps it is fairer to say that he gave Ted Heath, the leader of his party, who was dead set on Britain joining the Common Market, the benefit of the doubt. Sentiment in the party was slowly changing. By the time the Macclesfield by-election was held, in October 1971, the mood in the constituencies had become cautiously, if not enthusiastically, pro-Market. Perhaps if Britain joined the club, it could become a *better* club, one in which Britain could prosper. Nothing was certain, but there were grounds for hope.

Later that month, at the end of the first major debate that he attended in the House of Commons, my father was happy to march through the Aye lobby with Ted Heath and the rest of the Tory government, on a motion supporting British entry to the European Community on the terms which Heath had negotiated. The die was cast.

It did not escape his attention that Enoch Powell, his political hero, who was virulently anti-Market, had voted with the Opposition. Should he have followed Powell's lead? The idea certainly crossed his mind. But he was content, on balance, to support the party leadership – and to continue to support it right through to the 1975 referendum, which finally settled the Europe issue for a gen-eration. He simply never imagined – and not many other people did – a European Union of twenty-eight member states, with all the attendant problems. A bloated, dysfunctional, undemocratic organisation. A political basket case. A farce.

You could say that his subsequent journey from tepid pro-Marketeer to committed Eurosceptic mirrored the journey taken by Margaret Thatcher over the same period. As a member of Ted Heath's Cabinet, she had backed him, without great enthusiasm, while he was negotiating British entry to the European Community. By the time she became Tory leader in 1975, British membership was a *fait accompli*. In the referendum on Europe that summer, she even wore a naff pullover decorated with the flags of Common Market countries – *not* her most elegant fashion statement. (Replicas of it went on sale during the 2016 referendum, which would have mortified her.) But after that, her impatience with Brussels increased by the day – until her famous outburst in the House of Commons in October 1990. 'No! No! No!'

From the back benches, my father cheered her to the echo. He liked politicians who called a spade a spade: there had been too much pussy-footing about when it came to Europe. He could not foresee – *nobody* could foresee – that four weeks later she would be gone, sacrificed on the altar of European integration. Or that her chief assassin would be Geoffrey Howe, the dead sheep, the man who had taken exception to Dad's shouting twenty years earlier. Politics is a funny old game.

If my parents had needed any encouragement to fight the Maastricht Treaty every step of the way, the knowledge that their deposed leader was on their side – 'I could never have signed this treaty', she told the House of Lords – provided it. In its way, Maastricht was about far more than Maastricht: it was an opportunity for Thatcherite loyalists like my parents to show their loyalty to the old regime. Which, of course, only made the rows about Maastricht even more toxic. People who had been rising stars under the old leader were now embittered has-beens under the new one. It is one of the oldest sub-plots in politics.

If the third reading of the European Communities (Amendment) Bill in May 1993 had been the end of the matter, the Tory wounds might have been patched up before the party had to face the electorate at the polls again. But the Maastricht saga just dragged on and on, like a bad dream. In July 1993, a Labour amendment to postpone incorporation of the treaty until the Social Chapter had also been incorporated led to a tied vote in the House of Commons. 317–317. A parliamentary cliff-hanger! The Speaker, following precedent, voted with the government. Then someone noticed that the Tory whips had miscounted the votes. The final score should have been 316–317. Chaos! Fury! Points of order!

Why, oh why, hadn't John Major put the matter of Europe and sovereignty to the British people? My father must have asked himself that a thousand times. It just seemed so obvious – and would seem even more obvious in the years that followed. His constituents in Macclesfield had a far better grasp of the *real* issues than the Cabinet, stuck in their Whitehall offices. So why were they being ignored?

He and Mum were just forced to watch, helpless, as the parliamentary Conservative Party fell apart at the seams, disintegrating by the day. In July 1993 – in comments accidentally recorded in a television interview – John Major called some of his Eurosceptic colleagues 'bastards'. *Not* very statesmanlike! More chaos. More fury. More name-calling. The following week, the safe Tory seat of Christchurch fell to the Liberal Democrats, with a majority of 16,000, in one of the biggest swings ever recorded in a British by-election.

Things came to a head again in November 1994, when nine Tory MPs – including Christopher Gill, but not my parents – had the party whip withdrawn after voting against the EC Finance Bill. In July 1995, in a desperate effort to restore his authority, Mr Major called a leadership election. He won, seeing off John Redwood, but had no more authority than he had before. After that, all he could do was delay the inevitable – an absolute hammering at the polls, which duly happened in May 1997 – for as long as possible.

For my father, it was not just an acrimonious time, but a period of conflicted loyalties. On more than one occasion, if enough of the Maastricht rebels had joined the opposition in a vote of no confidence – or what was effectively a vote of no confidence – the government would have fallen, precipitating a general election. But Eurosceptic or not, that would have been a step too far for my father. 'I was never afraid to vote against my party on matters of principle,' he tells people today. 'My record proves that. I rebelled time after time for nearly forty years. But I was not prepared to bring down a Conservative government. I was often constructively disloyal. I was never destructively disloyal. It would have gone against everything I believed in.'

To which my mother will nod in agreement, but with a wicked glint in her eyes. She is such a natural mischief-maker that it is not impossible to imagine circumstances in which she *might* have brought down a Conservative government, just for the hell of it.

As Harold Wilson famously joked about Tony Benn, she has immatured with age – which is one of the reasons I adore her.

12.

FOR SERVICES TO PARLIAMENT

Apart from the Sir Humphrey Applebys of Whitehall, who clock every GCB and OBE, nobody bothers to read honours lists, still less the small print. So a small detail in the 2002 Queen's Birthday's honours list will have escaped all but the most eagle-eyed observer.

On the surface, the elevation of Nicholas Raymond Winterton Esq. to Sir Nicholas Raymond Winterton looks like the non-story to end non-stories. If you are a long-serving Tory MP, knighthoods go with the rations, and if Dad had been made to wait a few years longer than some of his contemporaries, that was presumably because of the time he had spent on the naughty step, after defying three-line whips.

But now look at the small print. In the ordinary course of events, when an MP is knighted, it is for 'political and public services', which covers a multitude of sins and is often just code for 'lick-spittle and time-server'. The same form of weasel words is used as a fig-leaf to cover the fact that someone has only been made a peer because they have written a fat cheque to a political party. My father's citation, in contrast, was for 'services to Parliament', a fact of which he is inordinately – and very properly – proud.

He got his knighthood under a Labour government, which was also unusual, as the Labour Party does not traditionally hand out gongs as enthusiastically as the Tories. If he had had to wait for the

Tory leadership to put him forward for the honour, he would still be waiting. My mother – who would be Dame Ann Winterton if there was any justice in the world – still *is* waiting. The plain fact is that serial rebels like my parents are overlooked in the honours process. That is how politics works.

So it was a Labour Prime Minister, Tony Blair, who put my father's name forward for the honour, prompted by the then Leader of the House, the late Robin Cook – himself a distinguished parliamentarian of independent outlook. Cook was a passionate pro-European, so on the opposite side to my father in the debate that raged after Maastricht, but he recognised the distinctive contribution which my father had made to British politics. The two of them had worked together productively on the Modernisation of the House of Commons Select Committee.

As my father tells the story, Cook asked him into his office for an informal chat early in 2002, and got straight to the point. 'Why have you never been recognised?' He then produced a wad of statistics to show that there were over forty Tory MPs who had been elected to Parliament later than my father and were now – despite, in many cases, having done nothing of political consequence – knights or dames. So why had my father been overlooked? An oversight in the Tory whips' office?

The two men exchanged sly glances. They both knew the real answer. It did not have to be spelled out. After that, one thing led to another and, a few weeks later, my father's name was on the list of names submitted to Buckingham Palace by Downing Street.

On a personal note, I have to say that my pleasure at his knighthood was slightly tempered by the fact that, owing to a very British piece of bureaucracy, there is a strict limit on the number of family members who can accompany recipients of honours to the official investiture ceremony at Buckingham Palace. A spouse and two children is fine. A spouse and three children is inadmissible. So if – improbable, admittedly – the Queen were to be awarded an MBE, to be bestowed by herself, she would have to decide which of her four offspring could attend the ceremony. All most odd. What happened to family values?

In our case, it was my two older brothers who got the nod. My parents argued that, unlike me, they had not had the opportunity to go to tea at Downing Street nor had they attended any Garden Parties at Buckingham Palace. So I had to sit outside Buckingham Palace in the car, twiddling my thumbs, while Dad was getting bonged on the shoulder by Her Majesty. It was an anxious wait. Suppose HM asked Dad a question and he spent ten minutes answering it, holding up the CBEs and OBEs? Luckily, the British have a genius for a compromise as well as for petty rules. After the formal ceremony – courtesy of Richard Luce, formerly a fellow Tory MP, who was Lord Chamberlain at the time – I was smuggled into a palace courtyard to pose for a post-knighthood family photograph. It was a slightly surreal occasion, but heart-warming all the same.

If I had had a ringside seat at the ceremony, I might have caught some of the dialogue, which was priceless, apparently. Like everyone else, I have watched these investiture ceremonies on television and wondered what the Queen actually says to the men and women she has honoured. You see her smile and say something to put the other person at their ease, and you love the way she does it so graciously, day in, day out, year after year. Just small-talk, of course, but small-talk with a regal touch.

So what did she say to my father after she had knighted him and he had tottered to his feet again? 'I hear your wife is also a Member of Parliament'? 'I believe Macclesfield is in Cheshire'? 'I have found your views on Zimbabwe most thought-provoking'? 'Do tell me more about the work of departmental select committees'? Nothing so banal. She just looked him straight in the eyes and, as if contemplating a much-loved Corgi of advanced years, said: 'You've been around a long time.'

My father was so nonplussed that he came within a whisker of saying: 'Not nearly so long as you, Ma'am!', which would probably have got him beheaded or sent to the Tower. Luckily, the moment passed, and soon the two old troupers were chatting amicably about a recent visit the Queen had made to the King's School, Maccles-field, at which Dad had also been present.

For my father, the knighthood was not just recognition of his long years of public service, but a consolation for recent disappoint-ments. If the early 1990s had been, in many ways, the pinnacle of his career, the high watermark of his particular brand of obstreperousness, the early Noughties were far more frustrating. It was as if his luck had turned and his political star was on the wane. He would have torn his hair out in clumps if Mother Nature had not already started to do it for him.

After the huge Labour landslide in 1997, he could see that he was likely to spend the rest of his days in Parliament on the opposition benches. So it was goodbye to any faintly lingering ministerial am-bitions. But he did nurse one last great political dream – to become the Speaker of his beloved House of Commons. In fact, 'nurse' is probably too weak a word. The dream burned stronger and stronger the longer he sat on the back benches. He was a parliamentarian, for God's sake! And in a parliament, it is the Speaker, not the Prime Minister, who is king of the castle.

He had served a long and loyal apprenticeship and, since 1986, had been a member of the Speaker's Panel, the select group of senior backbenchers who chair the standing committees that consider legislation – not to be confused with the *select* committees that hold inquiries and produce reports. (If you get confused by parliamentary committees, join the club. I was once told by a parliamentary official that standing committees are actually select committees and select committees are actually standing committees!) My mother was also a member of the Speaker's Panel, and loved every minute. The job involves keeping order in debate, selecting amendments for discussion etc., and is the best possible preparation for becoming a Speaker or Deputy Speaker of the House itself. (Incidentally, and for connoisseurs of political correctness gone mad, the Speaker's Panel has now been renamed the Panel of Chairs, which sounds like something you can buy in John Lewis. Do *not* get my father started on this one.)

For my father, with his passion for Parliament – a passion that ran much, much deeper than his love of the Conservative Party – the Speakership would have been a political prize to equal any of the great offices of state. He coveted it far more than he had ever coveted being Minister for Paper Clips under Margaret Thatcher or John Major. Would-be Speakers are not expected to advertise their ambitions, just as Catholic cardinals are not expected to drop hints that they would like a crack at the Papacy. In fact, by tradition, Speakers are dragged to the Speaker's chair upon their election, in a show of reluctance. But it does would-be Speakers no harm to discreetly demonstrate their credentials for the job – most important of all, of course, a capacity for political impartiality. Speakers of the House of Commons, by long custom, stand above the party fray and traditionally resign from their parties as soon as they are elected.

By that benchmark, my father scored very well. To some on the Labour benches, his views on some subjects were so outspoken, and expressed so vigorously, that they virtually ruled him out of contention as Speaker. But anyone who had seen him chair standing committees, and noted his determination to give everyone a fair hearing, recognised him as a House of Commons man to his bootstraps. He had also consistently demonstrated his independence of the party whips – which is, or should be, an indispensable part of the job description. Even Labour MPs who found him too right-wing for their tastes had cheered him to the echo when he gave Tim Renton & Co. a bloody nose.

His chance to have a shot at the Speakership – a slim one – came in October 2000, when the popular Labour Speaker Betty Boothroyd stood down, precipitating an election for her replacement. Should her successor be Tory or Labour? It was a moot point. Historically, Speakers had tended to come from the governing party. But the Boothroyd precedent – a Labour Speaker elected under a Tory government – also had obvious attractions. In the Tea Room, Tory MPs could be heard muttering, 'It's our turn', while Labour MPs could be heard muttering, 'We'll see about *that.*' Low politics, as they always do, muddied high principles.

The front-runner was Labour's less than charismatic Michael Martin, a decent enough man, but a political lightweight. He was a former whip and, as his party had a three-figure majority, the odds were stacked in his favour. But before his eventual coronation, MPs had the chance to vote on a number of other candidates, including my father, who was nominated by John Wilkinson, the Tory MP for Ruislip and Northwood, and Stephen Pound, the Labour MP for Ealing North, one of those colourful eccentrics who are the very soul of Parliament.

In a typically puckish intervention, Pound noted that one obvious advantage of making my father Speaker would be to shut him up. 'I have heard more than I wish to know about the Congleton to Macclesfield by-pass,' he admitted, to general amusement. But he added that my father had also been 'an original and fresh and idiosyncratic voice' on the back benches, and that he had pursued 'an unbroken line of integrity and unchanging and unflinching morality'. Best of all – and of greatest relevance to his suitability as Speaker – he had been his own man throughout his time at Westminster. As Pound put it, he had been 'a paid-up member, almost the shop steward, of the awkward squad'. Praise indeed, as far as my unrepentantly awkward father was concerned.

It was a nice try and, given that Stephen Pound was a Labour MP, a fine example of the House of Commons rising above petty partisanship. But his arguments, alas, fell on deaf ears. Dad got a respectable 116 votes, but lost out to Michael Martin, as expected, with the huge Labour payroll vote backing its man.

Did the House of Commons choose the wrong man? I know Dad privately thinks so, although he swallowed his disappointment as best he could and pledged his loyalty to the new Speaker. He had seen too many bad losers in politics – not least the Prime Minister when he was first elected, Ted Heath, the Sultan of Sulk – to go down that route. And by the time Michael Martin had gone, forced out after his mishandling of the expenses scandal, and been replaced by John Bercow – the House certainly chose the wrong man *there* – his dream had gone the way of 99 per cent of political dreams.

It is best not to ask my father about Speaker Bercow as most of his comments are unprintable. He actually helped and encouraged the man when he was starting out as a back-bench MP and, after Bercow had been sacked from the shadow Cabinet in 2004 and was at a low ebb, suggested he might consider joining the Speaker's Panel. But shortly after he had been elected Speaker, Bercow issued a pompous and cack-handed rebuke to my father from the Chair. Dad stormed into his private office after the sitting to complain that, as a senior backbencher, he was not prepared to be treated like that – at which point, Bercow flounced out of the room, slamming the door behind him.

After my father's failure to win the Speakership, it was just a case of managing his exit gracefully. Throughout the Blair years, he and Mum continued to serve their constituents to the best of their abilities. They remained very active at Westminster, chairing committees, asking questions, making speeches on their pet topics. In some ways, they rather liked being in opposition rather than government: after the internecine Tory warfare that followed Maastricht, it almost felt like a holiday. But even without the various bumps in the road which I have already related – notably the expenses scandal in 2008 – they had become conscious that Father Time was catching up with them. Gone were the days when elder statesmen could go on for ever – Churchill remained an MP till he was nearly 90 – without raising eyebrows in their constituency. They could almost smell the young Tory hopefuls itching to take their place. It had been one hell of a party, but they did not want to overstay their welcome.

'The years are taking their toll, and we can no longer represent Macclesfield and Congleton with the same level of energy and enthusiasm as in the past,' Dad wrote to David Cameron in May 2009, announcing my parents' decision to stand down at the next election. It was a melancholy letter, written with a heavy heart. The final curtain beckoned – and one last piece of parliamentary flummery.

Appropriately for a profession where so many high hopes end in disappointment, an MP's formal leave-taking of the House of Commons is far more low-key than his introduction as a new Member. In an earlier chapter, I tried to convey my father's pent-up excitement as he first took his seat in October 1971, before a crowded chamber: the rush of adrenaline as he joined the big beasts of British politics. His emotions when he retired at the 2010 general election, along with my mother, were very different.

After the formal dissolution of Parliament that is the starting gun for the election campaign, retiring MPs form a ragged queue in front of the Table of the House and shake the Speaker's hand before taking leave of the chamber for the last time. My parents, to be honest, had such a low opinion of John Bercow as Speaker that the hand-shaking was more of an ordeal than a pleasure. He has a rather creepy habit of grasping people by the hand, then not letting go of their hands, but clinging on to them in a clammy embrace, like a malevolent octopus.

But the other emotions swirling around in my father's head were so overwhelming that, as he took his final leave of the House, his eyes welled with tears and, somewhat to his embarrassment, he had to be comforted by one of the Clerks at the Table, David Natzler, who put an arm around his shoulder. For a few seconds, everything got a bit emotional, even un-parliamentary. Except that, as my father would be the first to testify, Parliament is, and should be, an emotional place.

In his own case, a great political love story – and it *had* been a love story, spanning nearly forty years, a near-perfect match between a man and the institution he strove so hard to serve – had run its course. Cause for tears indeed.

Had not his great political hero, Winston Churchill, been no-toriously lachrymose? Even his screen double, John Wayne, in his signature role as Captain Nathan Brittles, had brushed away a tear in the famous scene in *She Wore a Yellow Ribbon* when he bids farewell to his troops and rides off into the sunset.

So, yes, it was quite all right to cry. What were a few tears between friends? But perhaps it was fortunate that my mother, dry-eyed and stoical, was on hand to shepherd him towards a bar and the stiff drink that the situation demanded.

After that, it was just a case of clearing their offices and making the long drive up to Cheshire together. Right to the last, the Wintertons of Westminster – leaving the wicket with a combined score of sixty-six years of service – operated as a team.

* * *

The Winterton story is slowly drawing to a close. Knowing my in-defatigable parents, they will probably live till a hundred and still be telling anyone who cares to listen what is wrong with socialism and why getting out of the European Union was like escaping Colditz castle. They are as outspoken in their views as ever, probably more so. But their days as active politicians, engaged, committed, with their fingers on the national pulse, are largely over.

Things might have turned out rather differently if the Establish-ment, which my father had spent so many years challenging, had not conspired to deliver one final, brutal snub. Upon his retirement in 2010, he was considered for a peerage, but as an official at No. 10 explained to him, there was a question mark against his name – as there was against many other MPs who retired in 2010 – after the expenses scandal. Fair or unfair, some of the mud had stuck. And, with public anger over expenses still raw, the government was understandably wary of signalling that it was business as usual at the Palace of Westminster.

My father was quite irritated by this line of argument. Yes, he had garnered some unfavourable headlines. But, as he had since been cleared of any serious wrong-doing by the Standards and Privileges Committee, shouldn't that, not vague memories of headlines past, be the acid test of his suitability? But he tried to accept the setback stoically.

He would have adored a peerage, not just as a title to add to his other titles, but because he had always regarded the Lords as 'the House of knowledge and experience', able on occasion to force the elected Commons into a necessary rethink over legislation. He knew it was an arena in which he could continue to serve his country with energy and dedication. He could just see himself as Baron Maverick of Macclesfield, Dennis the Menace in ermine, making a nuisance of himself, lobbing a few hand-grenades into their Lordships' deliberations. He also believed it to be a more grown-up, less shrilly partisan, debating chamber than the House of Commons. But he was not prepared for the cruel twist in the tale.

A few weeks after the 2015 general election, the phone went in the hall of the family home in Cheshire. 'It's No. 10,' said my mother, passing the phone to my father. Soon afterwards, David Cameron was telling my father personally that he wanted to put his name forward for a peerage. My father's heart leapt and he stammered his thanks. The fact that the Prime Minister had made such an offer presumably meant that the question mark in the Downing Street files had been erased. He also felt chuffed that, with the EU referendum looming, Mr Cameron should have been prepared to offer a peerage to such a notorious Eurosceptic as him. It felt like an acknowledgement that his lifelong efforts to put his country first, and his party second, had borne fruit.

But in politics, as my father knows better than anyone, there is many a slip twixt cup and lip. Nomination for peerages by the Prime Minister have to be vetted by a body called the House of Lords Appointments Commission (HOLAC), a non-partisan body made up of the great and good. Which sounds all very well in principle. But how often do committees of the great and the good make great and good decisions? They certainly made a pig's ear of this one.

At the time HOLAC considered my father's nomination, it was chaired by Professor Lord Kakkar, an eminent surgeon whose knowledge of thromboembolic diseases is unrivalled, but whose knowledge of ex-MPs and their suitability for peerages is necessarily limited. So when my father received a letter from Lord Kakkar explaining that HOLAC had blocked his nomination for a peerage, without giving reasons, his emotions can be imagined. It was like being blackballed by a London club in the bad old days: all the stigma of rejection without the courtesy of an honest, face-to-face explanation. He wrote a number of follow-up letters to Lord Kakkar, in an attempt to get such an explanation, but was rebuffed or ignored. Ludicrous! How can anyone, in any walk of life, challenge a decision if they are not told the basis on which the decision was made?

My father was clearly not alone in his predicament. It was apparent from newspaper reports that several other former Tory MPs, unnamed, who had been nominated for peerages by the Prime Minister, had also been blocked by HOLAC, also for unspecified reasons. Other former Tory MPs who had blotted their copy-books – from Richard Spring, who had featured in a three-in-a-bed scandal, to Douglas Hogg, who had tried to claim expenses for the cleaning of his castle moat – had had their nominations rubber-stamped by HOLAC and were now sitting merrily in the Lords, their past misdemeanours forgiven. So who was not prepared to forgive Nicholas Winterton? And for which past misdemeanours? Paranoid suspicions swirled around in his brain. Was it because, unlike Hogg the moat-cleaner, he had not been to Eton? Stranger things had happened. And was it just a coincidence that one of the members of HOLAC was Lord Howard of Lympne – the former Tory leader, Michael Howard, who had had that big bust-up with my mother? There was a whiff of a secret vendetta about the whole episode.

To my father, it just felt patently unjust that, having satisfied the preliminary checks made by the Cabinet Office, and been personally recommended for a peerage by the Prime Minister, he should fall at the next hurdle without, as a bare minimum, the courtesy of a full face-to-face explanation.

Whatever your politics, or your views about an unelected House of Lords, it is not too difficult to sympathise with my father's indignation at being cheated of the peerage to which he feels his long record of public service entitled him. Like members of other professions, MPs watch their contemporaries like hawks, and every time an ex-MP is 'kicked upstairs' to the House of Lords, there are at least a dozen other ex-MPs wailing, 'Why him? Why not me?' And of that dozen, at least three will have an excellent, not to say unanswerable, case.

A particular bugbear of my father's is the way that, after just about every election, MPs who have been defeated at the polls – as distinct to ones like him, who have retired – are parachuted back into the House of Lords a few months later to tinker with legislation passed by the lower House. What must their constituents feel to have their decision to chuck out their MP – the very cornerstone of our parliamentary system – so cynically set aside? To add insult to injury, a lot of these recycled rejects have been in the Commons less than half as long as battle-hardened parliamentary veterans like my father, with nearly forty years' experience to call on. Rob Hayward and Anne McIntosh (now ensconced in the Lords) come to mind.

Peter Temple-Morris, the man my father pipped in the race to be the Conservative candidate in the Macclesfield by-election all those years ago, is also the subject of dark mutterings in the Winterton household. Not because he is a bad or unpleasant man. He is the soul of courtesy. But because his elevation to Baron Temple-Morris of Llandaff in the County of South Glamorgan, and Leominster in the County of Herefordshire, can be attributed to a cunning plan worthy of Baldrick himself. He simply defected to the Labour Party, the pinko swine!

I have tried to console my father with Groucho Marx's aphorism: 'I would never join any club that would have me as a member.' And I have tried to persuade him that a House of Lords composed of people who have had to go through such a capricious and secretive selection process is not fit for purpose anyway. But the incident rankles, my God, it rankles.

Even without the farce of the disappearing peerage, my parents would not have been able to make a clean break with the past. Ex-MPs do not simply vanish. They carry their past around with them. Mum drives a car with an XMP number-plate, which always gives the locals a giggle. To this day, she and Dad can hardly move in Macclesfield or Congleton without bumping into former constituents. Last year, rather touchingly, one star-struck octogenarian came up to my father, shook his hand and said: 'Ooh Sir Nicholas, when are you going to stand again?' There are ageing rock stars who do not get that sort of treatment.

Those meandering conversations in the street which I remember so well – starting in Westminster and ending up in Syria or Brussels or South Africa – are still a regular feature of their lives. They still get invited to scores of constituency functions every year, from dinners to church fetes, and Dad in particular finds it hard to say no. If there is a public meeting of some description – protesting, say, at the introduction of hospital car park charges – it is like a bugle to a war-horse. He wants to be in the fray, fighting his corner, joining in the debate. You can take Nicholas Winterton out of Parliament. You can't take Parliament out of Nicholas Winterton.

He and Mum are rightly scrupulous about not treading on the toes of their successors as MPs for Macclesfield and Congleton – David Rutley and Fiona Bruce, respectively – but if they can help their local parties in small ways, they do. Dad is still remarkably loyal to the Tory tribe – more so than my mother – even though the Tory tribe has not always been loyal to the Wintertons. That instinctive loyalty irritates my brothers. Andrew, in particular, thinks my parents should have raised two fingers to the Conservative Party a long time ago. But I can understand and respect it. My parents *are* tribal. Beneath the mavericks, the bolshie backbenchers, the serial rebels, are two surprisingly good team players.

Politically, their last glorious hurrah was the 2016 EU referendum. No prizes for guessing which side they were on. Their disenchantment with the EU had reached boiling point – they were hardly alone – and they threw themselves heart and soul into the Brexit campaign. Here, finally, was the chance to put right the disaster of the Maastricht treaty, which they had fought so hard to stymie. The British people had not been given their say then. But now they were being given their say. And not before time.

Who was it who had called on Tony Blair to give the people a referendum on membership of the EU, way back in 2007? It was Nicholas Raymond Winterton. If a politician cannot crow at times like that, when can he crow? He felt like Nostradamus and Mystic Meg rolled into one.

Never had Dad's conviction that Britain was a great nation, and better off alone, been more evident. Never had Mum's hostility to smooth-talking Old Etonians found a more fitting target than the disingenuous David Cameron who played the European statesman but tried to sell his country a pig in a poke.

The year before the referendum, like Olympic athletes going to a training camp, they travelled to Waterloo to mark the 200th anniversary of Wellington's great victory against Napoleon. For my father, swelling with patriotic pride, it was an emotional pilgrimage, a reminder of the great days of British nationhood, when only power-crazed French dwarves imagined they could be masters of all Europe. My mother, more prosaically, hunted down a good local restaurant. There are *some* things Europeans are good at.

In its way, the EU referendum was like my parents' careers in miniature. They were swimming against the political tide, in the sense that what they wanted was the polar opposite of what the Establishment wanted and what the pundits at Westminster were predicting. But they were also swimming *with* the tide: sensing the strength of grassroots feeling on the subject and giving full voice to that feeling. They could see that people in Cheshire were fed up with the EU, fed up with giving the bloated Euro-crats in Brussels one last chance to put their house in order. They were hungry for something better. Much better.

As the referendum campaign got under way, they did what they could to rally the doubters, attending local Brexit meetings and, more than once, travelling down to London. In early March, they could be seen helping hand out Leave campaign leaflets in Alderley Edge, the affluent Cheshire village where so many Premier League footballers have homes. 'Ordinary people on the street were so receptive,' Mum told me. 'You could just tell how little attachment they felt to the EU.'

The Brexit campaign had galvanised her. I had not seen her so politically engaged since she stood down at the 2010 election. Her last few years in Parliament had been so bruising, and left her so out of the sympathy with the party leadership, that she had become semi-detached from British politics. 'I don't really care any more,' I have heard her mutter under her breath. Here, suddenly, was something about which she *did* care: a simple cause, set to a simple patriotic refrain.

The following week, my father addressed a lunch for Tory patrons in the Staffordshire constituency of his fellow Eurosceptic, Sir Bill Cash. 'Do people really think a great nation like ours is not able to manage its own affairs and find new trading partners after leaving the EU?' he thundered, to murmurs of approval from his fellow lunchers. His passion for his pet causes is quite undimmed by the passage of time. He can still give a speech plenty of emotional welly. He still knows – better than poor David Cameron – how to find the Tory sweet-spot.

Did my parents foresee the stunning victory for the Brexit campaign? In all honesty, probably not. How many people did? They had believed, but were not sure how many fellow believers there were – enough to outnumber the faint-hearts, the safety-firsters, the people clinging on to nurse for fear of getting something worse.

From talking to people locally, they could see that opinion was split more or less down the middle. Congleton and Macclesfield were certainly not hotbeds of Euroscepticism, like some other parts of the country. When the votes were counted, East Cheshire had voted for Brexit, but by the narrowest of margins: 51.2 per cent to 48.8 per cent, which almost perfectly mirrored the result nationwide.

Turnout was high, however: over 77 per cent, well above the national average of recent general elections. My parents – who had done their bit to make sure that turnout *was* high, campaigning, chivvying people, putting leaflets through letterboxes, etc. – liked that statistic. It felt like grassroots democracy in action, a glorious culmination of their political careers and the values that had underpinned them.

Were they sorry to see the back of David Cameron? What do you think? Mum had never forgiven the man for what she saw as his flagrantly disloyal behaviour during the expenses scandal. Dad had a slightly higher opinion of Cameron, but could see that his political goose was cooked as soon as the referendum result was announced. As the Prime Minister fell on his sword, like an officer and a gentleman, there was a sigh of relief in the Winterton household, followed by the popping of champagne corks. Freedom from Brussels at last!

On the streets of their old constituencies, euphoria was a bit more muted because the result had been so tight. But there was no shortage of smiling faces, no shortage of people walking around with a renewed spring in their step. It felt like the sun coming up over the horizon.

A few days after the referendum, Mum and Dad were asked to re-open a newly refurbished post office in the village of Mossley. At the group photograph, when the photographer asked people to say 'Cheese!', Dad asked them to say 'Leave!' – which they duly did, at their top of their voices, scaring the birds from the trees.

All in all, it was a great time to be one of the famous Eurosceptic Wintertons of East Cheshire. The people had spoken and they had spoken in Winterton English, not Whitehall English.

After that, like everyone else, my parents sat back to see which great champion of the Eurosceptic cause would take David Cameron's place and lead Britain to the Promised Land. Winston Churchill would have been nice, if available. Enoch Powell, ditto. Margaret Thatcher could have done the job in her sleep, without taking the curlers out of her hair. Instead...

Oh dear, oh dear. To what question was 'Theresa May' the answer? My parents have still not quite worked that out. Even as veterans of several vicious Tory leadership contests, some of which had plumbed the depths of parliamentary skulduggery, they were astonished by the ferocious way the various candidates for the leadership stabbed each other in the back. But they had vaguely assumed, like the rest of the population, that if the country had voted in favour of Brexit, then the next Prime Minister would have to be someone who had done the same – not someone who had spent the referendum campaign saying as little as humanly possible. Theresa May was notionally a Remainer, but might as well have been a deaf-mute for all the contribution she had made to the debate.

The problem was, of course, the lack of credible contenders from the Brexit camp. Mum and Dad would have been prepared, at a pinch, to let Boris have a crack at the top job, but only with their fingers crossed very tight indeed. Better a pro-Brexit Old Etonian than a pro-Remain Old Etonian! Michael Gove – not so much two-faced as three-faced, with a fourth face for Sundays – hardly inspired confidence. Dad's head was briefly turned by mother-of-three Andrea Leadsom and, for a few sweet, deluded days – there is no fool like an old fool – he thought she was Margaret Thatcher brought back to life and imagined frolicking with her in the sunlit uplands. But he soon woke up from that little fantasy. They would have loved to see David Davis in No. 10. He had impeccable Eurosceptic credentials but also warmth, decency and maturity – he could have been a unifier in troubled times. Alas, his name was not even on the ballot paper.

As soon as George Osborne – the brains behind Project Fear, the evil genius with the dodgy haircut, the man who had spent three months trying to spook the electorate with ever-more blood-curdling predictions – had ruled himself out of contention, that only really left Theresa. Vicar's daughter, grammar schoolgirl, safe pair of hands, liked cricket, husband played golf, hadn't been a *total* disaster at the Home Office, and, er ... well that was about it, really. Shame she had called the Tory party the 'nasty party', but you can't have everything. Onwards and upwards. At least she hadn't been to Eton.

As you will gather from my sarcastic tone, my parents are not totally convinced that Theresa May will cover herself in glory, still less achieve a post-Brexit settlement acceptable to voters. She made a solid, confident start, a bit like an opening batsman seeing off the new ball. Her debut at Prime Minister's Questions was widely hailed as a triumph, with echoes of Margaret Thatcher in handbag-wielding mode. But there were blunders, too. Her choice of the most tactless politician in the country as Foreign Sec-retary – a job demanding high diplomatic skills as an entry-level requirement – was either a surreal masterstroke or the own goal of the century. It is always fun waiting to see who Boris will insult next, but how long will that particular joke last? These are serious, uncertain, delicate times. And what was Theresa May doing flying up to Scotland to kowtow to Nicola Sturgeon? My father's thoughts on that were largely X-rated.

Still, at least David Davis had been put in charge of negotiating the terms of Brexit – that went down well in Cheshire – and Dr Liam Fox, another shrewd appointment, given a key role in striking new trade deals. George Osborne and Michael Gove had gone, discredited and unmourned. And there were other interesting ap-pointments, too, including Justine Greening as education secretary – with an early pledge, later given a following wind by Mrs May, to be open-minded about paving the way for more grammar schools.

Greening also took the opportunity to out herself as gay in the aftermath of the referendum, making her Britain's first openly gay female Cabinet minister. In any other year, that would have been front-page news, not tucked away on page 23, next to the horoscopes and the gardening tips. But 2016 wasn't any other year. For political junkies like me and my parents, it was a true *annus mirabilis*, when politics, in all its brutal beauty, dominated the headlines for weeks on end, relegating football to where it belongs – on the back pages. There was a nice cartoon in the *Daily Mail* of a *Mastermind* contestant sitting in the famous black chair, with the voice of the quiz-master saying: 'And your specialised subject is British politics between 23 June 2016 and 7 July 2016.' Brilliant!

Weird minor characters skittered across the stage in delicious profusion – none more memorable than Michael Gove's wife, Sarah Vine, who quickly became known as Lady Macbeth, for obvious reasons. At one point, as her husband dithered before stabbing Boris Johnson in the back, she sent him a wonderfully Lady Macbeth-like email ending, 'Be your stubborn best'. Stubborner, Michael, stubborner, my little Scottish mule! You couldn't make it up.

Everything happened so fast, and still is happening so fast, that it is a racing certainty that any verdicts which political pundits come to now will be overtaken by events. But after a period of near-hysteria, sanity seems to have returned – and not before time.

In the Westminster village, all the talk has been of a seismic political event, after which things would never be the same again. In Cheshire, life carries on much as before. Earthquake? What earthquake? The furniture of day-to-day life has barely moved an inch. Any post-Brexit changes look as if they are going to be slow and incremental. Evolution, not revolution – which, as my father has been telling me since I was child, is far, far better. It really looks as if people have taken stock and realised that, in 2050, Britain will still be what it is today – a prosperous, civilised, tolerant, multicultural country where it rains on Bank holidays and queuing is the national religion.

Not that there is any room for complacency. My parents wish Theresa May and her colleagues well – they will need a vast reservoir of public good will if they are to succeed – but cannot see the way out of the woods yet. They have realised, as millions of others have realised, that the referendum vote was both an end – in their case, the happy culmination of a campaign they had been fighting for more than thirty years – and a beginning. A historic challenge. A blank piece of paper waiting to be written on.

Brexit means Brexit, but what does Brexit mean? It is a philosophical conundrum worthy of Aristotle or Descartes. The EU referendum was the most momentous decision voters had taken since the war, much further-reaching than any general election. But what, exactly, had voters decided? At general elections, the main parties put forward detailed manifestos that the other parties go through with a fine-tooth comb, seizing on any wild or irresponsible promises. The referendum was a good deal more nebulous, with very little by way of hard-and-fast promises to which politicians could later be held to account. As one pro-Brexit Tory MP joked: 'It's as if we've won the election and now have to write the manifesto.' A bit scary, if you are the one having to write that manifesto!

It was rightly a matter of celebration in the Brexit camp that over 17 million people had voted Leave – more than had ever ticked the same box at the polling stations in the whole of British history. But it was also evident, as the dust settled, that those 17 million voters had 17 million different reasons for voting Leave. Many obviously saw Brexit as the best way to curb immigration. They were not totally sure what an Australian-based points system was, but they liked the sound of it. Many had simply had enough of the EU and its expensive, inefficient, meddling bureaucracy. They liked the idea of getting their country back – it was a rousing battle-cry, speaking to something deep within them. But how many had far vaguer motives for voting the way they did? To give David Cameron a good kicking. To vent their fury at out-of-touch politicians. To show their contempt for experts and their predictions. To express their resentment at being patronised and bullied. To assert that their concerns *mattered*, even if they lived on run-down council estates hundreds of miles from Westminster.

So many voters, so many motives. To paraphrase the famous French saying about love, voters have their reasons which even voters themselves do not understand. And, given the very different priorities of the people who voted for Brexit, it will take super-human skill by Theresa May and her government to guide the ship of state towards a harbour where all, or even most, of the passengers feel happy.

In the immediate aftermath of the referendum result, it felt like the sweetest of vindications for my parents and people like them. Ever since Maastricht, they had been reviled as bastards and traitors and all the rest of it. Now the wheel had come full circle and, in the final, decisive battle, they had ended up on the winning side. But as the Brexit negotiations got under way, it soon became clear that, beneath the surface, the Tory party was as disunited as ever – and that Europe, which had already cost three Tory Prime Ministers their jobs, had lost none of its power to cause toxic divisions.

Some Tories seem to want Brexit-lite: disentanglement from the formal political structures of the EU, but with the minimum of other changes and many of the features of the old set-up retained. Others, like my parents, want the full Monty: a clean break from Brussels, the scrapping of all EU legislation and freedom of move-ment laws, and the suspension of our membership of the European Convention on Human Rights. The final settlement, inevitably, will be an ungainly compromise between the two. But if one thing has characterised the Tory Eurofanatics, on both sides, over the years, it is the fact that they regard compromise as a dirty word. Much blood will be spilt at Westminster before the two warring factions make peace again – if they ever do.

One of the arts the successful politician has to master is how to manage voters' expectations. There have been signs, post-Brexit, of a concerted effort by government ministers to downplay – not to say kick into the long grass – earlier Tory promises to reduce net migration numbers to 'tens of thousands'. But will voters be happy to have their legitimate expectations downgraded in that way? I wonder.

Luckily for my parents, they are, and always have been, optimists. They would not dream of predicting where Britain will find itself twelve months from now, but they are hopeful that the long-term benefits of the Brexit vote will far outweigh any disadvantages. Some of our neighbours in Europe may still be snapping and snarling, but further afield, in far-flung Commonwealth countries, the mood is more upbeat. Countries like Canada and Australia can see trading opportunities that were not there before.

All the talk of trade and tariffs – subjects on which we are all going to have become experts in the months and years ahead – recalls debates that once nearly split the Conservative Party down the middle in the early years of the last century. Joseph 'Radical Joe' Chamberlain, who had left the Liberal party to ally himself with the Tories, advocated erecting tariffs on foreign imports, in part because of feeling in his Midlands heartland that immigration was out of control and the wages of workers had been undermined by competition from overseas. *Plus ça change…* Chamberlain ended up on the losing side of the argument with the free-traders, but did bequeath one quotation which seems eerily prescient today. 'In politics, there is no use looking beyond the next fortnight.'

Whatever new trade arrangements are struck, they will take time to bed down. Bumps on the road, to coin a phrase. But the Wintertons have never been scared of bumpy roads. And, although the British economy has its ups and downs, like everywhere else, the British *brand* – to use the sort of marketing jargon my father hates – is still recognised and admired around the world.

England may lose to Iceland at football. Our entries in the Eurovision Song Contest may be an embarrassment. Our weather, and our moaning about our weather, may be a joke. Our trains may arrive the day after they were supposed to. The M25 may be the biggest car park in Europe. The Speaker of the House of the Commons may be a pompous buffoon. But what other country has given the world Shakespeare, Admiral Lord Nelson, the rules of cricket, Sir Winston Churchill, the Beatles, Sir Isaac Newton, rugby union, James Bond, Morris dancing, Mr Bean, Harry Potter, warm beer, Queen Elizabeth II, the Lake District, Dame Judi Dench, the BBC, the NHS, the Dam Busters, the Last Night of the Proms, Sir David Attenborough, Harrods, Cary Grant, Hugh Grant, the Cheltenham Gold Cup and fish and chips with salt and vinegar?

The year 2017 is not a bad time to be British. In fact, for my parents, in their farmhouse in Cheshire, and for me and my family, in our home in Kent, it is a particularly *good* time to be British. And if Brexit does indeed mark an exciting new chapter in our history, it would be a crying shame to miss it.

* * *

So what next for Team Winterton? At the time of writing, my parents are still living in the house in Cheshire which they bought nearly fifty years ago, when Dad was first elected an MP. They have been very happy there, and they adore the property and its tranquil rural situation. But I doubt if they will end their days there. There is a small voice in their heads whispering: 'Time to move on.' And it is slowly getting louder.

Their children and grandchildren live many miles away: Robert and his family in Nottinghamshire, Andrew and his family in Gloucestershire, me and my family in Kent. They are already starting to talk about moving closer to their grandchildren, like so many people of their age. It could happen in five years, or ten years, or not at all, but it is definitely on their radar. They have thrown themselves into the role of grandparents with all the enthusiasm you would expect from a couple who put such a high value on the family. And if one of their grandchildren were to go into politics – even joining a party they would not have touched with a barge-pole – they would be as pleased as Punch. It would feel like an affirmation of their own values. I am working on it with my seven-year-old son Jack, who already recognises a few political faces including Boris Johnson.

The House of Commons, perforce, will continue to be a major presence in their lives. Unlike people who have retired from other professions, ex-MPs get to see their former workplace on television almost every day. Surgeons are not bombarded with images of their old operating theatres or teachers with images of their old classrooms. But ex-MPs have no choice in the matter. To my mother and father, those famous green benches are a reminder of their great shared adventure at the heart of national life. What extraordinary memories, years and years of them, they hold.

It must be said that, not surprisingly, they do not always like what see when they tune in to Prime Minister's Questions. They hate the showboating, the snide laughter, the endless, petty point-scoring. They cannot stand those featherbrain MPs who cannot listen to a debate for five minutes without a furtive glance at their mobile phones. They preferred the old House of Commons in which they served for so long. Warts and all, it had more dignity, more gravitas, than the present House. But, if they get irritated at times, they are still, heart and soul, parliamentarians. They like to see government ministers put on the spot and challenged, morning, noon and night.

Mum and Dad will die as they have lived – through their passionate engagement with the issues of the day. Anyone watching them glued to the six o'clock news in their living room in Cheshire would be treated to the Winterton brand of Tory-ism in its purest, undiluted form. Next to the television, like a lucky mascot, is a stuffed bulldog in Union Jack colours, who sets the general tone. Depending on the day's news, the newsreader will then have to compete with sarcastic sedentary interventions from the ex-Member for Macclesfield and snorted expletives from the ex-Member for Congleton. Woe betide a news item that is couched in less than perfect English. My mother, like any good grammar schoolgirl, can spot a spelling mistake or split infinitive at a hundred yards.

As they have got older, inevitably, their years in the House of

Commons have gradually faded in the memory, to the point that they have to keep racking their brains to remember vital details. A fly on the wall of their kitchen would hear a patchwork of incomplete memories, comically fragmented, like something in a play by Beckett or Pinter.

'What *was* the name of that man who looked like a slug with glasses? He once told me...'

'I can't remember if it was Michael or Patrick McNair-Wilson...'

'I'm *sure* her constituency began with a P. If it wasn't in Sussex, it was in Hampshire.'

'Didn't Maggie offer him a job at Trade and Industry, just to keep him out of mischief?'

'Jeremy something or other? Tall man with a slight limp? Smelled of stale cigars?'

'Do you remember the time that bastard Peter whatshisface...'

'According to Cecil, or it may have been Norman...'

'No, it wasn't the Health Committee, it was the Social Services Committee.'

Sometimes, to resolve an argument, my mother will look up something on Google and give a little grunt of pleasure as the missing piece of the jigsaw falls into place. Five minutes later, the information will have flown out of her head again. It is not that she is forgetful. She is just the kind of person who remembers faces better than names, people better than dates, emotions better than facts.

Like others of their generation, Mum and Dad now go to more funerals and memorial services than christenings and weddings. But that does not seem to make them unduly depressed: they just regard it as a fact of life. In fact, I have often known them come back from memorial services re-invigorated, glad to have given an old colleague a good send-off, glad to have caught up with friends, glad to have had the chance to reflect on a life well lived.

Politicians who have reached the very top tend to become obsessed with their legacy. As their days in Downing Street or the White House draw to a close, the L-word colours everything they do. How will they remembered? Will their achievements stand the test of time? Or will they be disparaged by future generations? But you will not hear my parents fretting self-indulgently about their legacy. They are too realistic to think that their names will be remembered centuries after they are dead. They were proud to have been foot-soldiers in the Thatcherite revolution that was the defining political event of their generation. Proud to have championed Britishness and British values at a time when they were under continual siege. Proud, incredibly proud, to have been Brexiteers since before some other Brexiteers were born. But they are not expecting statues of themselves to be erected by public sub-scription in the squares and marketplaces of Cheshire. They simply want to be remembered by their local communities for speaking up for them, in good times and bad.

The success of political lives can be measured in a myriad ways, not all of them obvious on the surface. There are MPs who have held five different Cabinet posts but left not a ripple behind, others who have festered on the back benches but occasionally flared into brilliant life, making an indelible impression on their contemporar-ies. Some have talked the talk. Some have walked the walk. Some have done both, then tripped on a banana-skin while trying to talk and walk at the same time. There are almost as many types of politician as there are politicians.

So summing up the contribution made to British politics by Nicholas and Ann Winterton is not easy, but I will do my best. Perhaps one should start with the most distinctive part of my father's anatomy, the one I have teased him about so often – his mouth. Conrad's famous lines in *Heart of Darkness* could equally have been applied to my father or, for that matter, my mother: 'That is the reason why I affirm that Kurtz was a remarkable man. He had something to say. He said it.' Bulls-eye!

My parents were not brilliant wordsmiths. The *Oxford Dictionary of Quotations* is not peppered with extracts from their speeches. But they expressed their views, popular or unpopular, with an unvarnished candour unusual among practising politicians. If they had been a bit less forthright, a bit more circumspect, they might have progressed a few rungs higher up the Westminster career ladder. But they would also have betrayed what was probably their deepest shared conviction: that politicians *should* speak their minds. What was the point of politics otherwise?

Of course, if they had simply spoken their minds, and achieved diddly squat, their political legacy would have been so much hot air. But because they were so determined to make a difference, they managed to achieve things of real substance.

Some lives can be distilled into a single memorable accomplishment. Sir Roger Bannister was a distinguished neurologist and Master of Pembroke College, Oxford, but will be remembered for something that took less than four minutes – if it had taken more than four minutes, nobody would have heard of him. Other lives – and my parents and other long-serving back-bench MPs are classic examples of this – can only be understood and appreciated through the aggregation of thousands of smaller deeds, trifling in themselves, but cumulatively compelling.

Writers of newspaper headlines like to keep things simple. If an MP were to have sex in a wigwam, he would be 'the wigwam sex MP' for all eternity – unless another MP was daft enough to do the same. One cartoon figure among thousands, instantly recognisable. But I would hope that my parents, whatever mistakes they may have made, will escape that kind of glib pigeon-holing. It is the least they deserve for their tenacity and perseverance. They are just too complicated to be summarised in three or four words.

The word 'do-gooder' gets used pejoratively, which is a shame, as doing good, in all sorts of ways, was what my mother and father were all about. When Robert Baden-Powell was writing his historic *Scouting for Boys*, published in 1908, one of the passages he underlined for emphasis was his famous injunction to boy scouts to 'do a good turn to somebody every day'. My parents understood that simple philosophy perfectly. Little and often. Small kindnesses, not extravagant gestures. Service, not self-service. Actions, not words.

I chose for the first chapter in the book, the title: *Every Constituency Should Have One*. What kind of MPs do we want representing us at Westminster in the twenty-first century? Are the present lot good enough? We can always throw out the under-performing ones at election time. But are there deep-seated, systemic problems which we ignore at our peril?

At the time of writing – even with the party I support in power, God knows how I would feel if I were a Labour or Liberal Democrat supporter – British politics is not in good shape at all. It is not on the critical list, but it is looking a bit green around the gills. Never mind all the fall-out of Brexit, which will rumble on for years. There is a less than fully convincing government, led by a largely untested Prime Minister, an unelectable opposition and a clutch of smaller parties struggling to make themselves heard. Worst of all, in some ways, is the gradual decline in political discourse. Serious arguments have given way to easy slogans. Image trumps substance. The Downing Street machine has been hijacked by the PR industry. I work in the PR industry, so that shouldn't really bother me, but it *does* bother me, and I will try to explain why.

When my father first went into politics, it was the clash of *ideas* – fierce arguments between opposing ideological camps, each with passionate views, sincerely held – that was the glory of the House of Commons, and of British politics generally. Now, if the EU referendum is any guide, we are entering a new, debased, frankly rather depressing era – where the prize goes to the politicians who concoct the biggest, cleverest lies and sell them to the highest number of voters.

Remember that infamous £350-million-a-week figure – and the tacit promise that, if we left the EU, the money could be spent on the NHS? You could hardly miss that, wholly erroneous, claim. It was emblazoned in large letters on the Leave campaign's battle bus.

It was on millions of leaflets on millions of doormats. It was not true, it did not come close to being true, and Boris Johnson and the other authors of the claim knew that; but it was peddled hard, with cynical persistence, in the hope that enough halfwits could be found to believe it.

Similar slipperiness was displayed by the Remain campaign. Poor George Osborne thought he had come up with his trump card – the 'fact' that, if Britain voted for Brexit, every family in the land would be £4,300 a year worse off. How convincing it looked, that £4,300 figure! This was not a suspiciously round number, a back-of-an-envelope guess, but the fruit of solid, detailed research by impartial Treasury officials. There was only one snag. The £4,300 figure was not a fact, but a *forecast* – by an organisation with such a patchy forecasting record that, if it was a racing tipster, it would have been sacked years ago. Yet another lie, cooked up in the Westminster village, looking for suckers out in the country.

Project Fear became an absolute cadenza of gloomy economic forecasts, with the Governor of the Bank of England – sombre-faced, as if he was playing the Second Gravedigger in *Hamlet* – accompanying the Chancellor in a minor key. But the dark forecasts became steadily less credible. It was as if voters could *smell* the lies, even if they lacked the economic know-how to rebut them intellectually.

In the end, if one is being cynical about the EU referendum, Boris Johnson's £350-million-a-week whopper played George Osborne's £4,300-a-year whopper, and Boris's whopper won because it was more slickly presented and marketed. The referendum was about much, much more than that, of course, but what was sad, whichever side of the argument you were on, was the sheer mendacious cynicism at the very heart of the two campaigns. For my parents, old enough to remember John Profumo having to resign after lying to the House of Commons – a lie which today's politicians would regard as the tiniest of tiny porkies – it felt as if something they had valued was being slowly eroded.

A phrase you often hear among political pundits nowadays is 'post-truth politics'. It sounds scary because it *is* scary. Here is how it works. If you are standing for political office, you do not bother with the facts, unless they are facts convenient to your argument: you just make up facts that match the prejudices of your target audience. Then you repeat those facts, over and over again, brazenly and openly. Who cares if voters who hate lies despise you? They will be cancelled out by the voters stupid and gullible enough to swallow your lies.

The post-truth politician *par excellence* is Donald Trump, who was elected President of the United States in 2016 after a string of lies that, in the nineteenth or twentieth century, would have completely scuppered his chances. The lies ranged from a claim that Barack Obama had not been born in the USA to a claim that 9/11 had been celebrated by thousands of Muslims in New Jersey to a claim that he had started his business empire with the help of a 'small loan' from his father – when he had actually inherited $40 million! Each lie more baroque and ludicrous than the last, but each lodging in the brains of many voters, who solemnly repeated the lies to their neighbours.

My parents – particularly my mother, who still has a soft spot for a man with a full head of hair – quite like Donald Trump. He has said things that needed saying. He has appealed to voters who had lost hope that politicians could make a difference in their lives. His political mantra – 'make America great again' – echoed one of the key refrains of the Leave campaign during the EU referendum. It was as if, on the other side of the Atlantic, millions of people were thinking the same thing as people in Cheshire. But they cannot stand his cynical, huckster-like style of politics, where the truth goes out of the window and the punters are taken for mugs. If Trump was a populist heir to Ronald Reagan, he felt like a comically inferior model. With the best will in the world, it was hard to imagine Margaret Thatcher treating such an obvious charlatan as a political soulmate.

Trump's particular brand of phoney politics reached its apogee at the Republican convention in Cleveland in July, when he wheeled out his Slovenian wife Melania, an ex-model (well, *there's* a turn-up for the books!), to woo the Republican faithful with some fruity clichés – clichés lifted verbatim from a speech made by Michele Obama eight years earlier. And nobody in the Trump camp – least of all the Donald himself – seemed to *care* that the prospective First Lady had been humiliated and made to look like a Barbie doll reading an autocue. Scary.

It is difficult, thank God, to picture a Donald Trump in Downing Street. Our parliamentary system is less vulnerable to buccaneering outsiders than the American Presidential system. But post-truth politics – complete anathema to MPs like my parents, who never made up a fact or figure in their lives, but always tried to use *bona fide* evidence to advance their cases – seems to be creeping into British politics at an alarming rate.

Everyone knows the famous old maxim that a lie can get halfway around the world before the truth has got boots on. Well, it has never been more relevant than it is today, in the age of the internet. A Westminster MP can make an injudicious tweet at nine o'clock and delete it at five past nine but, but by five past nine, it is too late – people in Melbourne and Singapore will already be reading it. For politicians of a cynical disposition, the sheer runaway infectiousness of lies, half-lies and urban myths is ripe for exploitation.

In his more Eeyore-ish moments, my father worries that we are entering an age in which all political arguments, however intellectually complex, are reduced to tweets, soundbites and slogans – and in the process of being reduced, robbed of their validity. What happened to the more nuanced politics he remembers from his earliest days in Parliament – when Enoch Powell or Roy Jenkins or another of the big political beasts of the day would set out their arguments like master brickmasons building a wall, one brick at a time, and the House would listen intently, pondering every word, to see if the structure of the wall was sound?

He can remember preparing to make speeches in the House, marshalling his facts, perhaps pottering along to the House of Commons Library to dig up some killer statistic. Now he would simply think of a number and double it, and nobody would *mind* because the rules of the game have changed – perhaps irrevocably.

As human beings, the men and women who get elected to the House of Commons today are no different from their predecessors. They are idealistic. They see things wrong with the world, and they want to change them. I have already mentioned William Wragg, the Tory MP for Hazel Grove, for whom my father campaigned in 2015. He is ridiculously young, still in his twenties, and my father can see glimpses of his younger self in Wragg's determination to get on in politics and make a difference.

But he doesn't envy Wragg having to make his mark in an age when chasing headlines is often more important than getting things done – and when an MP can hardly open his mouth on some sub-jects without getting a volley of abuse on Twitter.

A lot of voters now hold politicians generally in such contempt that it is frightening. One of the saddest sights of the extraordinary summer of 2016 was David Cameron, two weeks after he resigned, being booed on Centre Court at Wimbledon after the men's singles final. Centre Court at Wimbledon, for God's sake! The epitome of old-fashioned English politeness and restraint. An oasis of good manners where, if Andy Murray's opponent double-faults, not a sol-itary spectator cheers. A famously well-behaved crowd – the object of bemused admiration around the world – who habitually give the chair umpire a round of applause when he asks for mobile phones to be switched off. And there they were, booing a Prime Minister who, whatever else he deserved, did not deserve to be kicked when he was down. It fell to Andy Murray, bless his little Scottish cotton socks, to do the decent thing, rebuke the boo-boys and remind them that, actually, the incumbent of 10 Downing Street has a tough, tough job to do.

The electorate deserves much better than what it is being offered at the moment. But it will only get it if the House of Commons regains the trust and respect it used to enjoy. Parliament may be sovereign – and more sovereign than ever post-Brexit, my parents would argue – but its sovereignty relies, ultimately, on the man and woman in the street accepting that it is sovereign and abiding by its decisions.

Arguably the single most shocking political event in Britain in 2016 – one of the most shock-filled years in our history – was the pig-headed determination of Jeremy Corbyn to carry on as Leader of the Opposition despite losing the support of 80 per cent of Labour MPs in a no-confidence motion. Ten or twenty years ago, never mind fifty years ago, he would have seen the writing on the wall in seconds – 80 PER CENT OF YOUR MPS, JEREMY – and resigned on the spot. (By way of historical context, just thirty-eight Tory MPs voted against the government in the famous Norway Debate in May 1940, but that was enough to force Neville Chamberlain to resign.) Not Comrade Corbyn, the self-styled people's champion. He just looked to his supporters outside Westminster to help him cling on to his job.

For my parents, it was more than an act of certifiable vanity and stubbornness: it felt like an attack on Parliament itself, according elected Members of Parliament no more weight in the democratic process than rank-and-file Labour members, accountable to nobody, some of whom had joined the party for the price of a pint of beer.

Corbyn was eventually challenged for the Labour leadership by a man called Smith who was so anonymous-looking he could have been a bank manager in Pontypridd. I have nothing against Pontypridd bank managers, I hasten to add. We could probably do with a bank manager in charge after all the excitements of the last six months. But what did we actually know about Mr Smith? Could we trust the man? He had only been an MP since 2010. He could talk the talk, in a bland, PowerPoint presentation sort of way, but could he walk the walk? Nobody had a clue. The Labour membership certainly didn't. They scratched their heads, held their noses, crossed their fingers and re-elected Comrade Corbyn – condemning the Labour Party to heaven only knows what. Parliamentary democracy in Britain had never seemed more fragile.

In the end, a country which despises its MPs – and a depressing number of people *are* contemptuous of Members of Parliament as a breed – can never call itself a great nation. It is no good just damning the Westminster village and all its works: if that village is dysfunctional, the whole body politic is dysfunctional. We need to cling on to the hope that, little by little, it can start to function a little better.

Putting Humpty Dumpty together again – rebuilding a House of Commons that is fit for purpose and commands public respect, which it signally fails to do at the moment – is the subject for another book. But one pre-condition for a more muscular, more dynamic, more accountable Parliament is surely worth stressing here, because it is so integral to the Winterton story: the importance of independent-minded backbenchers. And I do mean independent-minded, not the kind of Nervous Nellies who do the whips' bidding week in, week out, but once a parliament, make a token foray into the No lobby to protest against a clause in the Sunday Trading (Miscellaneous Provisions) (No. 2) Bill.

At local council level, it is commonplace for candidates to stand as independents and get elected. But at Westminster, there have only been a handful of genuinely independent MPs since the war. Everyone remembers Martin Bell, the Man in the White Suit, who unseated the Tories' Neil Hamilton in Tatton at the 1997 election. Richard Taylor, who represented Wyre Forest between 2001 and 2010, having stood as a single-issue candidate protesting at the closure of the A & E department at the local hospital, also deserves an honorary mention. By a nice coincidence, he and Bell were at school together. But other notable independent MPs – George Galloway, for example – were renegades from mainstream parties, not people who had never joined a political party in the first place.

Realistically, if you want to take your place on the green benches of the House of Commons, you first have to win the nomination of a national political party.

But *not*, and this is the crux, be the unthinking, uncritical mouthpiece of that party. Political parties leeched of internal dissent are sinister and totalitarian: no better than those trade union block votes which made such a mockery of democracy in the Labour Party in the 1980s. Better honestly aired differences than a pretence of party unity where no such unity exists. The Conservatives had to relearn that necessary lesson during the 2016 EU referendum campaign.

A lot of MPs, though they will not admit it publicly, have a simple mantra: 'My party right or wrong.' They are dull, predictable and, at their worst, dangerous. What the House of Commons needs is a healthy quotient of MPs who are what you might call semi-detached. The expression first gained currency in the 1980s, when the late John Biffen, an elder contemporary of my parents, and a man they much admired, was called semi-detached by Bernard Ingham, Margaret Thatcher's press secretary – a man who was so attached to his leader it was scary. Biffen – who thought being called semi-detached was a badge of honour and used the word as the title of his autobiography – was eventually sacked.

Obviously, if all 650 Members of Parliament were semi-detached, it would be a recipe for disaster. Nobody would know if they were coming or going. But what if around 30 per cent were? That is roughly the percentage of domestic properties in the UK that are semi-detached, as opposed to detached or terraced. There is nothing *wrong* with semi-detached, whatever the snobberies the word sometimes unleashes. More semi-detached MPs – like my parents, like John Biffen, like Frank Field, like Enoch Powell, like Kate Hoey, like David Davis, like Edmund Burke, if you go back far enough – might cause a few of the party whips to have coronaries.

As Members of Parliament, my parents were at their best when they were most themselves, and least Conservative with a capital C. That was one of the reasons their constituents treasured them.

Even as a fellow Tory, someone who shares their basic values, I have loved and admired them most when they have been at their most anarchic, spurning the conventional wisdom, throwing political hand-grenades, roughing up the Establishment.

I like to think of my mother at her most outspoken, mocking pinstriped twits, calling Old Etonians names from which even Old Harrovians would shrink – then throwing back her head and laughing out loud because, at the end of the day, the worst crime of all is to take yourself too seriously.

I like to think of my father striding through the middle of Macclesfield like a man half his age, stopping to say hullo to former constituents, asking after their health, asking after their families, asking what they think about so-and-so, bending their ears about anything and everything. Mr Macclesfield in person, bloodied but unbowed.

And I like to think of them together, staunchly supportive, rugged in their affections, bickering the way all couples bicker, constantly interrupting and correcting each other, but always, on the issues that matter, singing loud and clear from the same hymn sheet.

They have come a long, long way since that first chance encounter at the pony club, more than sixty years ago. It has been an extraordinary journey, bewildering in its variety, challenging them every step of the way. They have risen higher, in terms of public office, than they ever thought possible – and fallen lower, in terms of bad publicity, than in their worst nightmares. Regrets? They have had a few. Mistakes? They have made hundreds. But even at their lowest ebb, they have never stopped believing in the power and the beauty of parliamentary democracy – that miraculous distillation of the hopes and fears of millions of people into a crowded, noisy, unruly room the size of a tennis court.

And if there have been times when I wished I had more conventional parents, living blameless lives out of the limelight, I could not be prouder of what they have achieved, and of the battles they fought, side by side, like soldiers in a fox-hole.

They may not have been big beasts in the Westminster jungle. But for me, growing up in their shadow, their dogged exertions on the back benches were the stuff of heroism.

APPENDIX I

NOTABLE HUSBAND-AND-WIFE TEAMS AT WESTMINSTER

As Mr Macclesfield and Mrs Congleton, my parents hold two distinct parliamentary records. Neither their combined length of service, sixty-six years, nor their years of concurrent service, twenty-seven years, has been matched by any other husband-and-wife team of MPs in the entire history of the House of Commons. Their Tory contemporaries, Peter and Virginia Bottomley, are threatening to challenge the first of those records and, with parliamentary marriages becoming more frequent, the second might one day fall as well. But the husband-and-wife team is still a considerable rarity at Westminster, bringing a welcome touch of domestic comedy to our national parliament. Some couples have even met and married while sitting MPs, which is pretty mind-boggling. Did their hearts go boom-di-di-boom during a meeting of the Joint Committee on Statutory Instruments? At least – as I have tried to explain throughout this book – the various amorous interludes prove that MPs are *human beings*, not mere political robots.

Here is just a selection of husband-and-wife teams of MPs at the House of Commons, along with some statistics on their length of service. The 'maverick ratings' which I have awarded each couple – entirely subjectively! – reflect both their general bolshiness as individuals and the frequency or infrequency with which they have defied their party whips.

Mr Macclesfield and Mrs Congleton. As previously introduced.

- TOTAL COMBINED SERVICE: 66 years.
- TOTAL CONCURRENT SERVICE: 27 years.
- MAVERICK RATING: *****

Mr Swansea and Mrs St Ives. The first husband-and-wife MPs to sit concurrently in the House, which they did between 1928 and 1929, Walter and Hilda Runciman were prominent Liberals in the early years of the twentieth century. Hilda joined her husband, the MP for Swansea West, in the House of Commons after winning the St Ives seat in a by-election. She then gallantly relinquished her seat in favour of her husband – not something my mother would have done in a million years – at the general election of 1929.

- TOTAL COMBINED SERVICE: 26 years.
- TOTAL CONCURRENT SERVICE: 1 year.
- MAVERICK RATING: ***

Mr Ebbw Vale and Mrs Cannock. Probably the most celebrated of all British parliamentary marriages, and the subject of a forthcoming television drama. Labour heavyweight and architect of the NHS, Aneurin 'Nye' Bevan, represented the Ebbw Vale constituency from 1929 until his death in 1960. From 1945, he was joined in the House by his wife, Jennie Lee, minister for the arts under Harold Wilson, who continued to represent her Cannock constituency until the 1970 general election. Both children of miners, they had a famously tempestuous relationship, punctuated by blazing rows. One commentator wrote of Jennie Lee: 'She kept Nye socialist and would always have the last word on political matters' – *not* a scenario replicated in the Winterton household.

- TOTAL COMBINED SERVICE: 46 years.
- TOTAL CONCURRENT SERVICE: 15 years.
- MAVERICK RATING: ****

Mr Worthing and Mrs Surrey. Southern England's answer to the Wintertons, the Bottomleys have never given Tory whips as many headaches as my parents, but have also been the object of wry amusement to their colleagues. Sir Peter Bottomley, the energetic MP for Worthing West, has been in the House continuously since 1975, having previously represented Woolwich West and Eltham. He held various junior ministerial posts under Margaret Thatcher, but was eclipsed in the career stakes by his wife Virginia, now Baroness Bottomley, who was MP for South West Surrey from 1984 to 2005 and served as Health Secretary under John Major. The Baroness is famously well-connected and, for any conspiracy theorists out there, is a cousin of Jeremy Hunt, the present Health Secretary, who also inherited her former constituency.

- TOTAL COMBINED SERVICE: 63 years.
- TOTAL CONCURRENT SERVICE: 21 years.
- MAVERICK RATING: *

Mr Morley and Mrs Pontefract. If the electorate had taken leave of its senses in 2015, this pair of Labour bruisers might have been sitting next to each other around the Cabinet table – as they did, briefly, the first married couple to do so, when Gordon Brown was Prime Minister. In the event, voters had seen enough of Ed Balls, the pugnacious shadow Chancellor, who lost his Morley and Outwood seat at the 2015 general election. He had represented the seat since 2010, having previously been MP for Normanton. His wife Yvette Cooper, confusingly, has been MP for Normanton, Pontefract and Castleford since 2010, having represented Pontefract and Castleford since 1997. She stood unsuccessfully for the Labour leadership after the resignation of Ed Miliband in the wake of the election defeat.

- TOTAL COMBINED SERVICE: 30 years.
- TOTAL CONCURRENT SERVICE: 10 years.
- MAVERICK RATING: **

Mr Erdington and Mrs Peckham. In contrast to my parents, it was the woman in this marriage who got into Parliament before the man, and the man who has had to play catch-up. Veteran feminist Harriet Harman, one-time deputy leader of the Labour Party, has represented Camberwell and Peckham since 1997, having previously held the Peckham seat since 1982. Her husband Jack Dromey, a former trade union official, has been MP for Birmingham Erdington since 2010.

- TOTAL COMBINED SERVICE: 42 years.
- TOTAL CONCURRENT SERVICE: 7 years.
- MAVERICK RATING: *

Mr Pendle and Mrs Lewisham. The stresses of sitting in the House at the same time proved too much for Gordon Prentice, who represented Pendle from 1992 to 2010, and his wife Bridget, who represented Lewisham East over the same period. The couple, who had met at the University of Glasgow as students, got divorced in 2000.

- TOTAL COMBINED SERVICE: 36 years.
- TOTAL CONCURRENT SERVICE: 36 years.
- MAVERICK RATING: **

Mr Bracknell and Mrs Bromsgrove. Like my parents, husband-and-wife Tory MPs Andrew MacKay and Julie Kirkbride were in the eye of the storm during the parliamentary expenses scandal. They both stood down at the 2010 general election. They represented Bracknell and Bromsgrove, respectively, since 1997, the same year they got married. MacKay had previously been MP for Birmingham Stechford between 1977 and 1979 and for East Berkshire between 1983 and 1997.

- TOTAL COMBINED SERVICE: 42 years.
- TOTAL CONCURRENT SERVICE: 13 years.
- MAVERICK RATING: *

Mr Feltham and Mrs Brentford. Another couple to feel the full fury of the media during the expenses scandal were the Labour duo of Alan and Ann Keen, whom one newspaper dubbed 'Mr and Mrs Expenses'. Like the Wintertons, the Keens were lucky enough to represent neighbouring seats. Unlike the Wintertons, they did not have to spend long hours commuting between Westminster and their constituencies, as they sat for London seats. Alan Keen was MP for Feltham and Heston from 1992 until his premature death from cancer in 2011. His wife represented Brentford and Isleworth between 1997 and 2010.

- TOTAL COMBINED SERVICE: 32 years.
- TOTAL CONCURRENT SERVICE: 13 years.
- MAVERICK RATING: *

Mr Chippenham and Mrs Dumbarton. Does Cupid's arrow ever land on Liberal Democrats? Improbably, yes. In 2011, Lib Dem MP Jo Swinson, who had represented East Dunbartonshire since 2005, and been Baby of the House – the youngest MP – married fellow Lib Dem MP Duncan Hames, who had been MP for Chippenham since 2010. The couple had a baby boy two years later. As the distance between Chippenham and Dumbarton is 404 miles, Cupid's arrow had a long way to travel on this occasion. Would the couple even have met but for the glorious melting-pot of the House of Commons? Sadly, the electorate decided that they both needed to spend more time with their families after the 2015 general election.

- TOTAL COMBINED SERVICE: 15 years.
- TOTAL CONCURRENT SERVICE: 5 years.
- MAVERICK RATING: **

Mr Aberdeen and Mrs Deptford. If you think Chippenham to Dumbarton is a bit of a trek, you should ponder the logistical problems facing poor Frank Doran, the MP for Aberdeen North, who in 2010, married fellow Labour MP Joan Ruddock, whose Lewisham, Deptford constituency in south-east London was more than 500 miles away. Ruddock represented her seat for twenty-eight years, while Doran was MP for three different Aberdeen constituencies over the same period. Both retired at the 2015 election, with Doran joking, 'I don't want to be wandering around Westminster as a skeleton.'

* TOTAL COMBINED SERVICE: 51 years.
* TOTAL CONCURRENT SERVICE: 23 years.
* MAVERICK RATING: **

Mr Milton Keynes and Mrs Gosport. Another couple who got married while fellow MPs – both had previously been divorced – were Tories Mark Lancaster and Caroline Dinenage, who tied the knot in 2014. Lancaster has represented Milton Keynes North since 2010, having been MP for North East Milton Keynes between 2005 and 2010. Dinenage has represented Gosport since 2010. Both are now junior ministers.

* TOTAL COMBINED SERVICE: 19 years.
* TOTAL CONCURRENT SERVICE: 7 years.
* MAVERICK RATING: *

APPENDIX II

EXPENSES:
THE FINAL VERDICT

My parents' final years in the House of Commons were over-shadowed – and the same was true of many other MPs – by the expenses scandal. I have covered this episode in the main body of the text. But given the huge reputational damage done to my parents, I would like to reproduce below the conclusions of the Parliamentary Commissioner for Standards, John Lyon CB, the House of Commons official charged with investigating the matter. His conclusions were endorsed by the House of Commons Committee on Standards and Privileges, a back-bench all-party scrutiny committee.

As you will see, Mr Lyon did not absolve my parents from all criticism. Far from it. But I hope his conclusions will restore a sense of something that went badly missing at the time: balance.

House of Commons Committee on Standards and Privileges, Twelfth Report of Session 2007–08: Conduct of Sir Nicholas and Lady Winterton.

Conclusions of the Parliamentary Commissioner for Standards:

... 34. The arrangements under which Members claim allowances have changed substantially in recent years. They are likely to change again. Members are well advised to check their own arrangements against each succeeding version of the Green Book and other rules and guidance from the House authorities.

35. In this case I accept that Sir Nicholas and Lady Winterton consulted the House authorities, initially in 1998, before they established the trust arrangements for their property in February 2002. There was at that stage nothing in the Green Book's rules or guidance which prevented them from claiming the Additional Costs Allowance for rental payments to the trust of which they were two of the three trustees and of which their children were the beneficiaries.

36. I accept the view of the Director of Operations that the rules of the House are not legal documents and cannot easily be subject to normal legal analysis. They are a mixture of guidance for Members and rules established by the House. The spirit as well as the letter of the rules is important. Members have a responsibility to abide by both. I believe it is right that the latest version of the rules should be taken to apply to all serving Members. In equity, and to preserve consistency and clarity in the arrangements for Members, all Members should be subject to the same rules at the same time for the same set of circumstances, however long they have been in the House, unless for some reason it is impossible for them to be so. Except in certain specified cases, therefore, Members should expect to have to change their arrangements if, when new rules are introduced by the House, those arrangements no longer comply. But they should be given reasonable time to do so. Agreements between the Department and individual Members as to the interpretation of the rules of the House at a particular time should not normally be expected to override changes in the rules of the House. I conclude, therefore, that the successive changes to the Green Book should have been applied to the arrangements established by Sir Nicholas and Lady Winterton in 2002.

37. It is arguable that the change to the Green Book in 2003 put the arrangements established by Sir Nicholas and Lady Winterton

outside the scope of the rules. This was because it could be argued that Sir Nicholas and Lady Winterton were in some sense leasing the accommodation from themselves since they were the majority trustees in the trust. Sir Nicholas and Lady Winterton did not raise the issue at the time, and neither did the Department. I accept that it never occurred to Sir Nicholas or Lady Winterton to do so. I do not think it is productive or necessary at this remove to attempt to resolve this issue. It would be unfair to apply the standards of the current time to the actions and thinking of nearly five years ago. Nevertheless it is unfortunate that Sir Nicholas and Lady Winterton did not revisit the arrangements in 2003 with the help of the House authorities: it was an unusual arrangement when first entered into, it was one which benefited their family, their estate and assisted their personal inheritance tax planning and, in such circumstances, it would have been prudent for them to check, following each revision to the rules, whether the arrangements still met the changing circumstances of Members.

38. But whatever may have been the position in June 2003, I consider, and agree with the Director of Operations, that the arrangements were clearly not within the terms of the rules established in July 2006. The new provisions introduced then prohibit meeting from the Additional Cost Allowance the costs of leasing accommodation from any organisation in which a Member, a partner or family member has an interest. They also require Members to avoid any arrangement which may give rise to an accusation that the Member or someone close to them is obtaining an immediate benefit from public funds. In this case, the Members' children clearly had an interest in the trust and therefore in the benefits which the trust secured from public funds to meet the rental costs of the property. There is no evidence that the immediate financial benefit to the trust was greater than could have been secured by renting the property on the open market. But the trust did not have to carry the risks of renting the property on the open market. It must be presumed that

renting to the two Members must have been in the interests of the trust and its beneficiaries, otherwise the trustees would have risked being in breach of their fiduciary duty under the trust when they allowed the arrangement to continue. And the arrangement was, as I have said, beneficial to the family's inheritance tax planning and to the family members who benefited from the trust.

39. My finding on the complaint, therefore, is that the arrangement for using the Additional Costs Allowance to meet the costs of leasing accommodation from the trust established by Sir Nicholas and Lady Winterton was a clear breach of the rules of the House following the change to those rules in July 2006. I accept, however, that the rental costs made no additional calls on public funds as a result of the trust arrangement compared to alternative arrangement the Members might have rented. Had Sir Nicholas and Lady Winterton recognised that changes to the rules applied to their pre-existing arrangement, I am in no doubt that the Department would have advised them to bring this arrangement to an end and the resultant public criticism of their arrangements would have been avoided. It is unfortunate that the correspondence initiated by the then Department of Finance and Administration in February 2007 was, through an oversight in the Department, not followed to a conclusion. But the Department of Finance and Administration's initial letter should have alerted the Members to the problem and to the risks they ran in concluding that the rules did not apply to pre-existing arrangements. And the Department itself might have been more aware of the risks the Members were running if Lady Winterton's response to the Department of 11 February 2007 had given some information about the nature of the trust which owned the lease of the property they rented.

40. Nevertheless, I accept that Sir Nicholas and Lady Winterton have not at any stage attempted to conceal the arrangements they had entered into. And I recognise that Sir Nicholas and

Lady Winterton have recently taken significant action to rectify this situation. It is clearly undesirable that the Additional Costs Allowance should continue to be paid for a property managed under this trust arrangement for longer than is absolutely necessary. Equally, it would be unfair and unreasonable to terminate the arrangement without allowing the Members reasonable time to put alternative arrangements in place. 31 March 2009 has been agreed by the House authorities as the end date for continuing the current arrangement. I note that this is the last date and not the earliest date for ending the arrangement. I welcome the fact that Sir Nicholas and Lady Winterton are already looking for an alternative property. I recognise their heavy parliamentary and constituency commitments. I hope, however, that their search will be concluded successfully earlier rather than later in the months remaining of this arrangement.

9 June 2008

ACKNOWLEDGEMENTS

The Wintertons' story has had more extras than a Cecil D Mille movie, from dogs to libel lawyers, from horses to politicians who have become household names. I have woven many of them into the book but I know there are many others whose help, support, advice and encouragement (in good times and bad) my parents would like to acknowledge. So many were not just supporters but lasting and genuine friendships were formed:

Gillian Rogers, Agent to the Meriden Conservative and Unionist Association, whose experience and calm advice was so valuable to a new boy in active politics; Arthur Moss, Agent to the Newcastle-under-Lyme Conservative and Unionist Association, whose guidance and commitment was invaluable, with the kindness of his wife, Ann; Frank Horsfield DFC, Agent to the Macclesfield Conservative and Unionist Association who knew the constituency backwards and his experience and knowledge were critical at the by-election in 1971 when Dad was first elected to represent Macclesfield. Marguerite Shooter and Elizabeth Gilliland were his final two agents in Macclesfield, both emerging from the membership of the Macclesfield Association and both proving to be excellent, hardworking and efficient agents who you could trust with your life.

There was Sir William Dugdale, Leader of the Conservative Group on Warwickshire County Council, who signed Dad's application form for him to get on the official list of Conservative Party candidates; Clifford and Jane Vero, Teddy and Joan Corner, Ron and Kath Walling, all members of the local Atherstone Conservative Branch whose homes became a second home to Dad. David Oldacres, Secretary of the Atherstone Conservative Club, who became a good friend and enabled my father to use the club as a base not just at election time. And Richard Lewis from the Atherstone office of John German, land and estate agents from where Dad held his political surgeries.

In Newcastle-under-Lyme, Guy and Christine Cavenagh-Mainwaring were wonderful and are still close friends to this day; Neil and Betty Harrison were generous to a tee and opened up their home, Butterton House, for us to stay at during both the elections that Dad contested at Newcastle-under-Lyme.

In Macclesfield, Charles Legh was Chairman of the Association when Dad was chosen to fight the by-election (he later became President) and could not have been more committed, generous and helpful during what was a critical time in the hard-fought by-election. His daughter, Camilla (now Camilla Legh Williams), acted as candidate's aide at a number of subsequent general elections backed up by volunteer drivers like Ian Smart and Geoff Barber.

Hon. Alderman Margaret Duddy, Conservative Leader of the Macclesfield Council for sixteen years, Chairman of the Conservative Association and a truly wonderful person with inexhaustible energy; Frank and Mary Oxley from Disley. Frank founded the Think British, Buy British campaign. Oxley Threads Ltd was a successful thread manufacturer. Eddie and Kit Koopman of Prestbury whom my parents counted as two of their closest friends. They asked my father to chair the charity they established to provide a nursery class at the Prestbury Church of England Primary and Infant School in memory of their daughter, Marijke, which was officially opened by the Rt Hon. Margaret Thatcher MP, who was then the former Secretary of State for Education.

Jan Sztukowski, David and Sandra Blythe, Donald and Wendy Parr – Donald was Chairman of Baird Textile Holdings Ltd. Peter and Audrey Emerson Jones – Peter is Chairman of the Emerson Group. John Downes, entrepreneur and great friend.

Keith and Dorothy Littler from Macclesfield – Dorothy has been a good friend to my parents since 1971 and for some years ran Mum's office (most efficiently) in Congleton. Keith, her husband, was a fantastic canvasser and campaigner too. Eric and Jackie Corner.

Francis and Sheila Kirk. Councillor Paul and Judith Findlow. Mrs Marjorie McHugh, Richard and Annie May – Richard was President of the Sheep Dog Trials Association. Mrs Betty May, Barry and Jenny Jones – Barry was Chairman of the Macclesfield Conservative Patrons' Club (which Dad helped to set up) for some twenty years and has been an exceptionally close personal friend.

Eric and Jacqui Corner – Eric was constituency chairman; Mavice and John Ridgway and Don Porter's parents Richard and Bette Porter, whose support I know Dad particularly appreciated.

Diana Millett, wife of Freddie Millett, the former Cheshire Cricket Captain. Miss Carolyn Andrew; Councillor Barrie and Councillor Sue Hardern; Anthony and Councillor Mrs Hilda Gaddum. Brian and Margaret Ollier – Brian was an outstanding photographer and took many of the photographs which appeared in both Mum and Dad's election material. Douglas and Hilary Parker.

Mrs Maureen Henderson, Chairman of the Congleton Con-stituency Conservative Association and volunteer general election agent. Stephen Sebire MBE, a Vice-President of Fodens Band and a textile manufacturer. Sue Dale, who found us our house (most important!). Councillor Thelma Jackson and Parish Cllr Jimmy Jackson. Joe and Dorothy Gilman. James and Jane Gilman. Betty Bonson. Peter Hayes. John Knott, auctioneer and larger than life character! Norman Edwards and Dorothy Barnett, a stalwart friend to Mum. Lillian Bagnall, who became part of our family and looked after me so well, keeping the home fires burning.

We must not forget the fantastic farming communities in the

Macclesfield and Congleton constituencies including Michael Wright, past President of the British Veterinary Association.

Thanks to each and every constituent in both Macclesfield and Congleton who kept them on their toes and without whom I would not be where I am today.

I cannot forget my second family, the Malvern Girls who have been by my side through thick and thin – Alice, Katrina, Nicky, Bex, Jules, Lou, Shivy and Doyler. A particularly big thanks to the bestest of friends, Alice, Katrina and Claudia, who will go to the ends of the earth for me and vice versa.

Both my parents and I would like to acknowledge and thank Max Davidson, my able and entertaining 'ghost', a distinguished former House of Commons Clerk for his invaluable skill, advice and perception in helping to translate the careers of two controversial and determined individuals into an eminently readable yet personal and passionate memoir. It was been an immense pleasure to work with him and one hell of a lot of fun. When's the sequel?

After thanking their constituents, friends and supporters, I must finally thank Family Winterton. My husband, Marc, and my son, Jack, for whom I hope this book will be revelation. Thanks to my brothers and sisters in law – Robert and Jo, Andrew and Holly and their respective families, Nic, Alex, Will, Tom, Catherine, Henry and Robert. A particularly large thanks to Mum and Dad, Mav & V, as without them this book would never have been. Being part of our quirky family is a unique way of life and there is never a dull or quiet moment – not even one!

INDEX